Cassell's
Contemporary
SPANISH

Other titles in the Cassell Contemporary Language series:

Cassell's Contemporary French	Valerie Worth-Stylianou
Cassell's Contemporary German	Christine Eckhard-Black and Ruth Whittle
Cassell's Contemporary Italian	Noemi Messora

Cassell's Contemporary
SPANISH

A Handbook of Grammar, Current Usage, and Word Power

Angeles Pérez
Rafael Sala
Manuel Santamarina

MACMILLAN PUBLISHING COMPANY
NEW YORK

MAXWELL MACMILLAN INTERNATIONAL
NEW YORK   OXFORD   SINGAPORE   SYDNEY

Macmillan Publishing Company
866 Third Avenue
New York, NY 10022

Macmillan Publishing Company is part of the
Maxwell Communication Group of Companies.

Library of Congress Cataloging-in-Publication Data
Pérez, Angeles.
    [Spanish]
    Cassell's contemporary Spanish: a handbook of grammar, current
usage, and word power/Angeles Pérez, Rafael Sala, Manuel
Santamarina.
        p.   cm.
    Originally published: Spanish. London: Cassell, 1993.
    Includes index.
    ISBN 0-02-595915-8
    1. Spanish language—Textbooks for foreign speakers—English.
I. Sala, Rafael.   II. Santamarina, Manuel.   III. Title.
PC4129.E5P47   1994   93–29597   CIP
468.2'421—dc20

Macmillan books are available at special discounts for bulk purchases
for sales promotions, premiums, fund-raising, or educational use. For
details, contact:

Special Sales Director
Macmillan Publishing Company
866 Third Avenue
New York, NY 10022

10   9   8   7   6   5   4   3   2   1

Printed in the United States of America

Contents

Contents

Introduction

Cassell's Language Guides are designed to meet the needs of English-speaking learners and users of European languages. We are assuming that you, the reader, have some grasp of the basics of Spanish, and want to improve your command of the spoken and written language. You may be studying Spanish as part of your education, or it may be that in your professional capacity you have dealings with Spanish-speaking colleagues or customers, or you may simply enjoy using your Spanish when on holiday abroad. We believe that the unique three-part structure of our series is equipped to meet your needs.

Part 1 provides a concise reference grammar. We include all the main areas treated in full-length reference grammars, with a particular focus on those areas which cause problems to the English-speaking learner. Explanations are followed by examples from contemporary usage, and we make a point of indicating differences of usage between formal and informal Spanish. The index to the book enables you to locate sections on specific points easily.

Part 2 demonstrates how to use the contemporary language in specific contexts. There are fourteen sections on key functions of language, such as giving advice, expressing agreement, making apologies. These sections aim to make you aware of the importance of the sociolinguistic context in which you are speaking, i.e. that we adapt the way we express ourselves according to the situation we are in and the person to whom we are speaking. If you were asking for advice in English, you would be likely to express yourself differently when talking to a friend as opposed to an official whom you had never met before. Of course, similar nuances exist in Spanish, and for the foreign speaker it is important to develop sensitivity to the right expression for a particular context. So the 'register' or degree of formality of expression is indicated. The last six sections of Part 2 look at the language required for specific tasks: telephoning, writing letters, essays and reports. Generous illustrations are given, again with attention to the context in which you are speaking or writing.

Part 3 concentrates on building up your word power in Spanish. It offers a convenient bank of important idioms based on verbs, nouns, adjectives and adverbs. Other sections focus on particularly rich areas of vocabulary (synonyms, slang, false friends, proverbs), or deal with key thematic areas relevant to various groups of readers (e.g. travel, finance, literature). Part 3 can be used for reference, if you come across a particular expression and want to track down its meaning, or as a basis from which to build up your own active vocabulary.

Since the series is aimed at English-speaking learners of languages, one essential feature is the bilingual nature of the Language Guides. All examples, from short phrases to whole letters, are translated into English, so you can see at a glance what is being illustrated. Finally, all our examples are drawn from authentic contemporary situations. This is the 'real' Spanish that is spoken and written in Spain. To remind you of this, we include a number of illustrations which show Spanish in action.

We hope you enjoy using this book; *¡buena suerte!*

VALERIE WORTH-STYLIANOU

Series Editor

Acknowledgements

I would like to thank my departmental colleagues José Amodia and Dan Whitehouse: the former for having read the original manuscript and commented on various points, the latter for providing some useful hints for the translation of a few tricky examples.

R.S.

The Publisher wishes to thank the Series Editor, Valerie Worth-Stylianou, and Consultative Editors, Anthony Gooch and Pippa Mayfield, for their help in the preparation of this book.

Note to the reader

If you want to find out more about Spanish pronunciation in general, or to check the pronunciation of a given word in one of our examples, we suggest you consult *Cassell's Spanish–English / English–Spanish Dictionary*, which offers a key to pronunciation and gives the transcription of words according to the symbols of the International Phonetic Association.

English grammatical terms are kept to a minimum, but for further information consult Cassell's *English Usage*, edited by Tim Storrie and James Matson, which contains a grammatical survey of parts of speech and the rules of syntax.

The material presented in all three parts provides you with illustrations of key aspects of grammar, current usage and word power. If you would like to find out more about a particular topic, the list of books under 'Suggestions for further reading' (p.363) will be useful.

Abbreviations and symbols used

f.	feminine
m.	masculine
pl.	plural
sg.	singular
fut.	future
imp.	imperfect
indic.	indicative
subj.	subjunctive
coll.	colloquial
fam.	familiar
pol.	polite
< >	indicates the register of language, e.g. < formal >
X—X	indicates an incorrect usage, not to be followed
★	indicates an important note
! and !!	indicate vulgar or slang words or usage

PART 1

A concise reference grammar

Rafael Sala

PRONUNCIATION AND SPELLING

1 The Spanish alphabet

(i) The Spanish alphabet is as follows:

a	b	c	ch	d	e	f	g
h	i	j	k	l	ll	m	n
ñ	o	p	q	r	s	t	u
v	w	x	y	z			

Each of these counts as a letter, which means that words beginning with *ch* usually have their own section in a Spanish dictionary, and that a word like *cuchara* will come after *cucú* in the 'c' section. The same applies to *ll*.

Spanish is basically a phonetic language, where the same letter always represents the same sound. Once the pronunciation of the alphabet and the rules of stress have been learnt, no new word will present a problem. In the explanations that follow, as accurate a description as possible is given, but the student should bear in mind that this is only approximate and that a reliable spoken model is indispensable.

(ii) Each of the five Spanish vowels, *a, e, i, o, u*, has one clear sound which must be kept in all positions, stressed or unstressed. Their approximate value can be described as follows:

a: similar to the 'a' in 'father', but much shorter – rather like the 'u' in 'butter', as pronounced in the south of England
e: similar to the 'e' in 'set'
i: similar to the 'i' in 'machine', but shorter
o: somewhere between the vowels of 'pot' and 'port'
u: somewhere between the vowels of 'foot' and 'food'

(iii) A Spanish diphthong is the combination (in either order) of a strong vowel (*a, e, o*) and a weak vowel (*i, u*), or of two weak vowels. When two vowels form a diphthong, their individual sounds are kept and simply joined together.

(iv) Spanish consonants are pronounced as follows:

b: Similar to English 'b', but in most cases Spanish 'b' is pronounced with a little more friction, i.e. with the lips slightly open. In Spanish 'b' and 'v' are pronounced the same.

c: like English 'c' in 'car' before *a, o, u*; like English 'th' in 'thin' before *e* or *i*

ch: as in 'chin'

d: At the beginning of a word and after 'l' or 'n', Spanish *d* is similar to English, except that the tip of the tongue is a little lower behind the teeth; in other cases it is practically like the 'th' in 'then', pronounced very gently. In a final position, many Spaniards pronounce it like the 'th' in 'thin', or even drop it.

f: as in English

g: like English 'g' in 'get' before *a, o, u*, at the beginning of a word or after 'n'; in other cases it is pronounced in a relaxed way which has no English equivalent. The best advice is to pronounce it as in 'get', but as gently as possible.

Before *e* or *i* it is pronounced like the 'ch' in Scottish 'loch' or German 'nach'.

gu (with a silent 'u') is used in Spanish to keep the sound of 'g' in 'get' before *e* or *i: guitarra, guerra*. In the comparatively few cases when the *u* between *g* and *e* or *i* keeps its own sound, this is shown by a diaeresis: *pingüino, desagüe.*

h: always silent

j: like 'ch' in Scottish 'loch' or German 'nach' – i.e. the same as *g* before *e* and *i*, but with all vowels

k: as in English (a rare letter, except in *kilo[gramo], kilómetro*)

l: as in English

ll: like the 'lli' in English 'million'. Many native Spanish speakers pronounce it as 'y' (as in 'yes') instead.

m: as in English

n: as in English

ñ: like the 'ni' in English 'onion'

p: as in English, but pronounced more gently

q: This is only used with written silent 'u' to represent the sound of 'k' before *e* or *i: que, quitar.*

r: between vowels or at the end of a word, similar to the 'r' in 'very'; at the beginning of a word, after 'l', 'n', 's' or 'z', a strongly rolled 'r'. A rolled 'r' between vowels is written *rr*, and students should remember to make the distinction between, for example, these pairs of words: *caro, carro; pero, perro; cero, cerro.*

s: basically, as in 'bus'; only rarely as in 'rose', before a voiced consonant: *mismo, desde*
t: as in English, but, as in the case of *d*, with the tip of the tongue a little lower against the teeth
v: see *b*
w: strictly speaking, not a Spanish letter; pronounced as *b/v* in words of Germanic origin (*Wagner, Wenceslao*) and as *u* in the case of English words (*whisky, Washington*), with the exception of *water* where it is also pronounced as *v*
x: Although in careful speech *x* is pronounced 'ks', colloquially it is often just 's'. This is acceptable before a consonant, but should be avoided between vowels.
y: as in 'yes'
z: like 'th' in 'thin'

2 Stress and use of the accent

In Spanish, words of more than one syllable always have one syllable which is stressed – but remember that **all** vowels keep their full value. This stress may be shown by the written accent, as outlined in the following rules.

(i) Words ending in vowels, *-n* or *-s* take the natural stress on the penultimate syllable:

> *amigo*   *mesas*
> *cantan*

In words ending in vowels, *-n* or *-s*, if the stress does not fall on the penultimate syllable, then a written accent shows the stressed syllable:

> *café*   *melón*
> *rectángulo*   *estás*

(ii) Words ending in consonants other than *-n* or *-s* take the natural stress on the last syllable:

> *amistad*   *reloj*
> *dormir*

Again, in words ending in consonants other than -*n* or -*s*, if the stress does not fall on the last syllable, then the written accent shows the stressed syllable:

lápiz   *útil*

★ Remember that, as a result of these rules, some nouns have to gain or lose the written accent when changing from singular to plural, in order to keep the stress on the same part of the word:

joven but *jóvenes*
melón but *melones*

• Note also that for certain Spanish words the meaning depends on the stress: *revólver* revolver, *revolver* to stir; *cántara* pitcher, *cantara* (imp. subj. of *cantar* to sing), *cantará* (fut. indic. of *cantar*). Pay particular attention to the stress of verb forms such as *miro* I look and *miró* he / she looked.

• For the exceptional words *carácter*, *régimen* and *espécimen*, see section 11a(iv).

(iii) Diphthongs count as one syllable and follow the general rules, and the written accent (if required) is placed on the strong vowel:

habláis but *hablasteis*

On the other hand, when two vowels which could form a diphthong are pronounced as separate syllables, this is shown by a written accent on the weak vowel: thus, the accent on *país* shows that the word is to be read as *pa-ís*, two syllables.

(iv) In addition to the preceding rules, the written accent is used in a number of cases where it has no effect on stress.

• The accent is used to distinguish words – mostly monosyllabic – which are otherwise written the same:

mí	(personal pronoun)	*mi*	(possessive adjective)
tú	(personal pronoun)	*tu*	(possessive adjective)
él	(personal pronoun)	*el*	(definite article)
sí	yes, him / her / itself	*si*	if, te (musical note)
té	tea	*te*	(personal pronoun)
dé	from *dar*	*de*	(preposition)
sé	from *saber* or *ser*	*se*	(pronoun)
más	more	*mas*	but
aún	still, yet	*aun*	even, including
sólo	(adverb)	*solo*	(adjective)

• With words like *que*, *cuando*, *cuanto*, *como*, *donde* and *cual*, when used in questions or exclamations, even in indirect speech:

¿Dónde vive Juan? Where does Juan live?

No sé cómo se hace esto. I don't know how this is done.

¿Qué quieres? What do you want?

• Compound words keep their original accents if they are linked by means of a hyphen: *estudio histórico-crítico*. If they are written as one word, the resulting word follows the general rules: *décimo*, but *decimotercero*.

• Adverbs in *-mente*, however, keep the accent of the relevant adjective (if it has one), and are the only cases in Spanish of words usually pronounced with two stresses: *rápidamente*.

• A number of words, many involving diphthongs, can be stressed in two different ways, shown by the variation in spelling with or without a written accent. Some examples are: *cardíaco / cardiaco*, *zodíaco / zodiaco*, *período / periodo*.

3 Punctuation

The most striking differences between Spanish and English usage are summarized in the following sections.

(i) Question and exclamation marks are used both at the beginning and at the end of a sentence, and are inverted at the beginning:

¿Cómo se llama la esposa de Roberto?
What is the name of Roberto's wife?

¡Qué alto está este niño!   Hasn't this lad grown!

(ii) Dashes, not inverted commas, are used to separate direct speech from narrative in novels and similar contexts. The use of dashes is the same as inverted commas in English, but they are not used at the end of direct speech when nothing else follows as part of the same paragraph:

– Si quieres – dijo él – podríamos cenar juntos.
'If you like,' he said, 'we could have dinner together.'

This use is found is continuous conversation. If one single occurrence of direct speech is found in the middle of a narrative passage, inverted commas are also used:

> *Juan andaba lentamente, dándole vueltas al asunto. '¡Con lo fácil que sería, si tuviera un par de millones!', pensó con rabia.*
> Juan was walking slowly, going over and over it in his mind. 'Wouldn't it be easy if only I had a couple of million!' he thought angrily.

(iii) Full stops are used in Spanish instead of commas in figures, and commas instead of decimal points:

SPANISH	ENGLISH
4.350.278 ptas.	4,350,278 ptas.
7,5%	7.5%
23,40 libras esterlinas	£23.40

ARTICLES

4 Forms of the article

(a) Definite article

The definite article ('the') in Spanish has the following forms:

m. sg. *el*	m. pl. *los*
f. sg. *la*	f. pl. *las*
el libro the book	*los libros* the books
la casa the house	*las casas* the houses

(b) Indefinite article

The indefinite article ('a, an') in Spanish has the following forms:

m. sg. *un*	m. pl. *unos*
f. sg. *una*	f. pl. *unas*
un libro a book	*unos libros* (some) books
una casa a house	*unas casas* (some) houses

(c) Contracted forms

The prepositions *a* and *de* contract with the masculine singular of the definite article, giving the forms *al* and *del*:

> *Voy al jardín.* I'm going to the garden.
> *Vengo del jardín.* I'm coming from the garden.

The prepositions *a* and *de* do not contract with *el* when the article is part of a proper name:

> *un artículo de* El País an article from *El País*
> *Vamos a El Escorial.* We are going to El Escorial.

In these cases, the spoken language normally uses the contracted forms.

(d) *el* and *un* with feminine nouns

(i) As a result of the phonetic evolution of the language, the feminine singular of the definite article has a variant form, *el* –

9

looking the same as the masculine singular – which is used with feminine nouns beginning with stressed *a-* or *ha-*. The regular feminine plural form is used:

el agua the water	*las aguas* the waters
el área the area	*las áreas* the areas
el hacha the axe	*las hachas* the axes
el haya the beech tree	*las hayas* the beech trees

(ii) The form *el* just mentioned is not used in the following cases:

● When an adjective, not a noun, follows the article:

el área the area, but *la amplia área* the wide area
el haya the beech tree, but *la alta haya* the tall beech tree

● When, in colloquial registers, the definite article is placed before a proper noun: *la Ana*.

● With letters of the alphabet: *la a* 'a'; *la hache* 'h'

● In front of common-gender nouns beginning with stressed *a-*, where *el* could refer to the masculine (*la árabe*).

● In a few exceptional cases like *La Haya* The Hague.

(iii) Whereas the form *el* is always used before feminine nouns beginning with stressed *a-* or *ha-*, contemporary Spanish uses both *un* and *una* with these nouns, although the form *un* is by far the more frequent, particularly in formal literary style:

un / una alma a soul
un / una área an area
un / una hacha an axe

5 Uses of the definite article

(a) Abstract and general

(i) The definite article is used with abstract qualities:

La belleza es un don de los cielos.
Beauty is a gift from heaven.

(ii) The definite article is also used with nouns in the plural when used in a general sense:

No me gustan las lentejas. I don't like lentils.

• The definite article is used before the words *hombre* man and *mujer* woman when they are used in a generic sense.

El hombre fue creado para la mujer, y la mujer para el hombre.
Man was made for woman, and woman was made for man.

• Similarly, it is used with nouns of matter or substance, when they are used in a general sense:

El aire es necesario para vivir.
Air is essential for life.

El oro es más caro que el hierro.
Gold is dearer than iron.

(b) People

(i) The definite article is used with titles such as Mr, Mrs, Miss (though not when addressing a person directly) and with nouns that express title, rank or condition. Note that these nouns do not take a capital letter:

la señora Valdés Mrs Valdés
el capitán Téllez Captain Téllez
el conde Fernán González Count Fernán González
el rey Enrique III King Henry III

(See also section 6(i).)

(ii) The definite article is not used with proper names except in very colloquial registers, but it is obligatory if the noun is qualified by an adjective:

> *el pobre Juan* poor old Juan

The article is sometimes used with women's surnames. In the case of famous women, this practice is felt to be somewhat outdated (*la Pardo Bazán*, a well-known writer, 1851–1921); otherwise, it tends to be seen as very colloquial (*la Pantoja*) or – with the preposition *de* added, to mean 'Mrs' – somewhere between very colloquial and outdated (*la de Bringas, la de Fernández*).

(iii) When in English a noun is in apposition to 'we' or 'you', Spanish uses the definite article before the noun, whether or not there is a personal pronoun. When the pronoun is used, the noun may be enclosed in commas:

> *Nosotros (,) los españoles (,)* ⎫
> *Los españoles* ⎬ *somos muy orgullosos.*
> ⎭
> We Spaniards are very proud.

(iv) Spanish uses the definite article after *tener* followed by parts of the body, where English uses 'a' for the singular and no article for the plural:

> *Tiene la nariz pequeña.* She has a small nose.
>
> *Tiene los ojos castaños.* He has brown eyes.

The same rule applies where the English possessive is expressed by a reflexive verb:

> *Me preparo el desayuno.* I get my breakfast ready.

(c) Place

(i) Traditionally, the definite article has been used with the names of many countries: *la China, el Japón, el Perú, el Canadá, el Uruguay, la Argentina*, etc. This use, especially in journalistic style, is disappearing. In case of doubt, it is reasonably safe to use the name of a country without the article.

(ii) It is used when referring to the names of streets, squares, avenues, etc., as well as with some geographical names which do not need it in English:

la calle de Pérez Galdós Pérez Galdós Street
la avenida de América America Avenue
el Monte Everest Mount Everest
el lago Ontario Lake Ontario

(iii) Spanish does not differentiate, as English does, between phrases such as 'to school' / 'to the school'. The definite article is used in both cases and the context would clarify the meaning.

Voy al colegio. { I'm going to school.
                 { I'm going to the school.

(d) Time

(i) The definite article is used with expressions of time to refer to both general and specific points in time:

● General
    Los domingos vamos a misa.
    On Sundays we go to church.

● Specific
    Venga la semana próxima. Come next week.
    Se fue el mes pasado. She left last month.
    Te veré el lunes. I'll see you on Monday.

(ii) Telling the time requires the definite article in Spanish:
    Son las siete. It's seven o'clock.
    Termina a la una. It finishes at one o'clock.

See section 140 for other expressions used for telling the time.

(iii) The definite article is used to refer to parts of the day:
    por la tarde in the afternoon
    por la noche at night
    al amanecer at dawn
    al atardecer at dusk

(iv) It is also used with seasons:
    Me encanta el verano. I love summer.

(e) Number

As well as in expressions of time, the definite article is used in the following cases referring to numbers:

(i) Percentages
Percentages are usually preceded by the article, either definite or indefinite.

Los precios han subido el / un 9%.
Prices have gone up 9 per cent.

(ii) Prices

a 250 ptas el kilo 250 ptas a kilo

(iii) Page and number

Voy por la página ochenta. I'm on page eighty.
Tengo el número seis. I've got number six.

(f) Things

(i) The definite article is used with nouns belonging to certain categories.

● Diseases

El tifus es una enfermedad peligrosa.
Typhoid is a dangerous disease.

● Meals

El desayuno es a las siete y media, el almuerzo a la una y media, y la cena a las nueve.
Breakfast is at half past seven, lunch at half past one, and dinner at nine.

● Sports

¿Te gusta el fútbol? Do you like football?

● Games

Vamos a jugar al ajedrez. Let's play chess.

★ Note the use of *a* with the verb *jugar*.

(ii) With names of languages as the subject of the sentence, the definite article is required, but usage varies when the language is the object of verbs such as *hablar, saber, estudiar, aprender.*

> *El latín es una lengua indoeuropea.*
> Latin is an Indo-European language.
>
> *¿Hablas (el) inglés?*
> Do you speak English?
>
> *Mi primo sabe (el) francés y (el) alemán.*
> My cousin speaks (literally: knows) French and German.

On the whole, it is more common to omit the article, especially in long lists:

> *En poco tiempo aprendió inglés, francés, alemán e italiano.*
> In a short time he learnt English, French, German and Italian.

(iii) Spanish often uses a definite article followed by a noun plus *que* in exclamatory sentences. This emphasizes the noun:

> *¡Las penas que hay que aguantar en esta vida!*
> One has to endure so much in life!
>
> *¡La rapidez con que escribe!*
> She writes so fast! (literally: the speed with which she writes!)

(g) Other grammatical uses

(i) Sometimes the article is used with *de* or *que* without an intervening noun, when the context is clear, and the article is thus acting as a pronoun:

> *Déme el de ayer.* (for example, *el periódico*)
> Give me yesterday's (paper).
>
> *los de mi primo* (for example, *los zapatos*)
> my cousin's (shoes)

(ii) The definite article can also occur before infinitives used as nouns, although contemporary use tends to omit it:

> *El comer y el rascar, todo es empezar.* (traditional proverb)
> Once you start eating or scratching, there's no stopping.
>
> *(El) fumar perjudica la salud.*
> Smoking (i.e. to smoke) is harmful to your health.

6 Omission of the definite article

The following cases differ from English usage.

(i) In Spanish, the definite article is not said or written with ordinal numbers applied to kings, emperors or popes:

> *el rey Carlos Quinto* King Charles the Fifth
> *la emperatriz Alejandra Segunda* Empress Alexandra the Second
> *el papa Pío Nono* Pope Pius the Ninth

(ii) It is usually omitted, in formal registers, with nouns in apposition to well-known places:

> *París, capital de Francia* Paris, the capital of France

7 Uses of the indefinite article

There are a few cases where Spanish and English differ in the use of the indefinite article. The main ones are as follows:

(i) Some illnesses

> *coger una pulmonía* to catch pneumonia
> *coger una insolación* to get sunstroke

(ii) Percentages

Either the definite or indefinite article may be used (see section 5e).

8 Omission of the indefinite article

There are important differences between Spanish and English use of the indefinite article, and this section deals with the most common areas of difficulty.

★ **(i)** Spanish omits the indefinite article with nouns in the following categories referring to people.

- Religion
  > *Mi tío es católico.* My uncle is a Roman Catholic.

- Rank or status

  Es capitán del ejército. He is a captain in the army.

  Es concejal. He is a councillor.

- Profession

  Su padre es arquitecto. His father is an architect.

- Political persuasion

  Ella es socialista. She is a socialist.

(ii) With nouns in apposition to geographical places that are not well known, formal literary style omits the indefinite article:

Paramos en Bárcena Mayor, (un) pueblo pintoresco de aquella zona.
We stopped at Bárcena Mayor, a picturesque village in the area.

(iii) The indefinite article is not used with the following numbers:

cien hombres a hundred men
mil ejemplares a thousand copies
medio litro half a litre / a half-litre

(iv) The words *cierto* and *otro* also take no indefinite article:

cierto día (on) a certain day
otro vaso another glass

(v) The indefinite article is omitted with the object of *tener*:

Mi hermana tiene coche.
My sister has a car.

Esta puerta no tiene cerradura.
This door hasn't got a lock.

(vi) Spanish does not use the so-called partitive article (French *du*), which in English is expressed by means of 'some' or 'any':

¿Tienes dinero?
Have you got any money?

Voy a comprar pan.
I'm going to buy some bread.

¿Tienen rosas en el jardín?
Have they got any roses in their garden?

9 *Lo* – the neuter article

Apart from the forms we have already seen for the definite and indefinite articles, there is also the so-called 'neuter' article *lo*, which, although it does not quite belong to the same grammatical category, is usually classed with the other articles. Its main uses are as follows:

(i) With the masculine singular form of adjectives to express abstract qualities:

> *Lo bueno que tiene este pueblo son los restaurantes.*
> The good thing about this town is its restaurants.
>
> *Lo malo será cuando se dé cuenta.*
> The bad thing is (what will happen) when he realizes.

(ii) Followed by an adjective plus *que*, it is found in expressions where English uses 'how':

> *No sabe lo rico que es.*
> He doesn't know how rich he is.

(iii) It is used in the expression *lo de*, meaning 'the question of', or 'the business of':

> *¿Sabes lo de Teresa?*
> Do you know (the business) about Teresa?
>
> *No me vengas con lo de todos los días.*
> Don't start on the same old story.
>
> *Lo de ayer fue serio.*
> That business yesterday was serious.

18

NOUNS

In Spanish, all nouns are either masculine, or feminine, and their gender is usually clear from their meaning or – less often – from their ending.

10 Masculine and feminine nouns

This section deals with the basic rules. Sections 13 to 17 deal with more problematic cases.

(a) Masculine

(i) Nouns referring to men and male animals are usually masculine:

el caballo horse (stallion)
el hombre man
el padre father
el pastor shepherd
el primo (male) cousin
el toro bull
el vecino (male) neighbour

(ii) Other nouns that end in *-o* are usually masculine too:

el cambio change
el cuchillo knife
el escrutinio scrutiny
el hombro shoulder
el libro book
el periódico newspaper
el puerto harbour
el tesoro treasure

★ The main exceptions are *la mano* hand, and a few words which are shortened forms of a longer word ending in *-a*:

la foto(grafía) photo
la moto(cicleta) motorcycle
la radio(telefonía) radio

(iii) The following groups of noun are usually masculine:

- Numbers

    el cinco the (number) five
    el treinta the (number) thirty

- Colours

    el azul blue
    el rojo red

- For musical notes Spanish uses the sol-fa system ('doh-ray-me'):

    el re ray
    el si te

(iv) The following time expressions are masculine:

- Days of the week

    el miércoles Wednesday   *el viernes* Friday

- Months of the year

    el próximo febrero next February

- Years

    en el 88 in '88
    en el año 1880 in 1880

- Seasons

    el invierno winter
    el verano summer
    el otoño autumn
    (EXCEPTION: *la primavera* spring)

(v) Compound nouns are usually masculine:

    el altavoz loudspeaker
    el parabrisas windscreen
    el salvamanteles table mat

Compounds of *agua* have the occasional exception, like *aguanieve* sleet, which is officially feminine, but rarely so in practice.

(vi) Countries, regions and cities which do **not** end in unstressed *-a* are masculine:

el Canadá Canada
el Japón Japan
Santander es encantador en otoño.
Santander is charming in autumn.
(See also section 14(ii).)

(b) Feminine

(i) Nouns referring to women and female animals are usually feminine:

la madre mother
la mujer woman
la pastora shepherdess
la prima (female) cousin
la vaca cow
la vecina (female) neighbour
la yegua mare

(ii) Other nouns that end in *-a* are usually feminine:

la blusa blouse
la carta letter
la casa house
la entrada entrance
la mesa table
la montaña mountain
la pereza laziness
la ventana window

★ The main exceptions are *el día* day and a number of words of Greek origin ending in *-a* (many of them in *-ma*):

el lema motto
el mapa map
el morfema morpheme
el planeta planet
el problema problem
el sistema system
el telegrama telegram
el teorema theorem

(iii) The rule in (ii) also applies to names of countries, regions and towns, but see section 14(ii).

(iv) Letters of the alphabet are always feminine:

la eme (the letter) 'm'
la pe (the letter) 'p'

(v) Although there are exceptions, typical feminine endings are
-ción, -sión, -eza, -dad, -tad, -tud, -dez, -ie, -itis and *-umbre*. Here are
some examples:

acción action
precaución caution

misión mission
pretensión pretension

agudeza sharpness
pereza laziness

humildad humbleness
verdad truth

amistad friendship
libertad freedom

lentitud slowness
prontitud promptness

rapidez speed

especie species
superficie surface

apendicitis appendicitis
meningitis meningitis

muchedumbre crowd
pesadumbre sorrow

Endings other than those discussed are not reliable indicators of
gender: for example, *la leche* milk, but *el pie* foot; *la nariz* nose, but
el barniz varnish; *la sal* salt, but *el alcohol* alcohol.

(c) Abbreviations

(i) Care must be taken with the gender of abbreviations if an article
is used with them. The gender is always determined by the main
noun, which therefore has to be known before an article can be
used. In the photograph opposite the main noun is *universidad*, so
the abbreviation takes the feminine article.

la CEE	Comunidad Económica Europea
la OTAN	Organización del Tratado del Atlántico Norte
el PSOE	Partido Socialista Obrero Español

(ii) If the meaning of an abbreviation is totally unknown, people tend to use *el*, although usually there is some association of ideas that determines the gender of the article. Thus, it is *la TWA* (Trans World Airlines) even if the speaker does not know what the letters stand for, because of the association with *compañía aérea*, or *el IBM* (International Business Machines), if one is referring to a computer (*el ordenador*).

(d) Formation of the feminine

This section deals with the main ways of forming the feminine of a masculine noun. For details of more problematic cases of gender, and invariable nouns, see sections 13–17.

Nouns referring to human beings and to animals usually form the feminine by means of one of two possibilities:

(i) By changing *-o*, to *-a*, or adding *-a* to a masculine noun ending in a consonant:

abuelo	abuela	grandfather, grandmother
amigo	amiga	friend
ciervo	cierva	stag, hind

23

doctor	*doctora*	doctor
león	*léona*	lion, lioness
sobrino	*sobrina*	nephew, niece

(ii) By using a special ending:

abad	*abadesa*	abbot, abbess
actor	*actriz*	actor, actress
conde	*condesa*	count, countess
duque	*duquesa*	duke, duchess
emperador	*emperatriz*	emperor, empress
gallo	*gallina*	cockerel, hen
héroe	*heroína*	hero, heroine
marqués	*marquesa*	marquis, marchioness
poeta	*poetisa*	poet, poetess
príncipe	*princesa*	prince, princess
rey	*reina*	king, queen
tigre	*tigresa*	tiger, tigress

11 Singular and plural forms

(a) Formation of the plural

Most Spanish nouns form the plural by adding *-s* or *-es* to the singular, the choice being usually determined by the ending and the stress of the word.

(i) The general rule is to add *-s* to nouns ending in an unstressed vowel and to add *-es* to nouns ending in a consonant:

actor	*actores*	actor
ciudad	*ciudades*	city
dios	*dioses*	god
estante	*estantes*	shelf
jabón	*jabones*	soap
lápiz	*lápices*	pencil
libro	*libros*	book
mesa	*mesas*	table
país	*países*	country
papel	*papeles*	paper

(ii) Words ending in a stressed vowel vary.

● Those ending in stressed -e add -s:

café	*cafés*	coffee
pie	*pies*	foot
puré	*purés*	purée
té	*tés*	tea

● Those ending in another stressed vowel tend to have -es in formal registers but just -s at more colloquial levels:

hindú	*hindúes (-ús)*	Hindu
jabalí	*jabalíes (-ís)*	wild boar
paquistaní	*paquistaníes (-ís)*	Pakistani
rubí	*rubíes (-ís)*	ruby
tabú	*tabúes (-ús)*	taboo
no	*noes (nos)*	no (noes)
sí	*síes (sís)*	yes (ayes)

★ Note the following EXCEPTIONS:

champú	*champús*	shampoo
dominó	*dominós*	domino
mamá	*mamás*	mum / mummy
menú	*menús*	menu
papá	*papás*	dad / daddy
sofá	*sofás*	sofa

(iii) Words ending in an unstressed vowel plus -s are invariable:

el / los análisis	analysis, test
el / los atlas	atlas
la / las crisis	crisis
la / las dosis	dose
el / los lunes	Monday
la / las metamórfosis	metamorphosis
el / los paréntesis	bracket
la / las tesis	thesis
el / los virus	virus

The same rule applies to a few words ending in -x (*ántrax, bórax, dúplex, fénix, ónix, tórax*) and in a consonant plus -s (*bíceps, tríceps, fórceps*).

25

(iv) Three nouns have anomalous plural forms, in that the stress moves on one syllable when changing to the plural:

carácter	*caracteres*	character(s)
espécimen	*especímenes*	specimen(s)
régimen	*regímenes*	régime(s); diet(s)

(v) Words that have been taken from a foreign language and which have an unusual ending for Spanish offer a different kind of complication. The traditional plural of words such as *coñac, carnet, vermut* and *complot* has been in *-s*, and forms such as *coñacs, carnets, vermuts* and *complots* are still usual. However, since the spoken form of the singular usually loses the final consonant, the dictionary has progressively incorporated forms like *vermú* or *carné*, with the result that in present-day texts we come across two forms of the singular, *vermut / vermú*, and two forms of the plural, *vermuts / vermús*.

(vi) Latin words used in Spanish are in principle invariable, but usage varies. Thus *superávit, déficit, accésit, réquiem* do not usually change, while *referéndum* or *memorándum* – colloquially pronounced with a final *-n* – commonly have a plural in *-s*. (The original Latin plural in *-a* is not used in Spanish.)

(vii) A special category is the rapidly increasing number of compounds consisting of two nouns in juxtaposition, where the second qualifies the first: *hora punta, coche cama,* etc. Usage varies between putting both nouns in the plural or only the first (which is far more usual). Here are some examples:

niños prodigio child prodigies
peces espada swordfish
yeguas purasangre thoroughbreds

Some of these expressions can take both forms, but others will accept only one, and no clear-cut division into categories is possible. In case of doubt, it is safer to leave the second noun invariable.

(viii) Proper names are invariable:

Esta noche vienen los Ribalta.
The Ribaltas are coming this evening.

unless they are used in a figurative sense:

Aquí formamos a los futuros Picassos.
The Picassos of the future are trained here.

With names of royal dynasties usage varies, the plural being more usual:

la España de los Borbones
el imperio de los Austria(s)
la Castilla de los Trastámara(s)

(b) Nouns used only in the plural

As in English, many nouns which imply something made up of two equal halves are used only in the plural:

los auriculares headphones
los calzoncillos underpants
las gafas glasses, spectacles
los gemelos binoculars
las tenazas pliers
las tijeras scissors

Some of these appear in the singular in certain contexts, especially in the language of marketing:

chaqueta y pantalón
calzoncillo verano

★ Note that *pijama* pyjamas is singular in Spanish.

(c) Nouns with different meaning in the plural

A few words change meaning according to whether the singular or plural form is used. Some examples are:

el celo zeal	*los celos* jealousy
la esposa wife	*las esposas* handcuffs
la letra letter (of the alphabet)	*las letras* letters (literature)
la prez honour, glory	*las preces* prayers

(d) Initials in the plural

A peculiarity of Spanish is that the plural of some names expressed
by means of initials is formed by repeating the initials:

> *C.C.O.O., Comisiones Obreras* Workers' Commissions (Communist T.U.)
> *E.E.U.U., Estados Unidos* United States
> *F.C., F.F.C.C., ferrocarril, -es* railway(s)
> *R.M., R.R.M.M., Reverenda(s) Madre(s)* Reverend Mother(s)

12 Number agreement

(i) The masculine plural is normally used in a generic sense:

> *los abuelos* grandfather(s) and grandmother(s)
> *los hermanos* brother(s) and sister(s)
> *los hijos* children (i.e. sons and daughters)
> *los padres* parents
> *los primos* (male and female) cousins
> *los tíos* uncle(s) and aunt(s)

In the light of current debates about inclusive language, sentences
like *Los dos son viudos* or *Tiene muchos amigos* are attracting
criticism, if the meaning intended is 'He is a widower and she is a
widow', and 'He / she has a lot of friends (of both sexes)'.

(ii) Collective nouns such as *el gobierno*, *la policía*, *el ejército*, *la gente*, *el comité*, etc., are usually found agreeing in the singular:

El Gobierno ha tomado la decisión.
The Government has decided.

El comité no estaba de acuerdo.
The committee wasn't in agreement.

Occasionally, at more colloquial levels, or when the word strongly suggests the idea of individuals considered separately, the plural is also found:

La gente no sabe(n) lo que quiere(n).
People don't know what they want.

La mitad había(n) muerto por el camino.
Half of them had died on the way.

(iii) Spanish, contrary to English, tends to use the singular for references to parts of the body or personal objects if the underlying meaning is 'one each'. Thus, *Los niños se lavaron la cara*, 'The children washed their faces' (because each child has one face) but *Los niños se lavaron las manos*, 'The children washed their hands' (because each child has two). Similarly, *Entregaron el pasaporte*, 'They handed in their passports', *Recibieron el certificado*, 'They received their certificates', etc.

(iv) With a singular noun as the subject and a plural noun as the object, the verb *ser* to be usually agrees in the plural:

Mi infancia son recuerdos de un patio de Sevilla.
(Antonio Machado)
My childhood is (a collection of) memories of a courtyard in Seville.

Lo peor eran las chinches.
The worst thing was the bedbugs.

(v) With an intensifying adjective qualifying the noun, the singular is often found both with people and things in more colloquial registers:

Mucho intelectual hay por allí. < coll. >
There's a lot of intellectuals round there.

Estoy harto de tanto libro. < coll. >
I'm fed up with so many books.

GENDER

Section 10 was concerned with the straightforward masculine and feminine forms of nouns. Sections 13 to 17 deal with the more problematic cases of gender. These are the legacy of both linguistic and social evolution, and it is important to bear in mind that language is constantly changing.

⑬ Gender and sex

(a) Gender and professional occupations

(i) The gender of names of professions, other than invariable nouns ending in *-a*, is at present going through a process of adaptation as women become involved in activities which were previously male preserves. Traditionally, a word like *la médica* has meant 'the doctor's wife', and while this is now unusual, at least in the standard language, the fact is that there are still women doctors whose headed paper states *médico*. The real problem is inherent in the nature of language evolution: some feminines sound all right to most people, while others (still) do not. Thus, *médica, abogada, arquitecta* are probably acceptable to any educated person, but *testiga, fiscala, rea* (witness, counsel for the prosecution, defendant) sound odd, and *sargenta* or *generala* tend to have humorous connotations.

(ii) The problem becomes even more complicated if one looks at the possible masculine form of some professions traditionally associated with women. *Manicuro* is, at least for the time being, impossible both because of its overtones of the ridiculous and because there is no such thing as a male manicurist – although there are both *pedicuros* and *pedicuras* chiropodists. On the other hand, *modista* dressmaker for a male has steadily gained ground over the older form *modisto* – one of the rare triumphs, incidentally, of purist insistence. Again, *azafato* air steward is just beginning to appear and sounds rather ludicrous to many people. The English speaker simply has to keep up with the latest examples of good writers or progressive papers such *El País* and follow up the recent evolution of examples already well known, such as *la primer ministro*, through intermediate stages such as *la primera ministro*, finally becoming *la primera ministra*.

(iii) An older problem is the question of the feminine of nouns having the ending *-ante / -(i)ente* of the old present participle (see section 48d). For historical reasons, this ending has been invariable, gender – strictly speaking, sex – being shown by means of the article:

> *el / la agente* agent
> *el / la cantante* singer
> *el / la contribuyente* taxpayer

On the other hand, the process of linguistic wear and tear has made some of these nouns such a part of standard usage that the final *-e* has changed to *-a* for the feminine. Some of these *-anta / -(i)enta* endings have been officially incorporated in the dictionary for a long time: *dependienta* shop assistant; others are of recent adoption and may still be considered inelegant by some speakers: *clienta* customer; and others are still thought to be definitely substandard by educated speakers: *creyenta* believer. However, plenty of border-line cases occur, such as *estudiante*, still invariable among careful speakers, but with *estudianta* gaining ground at more colloquial levels. No doubt forms like *representanta* (within the category of new female professions) will eventually be accepted.

(iv) There is also a group with words such as *policía* that used to vary from masculine to feminine, where the masculine referred to a person (e.g. a policeman) while the feminine meant the profession (e.g. the police force) or something related to it. As a result of new professional openings for women, the feminine form has acquired an extra meaning:

> *el guardia* policeman
> *la guardia* duty (of soldier, etc.); policewoman
>
> *el guía* (male) guide
> *la guía* guide-book; (female) guide
>
> *el policía* policeman
> *la policía* police / police force; policewoman

(b) Gender of animals

(i) Just as in English, for many animals only one gender is used when the sex is irrelevant:

el escarabajo beetle	*la pantera* panther
el gato cat	*el pez* fish
la mosca fly	*la rana* frog
la oveja sheep	*el ratón* mouse

(ii) If the sex has to be specified and there is no other form (for example, *oveja*, strictly speaking, is feminine by gender but also the female form, the masculine / male being *carnero*), the words *macho* male or *hembra* female are added: *una pantera macho, un ratón hembra*.

14 Words with two genders

(i) There are some nouns that can be used as either masculine or feminine. In these cases, usage tends to favour one of the genders. Examples include:

el / la agravante aggravating circumstance (*la* more usual)
el / la armazón frame (*la* more usual)
el / la aroma aroma (usually *el*)
el / la arte art (*el* in the sg.; *las* in the pl.)
el / la atenuante extenuating circumstance (*la* more usual)
el / la azúcar sugar (*el* in normal use, but *la* in the trade)
el / la mar sea (*el* in standard usage; *la* in nautical and meteorological usage, and in more poetical registers)
el / la vodka vodka (*el* more usual)

(ii) In the case of cities, while names ending in *-a* are usually feminine and names ending in *-o* are usually masculine (and other endings have usually also been masculine), there seems to be a trend towards the feminine, presumably because of the underlying word *ciudad*. In some cases, usage has established one specific gender: *la imperial Toledo* (but *el Toledo desconocido*, in a recent newspaper article); in others it is more difficult to decide: *la amurallada Lugo / el amurallado Lugo*. Grammarians cite anomalous examples such as *No es verdad que Bilbao sea fea, torcida, negra* and – certainly more striking – *El otro Pamplona*. Borderline cases abound, and you will find examples that contradict each other.

15 Words with two genders with different form and meaning

(i) There is another group of words where the difference between masculine and feminine tends to be one of size, in which case the feminine form tends to imply the larger size:

bolso / bolsa bag	*jarro / jarra* jug
cesto / cesta basket	*saco / saca* sack
cuchillo / cuchilla knife	

The meaning, however, may change slightly; thus, while *bolsa* implies the general idea of 'bag', *bolso* is 'handbag', and while *cuchilla* can mean a bigger instrument than an ordinary knife, it can also mean 'razor blade'. An exception to the usual rule is *barco / barca* ship / boat, where the masculine form denotes the larger size.

(ii) There are several words which refer to a tree in the masculine and to its fruit in the feminine:

el almendro / la almendra almond
el cerezo / la cereza cherry
el ciruelo / la ciruela plum
el manzano / la manzana apple
el naranjo / la naranja orange

Some words in this category may change slightly in their morphology: *el peral / la pera* pear; others change their morphology but not the gender: *el melocotonero / el melocotón* peach; or change completely: *el olivo / la aceituna* olive (though *oliva* also exists, for the fruit, in colloquial registers).

16 Words identical in form but different in gender and meaning

In a different category are those words whose meaning totally changes depending on whether the word is masculine or feminine:

el capital capital (money)	*la capital* capital (city)
el cólera cholera	*la cólera* anger
el cometa comet	*la cometa* kite (children's)
el corte cut	*la corte* court (royal)
el cura priest	*la cura* cure

el frente (fore)front	*la frente* forehead
el Génesis Genesis	*la génesis* origin, beginning
el margen margin	*la margen* (river) bank
el orden order (position)	*la orden* command
el pendiente ear-ring	*la pendiente* slope
el pez fish	*la pez* pitch (chemical)
el radio radius; radium	*la radio* radio

17 Invariable nouns

(i) Some nouns have only one gender whether they refer to men or women:

el ángel angel
el genio genius
el personaje character (in literature)

la estrella star (i.e. 'actor, actress' – although *astro* also exists for a male actor)
la persona person
la víctima victim

(ii) Some nouns ending in *-a* are invariable and use *el* or *la* depending on whether they refer to a man or a woman:

artista artist
atleta athlete
colega colleague
espía spy
guía guide
policía policeman, -woman
turista tourist

ADJECTIVES

18 Forms of the adjective

(a) Gender

(i) Adjectives ending in -o in the masculine singular change to -a for the feminine singular:

> *bueno, buena* good
> *griego, griega* Greek
> *hermoso, hermosa* beautiful
> *piadoso, piadosa* pious
> *rojo, roja* red

(ii) Adjectives ending in -a, -e, -ú, -í are common to both genders:

> *belga* Belgian
> *noble* noble
> *verde* green
> *hindú* Hindu
> *israelí* Israeli

(iii) Adjectives ending in a consonant vary in the way the feminine is formed.

● They add -a (and lose the written accent) if the masculine ends in -án, -ín, -ón, -or, or if they indicate geographical origin (except those ending in -al, -ar):

> *alemán, alemana* German
> *andaluz, andaluza* Andalusian
> *cantarín, cantarina* singing, sing-song
> *comodón, comodona* fond of comfort
> *encantador, encantadora* charming
> *holgazán, holgazana* lazy
> *portugués, portuguesa* Portuguese

★ The main EXCEPTIONS are *marrón* brown and adjectives ending in -or which are historically comparatives but are no longer felt to be so: *anterior, exterior, inferior*, etc.

- All other such adjectives have no feminine form:

  balear Balearic
  fatal fatal
  feliz happy
  feroz fierce
  provenzal Provençal
  singular singular, unusual
  sutil subtle
  útil useful

(b) Number

(i) If the singular ends in an unstressed vowel, the plural is formed by adding -*s*:

  belga, belgas Belgian
  buena, buenas good
  hermoso, hermosos handsome
  verde, verdes green

(ii) If the singular ends in a consonant or a stressed vowel, the plural is formed by adding -*es* (but, as with nouns, there is some variation with the plural of stressed vowels):

  alemán, alemanes
  andaluz, andaluces
  encantador, encantadores
  hindú, hindúes (-dús)
  israelí, israelíes (-lís)

Note too that a written accent will be lost where the natural stress now falls on that syllable.

(iii) Adjectives of colour which were originally nouns are usually invariable. The reason is that *(de) color (de)* is still implied between the noun and the adjective:

  blusas naranja orange blouses
  botones rosa pink buttons
  cintas violeta purple ribbons

but other adjectives of colour agree in number:

  aceitunas verdes green olives
  calcetines grises grey socks
  ojos azules blue eyes

Occasionally, the invariable colour adjectives may appear in the plural, but this is rare in careful writers.

(c) Shortened forms (apocopation)

(i) The following adjectives lose their final -o before a masculine singular noun: *bueno, malo, alguno, ninguno, uno, primero* and *tercero*.

> *un buen libro* a good book
> *un mal estudiante* a bad student
> *algún día* some day
> *ningún hombre* no man
> *un café y dos cervezas* one coffee and two beers
> *el primer piso* the first floor
> *tercer piso* third floor

Note the addition of the written accent in *algún* and *ningún*.

(ii) *Grande* becomes *gran* before a singular noun, either masculine or feminine:

> *un gran hombre* a great man
>
> *Es una gran pianista.* She is a great pianist.

In formal high registers the full form is sometimes kept, although this now sounds affected or archaic.

(iii) *Santo* loses its final syllable before the names of male saints, except those which begin *Do-* or *To-*:

> *San Antonio*
> *San Eugenio*
> *San Juan*
> *San Miguel*

but:

> *Santo Domingo*
> *Santo Tomás*
> *Santo Toribio*

(iv) *Ciento* loses its final syllable before a noun:

> *cien casas* a hundred houses
> *cien ovejas* a hundred sheep

The short form is also often found in percentages – especially in the expression *cien por cien* – and practically always in sentences where the noun is not stated:

> *Déme cien.* Give me a hundred.
>
> *Quedaron más de cien.*
> More than a hundred were left over.
>
> *Aquí caben cien.*
> There is room for a hundred here.

In all these cases, only very careful speakers systematically use the full form.

19 Agreement of nouns and adjectives

(i) If they accompany one noun, adjectives agree with it in gender and number:

> *el libro barato* the cheap book
> *la casa blanca* the white house
> *retratos maravillosos* wonderful portraits
> *altas colinas* high hills

(ii) If they accompany more than one noun, the feminine plural is used if all the nouns are feminine, and the masculine plural if all the nouns are masculine or if both genders occur:

> *playas y aldeas españolas* Spanish beaches and villages
>
> *vino y coñac caros* expensive wine and brandy
>
> *Tanto los hombres como las mujeres estaban cansados.*
> Both the men and the women were tired.

In practice, however, this rule is not always followed, and, either because the two nouns are perceived as one unit or because of the attraction of the gender of the last noun, a singular adjective can also be found, for example:

> *lengua y literatura española* Spanish language and literature
>
> *la poesía y el teatro isabelino* Elizabethan poetry and drama

20 Comparative and superlative forms

(a) Comparisons of equality or inequality

(i) Equality (English 'as . . . as') is expressed by *tan . . . como*:

Elena es tan guapa como su madre.
Elena is as pretty as her mother.

Este paño es tan bueno como el otro.
This cloth is as good as the other.

Tan becomes *tanto* before a noun (English 'as much . . . as'):

Miguel tiene tanto dinero como Enrique.
Miguel has got as much money as Enrique.

Necesitamos tantas sillas como mesas.
We need as many chairs as tables.

★ *Tan . . . como*, expressing comparison, is not to be confused with *tan . . . que* so . . . that:

Era tan tarde que tuve que coger un taxi.
It was so late that I had to take a taxi.

(ii) Inequality is expressed by *más . . . que* or *menos . . . que*, literally 'more . . . than' or 'less . . . than', although English also has the comparative form in '-er':

Esta blusa es más barata que aquella.
This blouse is cheaper than that one.

Los edificios son menos altos que los de Nueva York.
The buildings are not as tall as those in New York.

When the word that follows is a number, *más / menos . . . que* becomes *más / menos de*:

Ese armario tiene más de cien volúmenes.
That cupboard has more than a hundred volumes in it.

El piso le costó menos de veinte millones.
The flat cost him less than twenty million.

(iii) 'More and more' and 'less and less', or equivalent constructions with '-er', are usually expressed by *cada vez más* and *cada vez menos*:

Se está haciendo cada vez más rico.
He is getting richer and richer.

39

Está cada vez menos tímida.
She's getting more confident (less timid) all the time.

(iv) 'The more ... the more ...' or 'the less ... the less' is expressed by *cuanto más / menos ... más / menos ...*:

cuanto más rico, más orgulloso the richer, the prouder

- *Cuanto* is invariable if an adjective or a verb follows *más* or *menos*. If a noun follows, then *cuanto* agrees with it in gender and number:

Cuantas más personas vengan, más divertida será la fiesta.
The more people that come, the more enjoyable the party will be.

(b) Irregular comparatives

The following adjectives have irregular comparative forms:

bueno, mejor good, better
malo, peor bad, worse
grande, mayor big, bigger
pequeño, menor small, smaller
mucho, más much, more
poco, menos little, less

- Of these, *más* and *menos*, which can also act as adverbs, are invariable; the others do not change in the singular, and form the plural in *-es*:

Tomás come muchas patatas, pero yo como más.
Tomás eats a lot of potatoes, but I eat more.

La cocina es mayor que el cuarto de baño.
The kitchen is bigger than the bathroom.

Isabel y Lola son mejores alumnas que Pepa.
Isabel and Lola are better students than Pepa.

Tus notas son peores que las de Jaime.
Your marks are worse than Jaime's.

- *Bueno, malo, grande* and *pequeño* can also form the comparative in the regular way. On the whole, the irregular form tends to sound more formal, and the connotations can also be different. For example, *Juan es más bueno* would be more usual in a moral sense ('kinder', 'nobler', etc.), while *Juan es mejor* would be more usual when intellectual or physical qualities are implied (i.e. as a candidate, student or sportsman). Similarly, a child can be *más malo* than another in the sense of 'naughty', but *peor* would be used when comparing intellectual or physical qualities.

• *Mayor* and *menor* also have some specific uses. To begin with, they are used for age (older / elder, younger):

mi hermano mayor my older brother
su hija menor his / her younger daughter
Juan es mayor que Pedro. Juan is older than Pedro.

However, the choice between *mayor / menor* and their corresponding regular comparative forms is rather complicated, and not every option is correct.

Más pequeño for *menor* is possible (and more usual), whereas *más grande* in place of *mayor* is not:

Igor es más pequeño que su hermana.
Igor is younger than his sister.

but:

X *Juncal es más grande que Íñigo.* X
Juncal es mayor que Íñigo.
Juncal is older than Íñigo.

(The use of *más grande* in this context would imply size rather than age.)

• As the previous note on *más grande* implies, both *mayor* and *más grande* can be used when referring to size:

Este dormitorio es mayor / más grande que el otro.
This bedroom is bigger than the other one.

but in the same context, one would almost certainly find *más pequeño* and not *menor*.

(c) Superlative

(i) To express 'the most ...' or 'the –est' (the so-called relative superlative), Spanish uses the following construction: definite article + comparative adjective + *de* (*que* in front of a clause):

el más alto de los hermanos the tallest of the brothers
la mejor de las alumnas the best of the (female) students
los mejores años de nuestra vida the best years of our lives

When irregular comparative forms are involved, the same variation mentioned in (b) may occur:

Es la peor película }
Es la película más mala } *que he visto en mi vida.*
It is the worst film I have ever seen.

41

(These examples show the most usual position for the adjectives, but individual style and preference can prevail. See section 25.)

(ii) The 'absolute superlative', which strictly speaking does not compare but intensifies a quality in itself, is formed either by placing the adverb *muy* very before the adjective or by adding the ending *-ísimo* to the adjective:

Este libro es { *muy interesante.* / *interesantísimo.*
This is a very interesting book.

Su padre es { *muy alto.* / *altísimo.*
His / her father is very tall.

While *muy* translates the English 'very', the ending *-ísimo* is rather like the absolute 'most' in sentences like 'This is a most interesting writer', or intensifiers such as 'exceedingly', 'highly', 'extraordinarily', etc. Care, however, must be taken with *-ísimo* because it cannot be used with all adjectives, either because of phonetic clashes or semantic incompatibility, or both. The result may be a very odd-sounding word or one with ludicrous connotations. Because of this, *-ísimo* is sometimes used for comic effect: *El caso de la mujer asesinadísima* The case of the very murdered woman, or, as Franco's brother-in-law (*cuñado*) and trusted confidant used to be popularly known, *el cuñadísimo*.

(d) Irregular superlatives

The following adjectives have irregular comparatives and super-latives, which are learned forms and which have also come to be used as independent adjectives:

bueno, mejor, óptimo
malo, peor, pésimo
grande, mayor, máximo
pequeño, menor, mínimo
alto, superior, supremo
bajo, inferior, ínfimo

Lo adquirió en óptimas condiciones.
He bought it on very good terms.

Estaba de un humor pésimo.
He was in an awful mood.

El gobierno establecerá el precio máximo y el precio mínimo de los hoteles.
The government will fix the highest (maximum) and the lowest (minimum) price for hotels.
Haciendo un supremo esfuerzo, consiguió llegar a la orilla.
With a supreme effort, he managed to reach the shore.
Esto es de calidad ínfima. This is (of) very low quality.

21 Numbers

(a) Cardinal numbers

For a full list of numbers, see section 139.

(i) *Uno* drops the final -o before masculine nouns. As a result, it is not always clear whether 'a(n)', or 'one' is meant:

En la mesa hay un libro.
There is a / one book on the table.

(ii) *Ciento* drops the final syllable before nouns (see section 18c), and before numbers higher than itself (*ciento diez*, but *cien mil*; *ciento cinco millones*, but *cien millones*).

(iii) *Cien* and *mil*, contrary to English usage, are never preceded by the article, although *millón* and *billón* are preceded by *un* and followed by *de* if a noun, not another numeral, follows immediately:

cien hombres a hundred men
mil soldados one thousand soldiers
un millón doscientas cincuenta mil libras £1,250,000
dos billones de pesetas two billion pesetas

(iv) The meaning of *un billón* has always been *un millón de millones*, that is, 1,000,000,000,000, but under the pressure of American English, and as has happened in British English, it is now increasingly used to mean *mil millones*, that is, 1,000,000,000.

(v) As mentioned in section 3, the use of points and commas with numbers is the opposite of English usage:

2.500 libras £2,500
25,75 dólares $25.75
7,5% 7.5%
3,5° bajo cero 3.5° below zero

(b) Ordinal numbers

(i) Ordinal numbers agree in gender and number with their nouns:

el cuarto centenario the fourth centenary
la segunda vez the second time
sus primeras novelas his first novels

(ii) As mentioned in section 18c, *primero* and *tercero* lose their final *-o* before masculine singular nouns:

el primer volumen volume one
el tercer hombre the third man

(iii) *Noveno* has a variant *nono* traditionally used with the names of Popes:

Pío Nono Pius IX

(iv) In ordinary use, ordinals above ten – especially above twenty – except *centésimo, milésimo* and *millonésimo* are very unusual, and cardinals are used instead:

Carlos tercero Charles III
Felipe quinto Philip V
Alfonso trece Alfonso XIII
el siglo dieciocho the eighteenth century

As seen here and in section 6(i), no article is used with ordinals accompanying the names of monarchs, emperors or popes.

(c) Collective numbers and fractions

(i) Here are some common collective numerals:

un par a pair, a couple
una decena ten
una docena a dozen
una veintena twenty, a score
una treintena thirty
una centena / un centenar a hundred
un millar a thousand

These are really nouns, with regular plural forms and are joined to the noun they determine by the preposition *de*:

dos pares de zapatos two pairs of shoes
tres docenas de huevos three dozen eggs
centenares de hormigas hundreds of ants

The ending *-ena* can be added to the other multiples of ten in exactly the same way as *veintena, treintena* (e.g. *sesentena, ochentena*) but the higher up the scale, the less usual they are.

(ii) *Medio* half acts like a normal adjective with regular agreements of gender and number:

medio litro half a litre
media naranja < coll. > other half

Other fractions are as follows:

un tercio one-third	*un séptimo* one-seventh
un cuarto one-fourth	*un octavo* one-eighth
un quinto one-fifth	*un noveno* one-ninth
un sexto one-sixth	*un décimo* one-tenth

● These follow the same syntactical pattern as the collectives mentioned above (*un cuarto de litro* a quarter of a litre) and are often replaced by the feminine plural of the ordinals followed by *parte(s)*:

una tercera parte de la novela one-third of the novel
tres quintas partes del terreno three-fifths of the land

● After *décimo*, fractions are usually stated by adding the ending *-avo* (which has regular gender and number) to the cardinal numerals:

un onceavo / una onceava parte one-eleventh
cinco quinceavos / cinco quinceavas partes five-fifteenths

22 Demonstrative adjectives

(i) Spanish demonstratives are as follows:

MASCULINE SINGULAR	FEMININE SINGULAR	
este	*esta*	this
ese	*esa*	that
aquel	*aquella*	that

MASCULINE PLURAL	FEMININE PLURAL	
estos	*estas*	these
esos	*esas*	those
aquellos	*aquellas*	those

The neuter forms *esto, eso, aquello* can function only as pronouns and have no plural; all the others can be either adjectives (used with a noun) or pronouns (used instead of a noun). See section 33.

(ii) Spanish has two forms corresponding to the English 'that' and 'those'. The traditional explanation of the difference between *ese* and *aquel*, and between their plurals, is linked to the speaker's point of view. Thus, *este* refers to something near me / us; *ese* refers to something near you; and *aquel* refers to something near him / her / it / them (or to something further away from me / us / you). From the English speaker's point of view, *ese* corresponds to 'that', and *aquel* has to be explained by comparing it with something like 'over there':

Este libro es muy interesante.
This book is very interesting.

Esa camisa que llevas te está muy bien.
That shirt you are wearing suits you.

Sigamos hasta aquellos árboles.
Let's go on as far as those trees (over there).

See also section 33.

(iii) The idea of proximity or distance expressed by the demonstratives may also apply to time:

Esta semana iré al cine.
This week I'll go to the cinema.

Aquel año llovió mucho.
It rained a lot that year.

In this case, the contrast is usually established by means of *este* and *aquel*, *ese* being little used in respect of time.

(iv) *Ese* is used to refer to something more or less indeterminate, or even with openly pejorative connotations:

uno de esos insectos que hay en el campo
one of those insects in the countryside

¿Qué se ha creído ese idiota?
What does the stupid fellow think?

Esa no se merece nada.
That woman doesn't deserve a thing.

(v) As with the use of *el* before feminine nouns beginning with a stressed *a-* or *ha-*, and the use of *un* in the same circumstances, the demonstratives *este*, *ese*, *aquel* are often found accompanying such nouns (*este agua*, *aquel hambre*, etc.). Although this is common, even among educated speakers, it is not accepted as correct Spanish and careful writers (and speakers) avoid it.

23 Possessive adjectives

The main point to remember is that Spanish possessive adjectives agree with the thing(s) possessed, not the possessor.

(i) Spanish possessives have different masculine and feminine forms for the first and second persons plural only.

SINGULAR		PLURAL		
MASCULINE	FEMININE	MASCULINE	FEMININE	
mi	*mi*	*mis*	*mis*	my
tu	*tu*	*tus*	*tus*	your (*tú*)
su	*su*	*sus*	*sus*	his / her / its / your (*Vd.*)
nuestro	*nuestra*	*nuestros*	*nuestras*	our
vuestro	*vuestra*	*vuestros*	*vuestras*	your (*vosotros / -as*)
su	*su*	*sus*	*sus*	their, your (*Vds.*)

su carta his / her / your / their letter
mis libros my books
tu perro your dog
nuestros padres our parents
vuestras camas your beds

(ii) Given the various possible meanings of *su*, as in the above example *su carta*, when the context is not obvious, the ambiguity is usually avoided by adding *de él, de ella, de usted, de ellos, de ellas, de ustedes*. In this case, the possessive adjective sounds a little stilted or old-fashioned and tends to be replaced by the article: *la carta de ella* (for *su carta de ella*), *la carta de ustedes* (for *su carta de ustedes*), etc.

(iii) With parts of the body, clothes and some possessions, English normally uses possessive adjectives: 'I washed my hands', 'He hurt his arm', 'She put her coat on', 'They raised their hands', etc. In Spanish, unless there is the risk of ambiguity or some emphasis is required, possessives are not used in this type of sentence. Instead, the definite article is used, either by itself, if the meaning is obvious, or accompanied by a reflexive verb:

Me lavé las manos.
I washed my hands.

Se hizo daño en el brazo.
He / she hurt his / her arm.

Se puso el abrigo.
He / she put his / her coat on.

Abrió los ojos.
He / she opened his / her eyes.

Levantaron la mano.
They raised their hands.

(For the use of the singular for parts of the body see section 12(iii).)

24 # Indefinite adjectives

In Spanish, as in other languages, there are many words which, depending on their grammatical function, can be classed as adjectives, pronouns or adverbs. As adverbs they are invariable; as adjectives or pronouns these words vary in that some mark gender and number, some mark either gender or number, and some are invariable. They usually have something to do with quantity, but in a more or less indeterminate way; hence their grammatical category of 'indefinites'. Here are some of the most common in their adjectival function:

alguno, -a, -os, -as some / any / a few

As seen in section 18c, the final *-o* of the masculine singular is dropped before a noun, and a written accent is required:

¿Tiene algún periódico?
Have you got any newspapers?

He leído algunas novelas.
I have read some novels.

In negative sentences, *alguno, -a,* placed after the noun means the same as *ninguno, -a,* and is usually preferred by good writers:

No vi a persona alguna. = No vi a ninguna persona.
(also *No vi a persona ninguna.*)
I didn't see anyone.

ambos, -as both

En ambos casos la solución es la misma.
In both cases the answer is the same.

Ambas mujeres vivían solas.
Both women lived alone.

Ambos, -as has rather a literary ring and, especially in the spoken language, is usually replaced by *los dos / las dos*:

> *Los dos tenían el mismo libro.*
> They both had the same book.

cada each / every

Cada is invariable:

> *Cada día te quiero más.*
> I love you more every day.
> *Cada soldado fue un héroe.*
> Each soldier was a hero.
> *Llevaba una carrera en cada media.*
> She had a ladder in each stocking.

Todos los / todas las should be used instead of *cada* when the sentence describes something which occurs regularly. Thus to say, 'I go to (the) University every day', *Voy a la Universidad todos los días* would be preferred to *Voy a la Universidad cada día*. In practice, however, *cada* for *todos los* seems to be on the increase. For 'Every day I catch the bus', *Cada día cojo el autobús* would probably be rejected in favour of *Todos los días cojo el autobús* by most educated speakers, but for 'Every time I look at you, I feel happy' *Todas las veces que te miro me siento feliz* would probably be felt more cumbersome than *Cada vez que te miro me siento feliz.*

cierto, -a, -os, -as (a) certain

> *Me lo ha dicho cierta persona.*
> A certain person told me.
> *Ciertas películas deberían prohibirse.*
> Certain films ought to be banned.

• In Spanish, the indefinite article is not used with *cierto*, at least by careful speakers, unless the implication is 'a so-called':

> *Un cierto señor González pregunta por usted.*
> A certain Mr González would like to talk to you.

• For the semantic implications of *cierto* before or after the noun, see section 25c.

cualquiera, *pl.* ***cualesquiera*** any

As an adjective, this is usually found as *cualquier* before a noun, and *cualquiera* after it:

> *Cómpralo a cualquier precio.*
> Buy it at any price.
>
> *cualquier día / un día cualquiera* any day
> *cualquier hombre que encuentres* (subj.) any man you come across

For the use of the subjunctive here, see section 46b.

• When referring to people, *cualquiera* may acquire pejorative connotations if placed after the noun: *una mujer cualquiera* any woman or a prostitute. These pejorative connotations are blatant when *cualquiera* is used pronominally: *una cualquiera* a prostitute.

• The plural form tends to be literary.

demasiado, -a, -os, -as too much / too many

> *Ha bebido demasiado vino.*
> He has drunk too much wine.
>
> *Has comprado demasiadas naranjas.*
> You have bought too many oranges.

mismo, -a, -os, -as same

> *el mismo hombre que vimos ayer*
> the same man we saw yesterday
>
> *las mismas historias de siempre*
> the same old story (literally: the same stories as always)

mucho, -a, -os, -as much / a lot of / many

> *No tengo mucho dinero.*
> I haven't got much money.
>
> *Aún tenemos mucho tiempo.*
> We still have a lot of time.
>
> *He estado allí muchas veces.*
> I have been there many times.

ninguno, -a, -os, as no / not any

As seen in section 18, the final *-o* of the masculine singular is dropped before a noun, and a written accent is required:

> *Ningún hombre haría eso.*
> No man would do that.

> *No me queda ninguna botella.*
> I haven't got any bottles left.

● In modern Spanish, the plural *ningunos, -as*, is rarely, if ever, used:

> *En su casa no hay ningún cuadro.*
> There are no pictures in his house.

● For the use of the double negative here, see section 59(iii).

otro, -a, -os, -as other / another

> *Iremos a la playa otro día.*
> We'll go to the beach another day.

> *Otras veces se quedaba en casa.*
> At other times he / she remained at home.

> *La otra cerveza es mejor.*
> The other beer is better.

> *Trae las otras cajas.*
> Bring the other boxes.

As seen in section 8, *otro* never takes the indefinite article in Spanish. Thus:

> *Trae la otra silla.*
> Bring the other chair.

> *Trae otra silla.*
> Bring another chair.

poco, -a, -os, -as a little / few

> *Queda poco pan.*
> There is (only a) little bread left.

> *Es hombre de pocas palabras.*
> He is a man of few words.

The same shade of meaning implied by 'few' and 'a few' usually applies in Spanish:

Aquí hay pocas diversiones.
There are few sources of entertainment here.

Más arriba hay unos pocos árboles.
There are a few trees higher up.

solo, -a, -os, -as alone / by oneself / on one's own

Estaba sola. She was alone.
café solo black coffee (literally: by itself)
Dos hombres solos no podrán hacer mucho.
Two men on their own will not be able to do much.

The last example shows the close relationship between this adjective and the adverb *sólo*, meaning 'only';

Sólo dos hombres no podrán hacer mucho.
Only two men will not be able to do much.

Since the adverb is invariable, confusion can only arise between it and the masculine singular of the adjective. A sentence such as *Vino Juan solo* could mean either he was the only one who came, or that he came unaccompanied. The *Real Academia Española* prescribes that the adverb is to be written with an accent only when confusion might arise (*Vino Juan solo* Juan came by himself; *vino Juan sólo* Only Juan came), but most writers systematically use the accent with the adverb. Another possibility is to use the adverb *solamente* – which never has an accent – which means the same as *sólo* and is unambiguous:

Solamente dos hombres ⎫
Dos hombres solamente ⎬ *no podrán hacer mucho.*

Solamente vino Juan. / Vino Juan solamente. / Vino solamente Juan.

tal, -es such (a)

Jamás hubiera creído tal cosa.
I would never have believed such a thing.

Tales suposiciones son ridículas.
Such suppositions are ridiculous.

The expression *un tal* is similar in meaning to *un cierto*, 'a so-called' or 'some . . .'

una tal Fernández some Fernández woman

varios, -as several

> *Te lo he dicho varias veces.*
> I have told you several times.

> *En esta calle hay varios restaurantes.*
> There are several restaurants in this street.

25 Position of adjectives

The position of adjectives in Spanish, especially those usually classed as descriptive, is one of the most complex aspects of Spanish grammar. Some adjectives precede the noun, some follow it, and some adjectives can go either before or after – in which case the meaning or stylistic implication may change. With a few exceptions, it is not possible to lay down categorical rules, but the following explanations offer some guidance.

(a) Adjectives following the noun

(i) The first general rule is that descriptive adjectives (such as those indicating size, shape, colour or character) follow the noun. This has the effect of stressing the specific characteristic of the noun in question, setting it apart from other similar nouns:

> *una mesa grande* a big table (not just any sort of table)

This is particularly the case when the adjective places the noun in a distinct category:

> *agua mineral* mineral water
> *vino francés* French wine

(ii) However, placing the adjective after the noun can have other implications. In the example:

> *Sonrió, mostrando sus dientes blancos.*
> She smiled, showing her white teeth.

the problem lies in that *dientes blancos* would tend to imply that she had other teeth that were not white! Where such a confusion is possible, the noun and adjective might well be reversed.

Unfortunately, it is not a straightforward matter of deciding whether there is an alternative implication that must be avoided.

For example, it would be correct to say *Me gusta su pequeña nariz* (and not *nariz pequeña* for the same reason as *dientes blancos*) but *Me gustan sus azules ojos* would be very unusual indeed. As with many areas of language, usage is the only guiding rule.

(iii) Ordinal numbers with the names of emperors, monarchs and popes always follow the noun:

> *Catalina primera*
> *Carlos quinto*
> *Pío nono*

(b) Adjectives preceding the noun

(i) Placing a descriptive adjective before the noun does not single out the specific characteristic of that noun, but is more like a comment added to it. It tends to be used as a literary, stylistic ornament. Thus, *Subió por la amplia escalera* implies the grandeur of the wide staircase, whereas *Subió por la escalera amplia* implies that there was a narrower staircase, too.

(ii) Demonstrative adjectives usually precede the noun:

> *este libro* this book
> *esa falda* that skirt
> *aquellas casas* those houses (over there)

In colloquial registers, demonstrative adjectives placed after the noun take on shades of irritation, irony or surprise which only the context clarifies. Thus a sentence like *¡Vaya con la niña esta!* < coll. > could mean anything from 'God, what a pain she is!' to 'I would never have thought she had it in her!'

(iii) The following also precede the noun:

- Possessive adjectives

> *mi trabajo* my job
> *nuestros hijos* our children

- Indefinite adjectives

> *ninguna razón* no reason
> *mucho dinero* a lot of money
> *pocas ideas* few ideas
> *cada día* every day

Note that *otros muchos* and *muchos otros* are both possible, to express 'many others'.

● Numbers

Both cardinal numbers and ordinal numbers (except those mentioned in a(iii) precede the noun:

dos gatos two cats
el primer paso the first step

(c) Adjectives with different meaning depending on their position

Some adjectives change meaning depending on their position. Common examples are:

hombre bueno good man (in the more noble sense of the word)
buen hombre decent fellow (often 'simple character' too)

hombre malo evil, wicked
mal hombre bad, untrustworthy

noticia cierta true news
cierta noticia a certain piece of news

hombre pobre poor man (in the sense of 'needy')
pobre hombre wretch

hombre medio average man
medio hombre half a man

Whatever the semantic nuance, it will be seen that the adjective following the noun tends to keep a more literal meaning. But there are exceptions. *Un viejo amigo* an old friend is somebody we have known a long time, as opposed to *un amigo viejo*, who is a friend who happens to be old; but *un nuevo coche* is 'a new car', in the sense of 'another one', whereas *un coche nuevo* can mean brand-new or also a different one, especially in colloquial spoken language:

– *Tiene un coche nuevo.*
– *¿Otro?*
– *Sí, lo compró ayer de segunda mano.*
'He's got a new car.'
'Another one?'
'Yes, he bought it yesterday second-hand.'

(d) Position of two or more adjectives

(i) When a Spanish noun is qualified by two adjectives, these are usually linked by the conjunction *y*:

un hombre alto y delgado a tall thin man
una habitación amplia y soleada a large sunny room

(ii) If one of the adjectives is felt to be more closely linked to the noun (or, simply, more 'ornamental') then it is placed before the noun and the other adjective follows:

el buen vino riojano the good Rioja wine
cómodos plazos mensuales easy monthly instalments
una enorme casa blanca a huge white house

The exception to this is in cases where the first adjective places the noun in a different category (e.g. *agua mineral*). Here, the first adjective already has to come after the noun because of its own individualizing role, and the conjunction *y* is not used:

agua mineral gaseosa fizzy mineral water
países europeos industrializados industrialized European countries
central térmica convencional non-nuclear power station

(iii) When more than two adjectives follow – not very usual, except in literary registers – the rule of placing *y* before the last also applies, except where, in elevated style, descriptive adjectives may also appear without any linking conjunction.

una habitación pequeña, fría y húmeda a small, cold, damp room
Unas notas suaves, lentas, melancólicas, llegaron hasta él.
A gentle, slow, melancholy strain reached his ears.

(e) Expressing English nouns used as adjectives

In English, many nouns can be used as an adjective simply by placing them in front of another noun. In Spanish, either an appropriate adjective or a prepositional phrase must be used:

gold watch *reloj de oro*
lung disease *enfermedad pulmonar*
picnic site *zona de picnic*
population movements *movimientos demográficos*

sea trade *comercio marítimo*
station-master *jefe de estación*
stomach ulcer *úlcera de estómago*

ADVERBS

Adverbs qualify or determine the meaning of verbs, adjectives or other adverbs, and thus fall within two basic categories: those which tell us how something takes place or is done (traditionally known as adverbs of manner), and those which restrict the circumstances stated in the sentence (traditionally classed as adverbs of time, place, quantity, etc.). Adverbs are invariable in form.

26 Adverbs of manner

These adverbs basically answer the question 'How?'

(i) The most usual way of forming adverbs which describe the way in which something is done is by adding the ending -mente (English '-ly') to an invariable adjective or to the feminine form of a variable one:

feliz happy	*felizmente* happily
fuerte strong	*fuertemente* strongly
hábil skilful	*hábilmente* skilfully
bondadoso kind	*bondadosamente* kindly
estricto strict	*estrictamente* strictly
honrado honest	*honradamente* honestly
lento slow	*lentamente* slowly

For stress and use of the accent in -mente adverbs, see section 2.

(ii) The adverbs corresponding to the adjectives *bueno* and *malo* are *bien* and *mal*:

No me siento bien.
I don't feel well.

Juegan muy mal.
They play very badly.

(iii) When two or more adverbs in -mente are joined by a conjunction such as *y, o, ni or pero*, only the last one usually has the adverbial ending:

Se lo dijo clara y llanamente.
He told him quite plainly.

La hizo salir cortés, pero firmemente.
He showed her out politely but firmly.

El país no había cambiado mucho ni social, ni política, ni económicamente.
The country had not changed a lot socially, politically or economically.

(iv) Very often, the adjectival form is used as an adverb:

Hazlo rápido. Do it quickly.

Le pidió que hablase claro.
He asked her to speak plainly.

In cases like these, the masculine singular is used as an invariable form. However, after many verbs which express a state, condition or result, the adjective very often agrees in gender and number with the subject of the sentence, thus acting both as an adverb (qualifying the verb) and as an adjective (qualifying a noun or pronoun):

Marido y mujer vivían felices.
Husband and wife lived happily.

(v) When translating from Spanish into English, note that the precise meaning of a *-mente* adverb is not necessarily the same as the corresponding English adverb in '-ly', and the most appropriate equivalent has to be gathered from the context. Thus, for example, *cristianamente* as a Christian, in a Christian fashion, in accordance with Christian principles, out of Christian charity, etc.

(vi) Spanish also has an endless fund of adverbial phrases of manner, ranging from simple prepositional phrases to expressions that would perhaps be more adequately described as idioms. Here are a few examples:

a ciegas blindly
a diestro y siniestro right, left and centre
a oscuras in the dark
a pies juntillas (creer) implicitly (to believe)
a tontas y a locas thoughtlessly
de hito en hito (mirar) to stare
de memoria by heart

de pies a cabeza from head to foot
en pelota(s) stark naked
en vano in vain
por poco almost
sin más ni más for no reason

A number of adverbial phrases of manner are constructed with the preposition *a* and the article *la* or *lo* plus an adjective. In a few cases both forms are possible, but usually only one is used, *la* being much more frequent:

a la antigua / a lo antiguo (in an) old-fashioned way
a la moderna / a lo moderno (in a) modern style
a la francesa (in the) French fashion
a la ligera carelessly
a lo loco in a crazy manner

27 Determining adverbs

For these adverbs there are usually no corresponding adjectives, and the adverbs must therefore be learned in their own right. This section deals with particular points of usage.

(a) Adverbs of time

These answer the question 'When?' Examples are:

hoy today   *siempre* always
nunca never   *temprano* early

cuando

When *cuando* is used as a relative adverb in restrictive clauses, *en que* usually replaces it:

el día en que te conocí the day (when) I met you

recientemente

Recientemente not only becomes *recién* before past participles, but it also expresses a more immediate past than the form in *-mente*:

recién casados newlyweds
recién pintado just painted / fresh paint
La paella hay que comerla recién hecha.
Paella has to be eaten as soon as it is cooked.

todavía and *ya*

Students often confuse *todavía* and *ya*. When the English translation would be 'still' or 'already', there is no problem:

> *Está aquí todavía.* She's still here.
> *Ha salido ya.* She's already left.

The problem arises because they can both mean 'yet' in some types of sentence:

> *Todavía no ha venido.* He has not come yet.
> *¿Ha venido ya?* Has he come yet?

The important difference to note here is that *todavía* can only be used in the negative as 'not . . . yet', *todavía no* or *no . . . todavía*. This is similar to English 'still . . . not' or 'not . . . yet'.

Whereas *todavía no* translates 'still . . . not' or 'not . . . yet', *ya no* translates 'no more', 'no longer':

> *Todavía no me quieres, pero un día me querrás.*

You { still don't love me, } but you will love me one day.
{ don't love me yet, }

> *Me querías, pero ya no me quieres.*
> You loved me, but you no longer love me.

(b) Adverbs of place

These answer the question 'Where?' Examples are:

> *arriba* up(stairs)   *encima* above
> *delante* in front   *lejos* far

aquí, ahí, allí

Aquí, ahí and *allí* (or *allá*) correspond to the three levels of demonstrative adjectives (see section 22) and pronouns:

> *este libro que tengo yo aquí* this book I have here (where I am)
> *ese libro que tienes tú ahí* that book you have there (where you are)
> *aquel libro que tiene él allí* that book he has there (where he is)

Although there are some colloquial and idiomatic uses of *ahí*, as a rule it is better to distinguish carefully between *ahí* and *allí* in the way shown above, and avoid the use of *ahí* when referring to something away from both 'I' and 'you'.

Acá means 'here' in the sense of the literary 'hither' – *Ven acá*, 'Come here' – although sometimes it is used colloquially instead of *aquí*.

dentro or *adentro*?

Careful speakers normally use *dentro, fuera, donde* for position, and *adentro, afuera, adonde* for motion towards. Strictly speaking, *adonde* should be written as one word when the antecedent has been stated and as two words when it is understood:

> *el pueblo adonde nos dirigimos*
> the village we are heading for
>
> *Nos dirigimos a donde fuimos ayer.*
> We are heading towards the place where we went yesterday.

However, *adonde* is often found in both cases.

dondequiera

Dondequiera (also *doquier / doquiera*), meaning 'wherever', is literary; everyday Spanish uses *en / por todas partes*.

(c) Adverbs of quantity

These answer the question 'How much?' Examples are:

casi almost	*más* more
demasiado too	*menos* less

(i) Note that some of these adverbs can also be adjectives and qualify nouns. Compare the following examples and note the adjective agreement:

> *Tiene muchas casas.*
> He has many houses.
>
> *Ellas no hablan mucho.*
> They don't talk very much.
>
> *Te lo he dicho demasiadas veces.*
> I have told you too many times.
>
> *Habláis demasiado.*
> You talk too much.

For *sólo*, see section 24.

(ii) *Muy* is the adverbial form of *mucho* before adjectives and adverbs; with verbs or by itself, *mucho* is used:

> *Son muy altas.*
> They are very tall.
>
> *Anda muy lentamente.*
> She walks very slowly.
>
> *Hablaba mucho.*
> He was talking a lot.
>
> *– ¿Es muy tarde? – Mucho.*
> – Is it very late? – Very.

(iii) *Algo* and *nada* are only adverbs when they qualify an adjective:

> *Es algo cínico.*
> He is somewhat cynical.
>
> *No es nada tonta.*
> She is not at all stupid.

As the object of a verb, they are indistinguishable from indefinite pronouns:

> *¿Has dicho algo?* Did you say something?
>
> *No he dicho nada.* I didn't say anything.

28 Comparative and superlative forms

(a) Comparative

(i) Adverbs follow the same pattern as adjectives:

> *Cerró la puerta más suavemente para no despertarle esta vez.*
> He shut the door more quietly in order not to wake him up this time.
>
> *Esta niña come tan lentamente como su prima.*
> This child eats as slowly as her cousin.
>
> *Les trataron menos severamente.*
> They treated them less severely.

(ii) The comparatives of *bien* and *mal* are the same as their corresponding adjectives, *mejor* and *peor*:

> *Hay que trabajar mejor.*
> One should work better.

Lo han hecho peor de lo que esperaba.
They have done it worse than I expected.

★ *Más bien* usually means 'rather':

Me gusta ver la televisión, más bien que ir al cine.
I like to watch television, rather than going to the cinema.

(iii) Expressions of the type 'the more ... the more', 'the more ... the less', etc., are translated by *cuanto más ... (tanto) más, cuanto más ... (tanto) menos*, etc. The *tanto* is not normally used in everyday registers:

Cuanto más tiene, más quiere.
The more he has, the more he wants.

Cuanto más leo, menos sé.
The more I read, the less I know.

(b) The superlative

(i) To intensify the meaning of an adjective, the adverb *muy* or the ending *-ísimo* can be used (see section 20c). This also applies to many adverbs, especially those of time and manner. In the case of adverbs ending in *-mente*, this ending is added to the *-ísima* form of the adjective:

Llegaron muy temprano.
They arrived very early.

Se levanta tardísimo.
He gets up ever so late.

El tren avanzaba lentísimamente.
The train was making its way very slowly.

(ii) However, the superlative form of an adverb, in a strict sense, occurs when the adverb is preceded by *lo más* and some further qualification:

Ven lo más pronto que puedas.
Come as soon as you can.

Hazlo lo más silenciosamente posible.
Do it in the quietest way possible.

As can be seen, this structure seems a comparative from a purely structural point of view, but is superlative in its implied meaning.

29 Position of adverbs

Adverbs usually come before or after the word, phrase or clause they refer to, but the choice of position depends on a number of factors which range from a few precise rules to issues of sentence length, balance, rhythm or usage.

(i) An adverb usually precedes an adjective or another adverb:

> *Esto es muy fácil.*
> This is very easy.

> *Llegó bastante tarde.*
> He arrived rather late.

> *Es demasiado pronto para salir.*
> It is too soon to go out.

> *Resultó totalmente falso.*
> It turned out to be quite untrue.

(ii) An adverb that qualifies a whole sentence usually comes at the beginning:

> *Afortunadamente, consiguió llegar a la costa.*
> Luckily, she managed to reach the shore.

(iii) An adverb must normally come before an auxiliary verb or after the past participle, but **never** in between them:

> *También han venido* ⎞
> *Han venido también* ⎠ *Juan y Pablo.*
> Juan and Pablo have come too.

(iv) Adverbs of time are usually placed at the beginning of the sentence:

> *Ayer fuimos al cine.*
> We went to the pictures yesterday.

> *Mañana va a llover.*
> It is going to rain tomorrow.

At the end of the sentence, they are emphatic, often to correct a misunderstanding:

> *¡No! Te dije que fuimos ayer.*
> No! I said we went yesterday.

(v) In general, it is much more usual in Spanish than in English to put the adverb first. As a result, there are cases where a final position signals emphasis, and cases where a final position is very odd:

Pasaré por tu casa mañana.
I shall call on you tomorrow. (precisely tomorrow)

Saludó atentamente a toda la familia.
(more straightforward than *Saludó a toda la familia atentamente.*)
He greeted the whole family courteously.

Me gustan mucho los helados. (not X ~~Me gustan los helados mucho.~~ X)
I like ice-cream very much.

PRONOUNS

 Personal pronouns

Spanish personal pronouns have the following forms:

	SUBJECT	DIRECT OBJECT	INDIRECT OBJECT	WITH PREPOSITIONS	REFLEXIVE
I	yo	me	me	mí, conmigo	me
you sg.< fam. >	tú	te	te	ti, contigo	te
he, she, it	él, ella, ello	lo / le, la, lo	le	él, ella, ello, sí, consigo	se
you sg.< pol. >	usted	lo / le, la	le	usted, sí, consigo	se
we	nosotros, -as	nos	nos	nosotros, -as	nos
you pl.< fam. >	vosotros, -as	os	os	vosotros, -as	os
they	ellos, -as	los / les, las	les	ellos, ellas, sí, consigo	se
you pl.< pol. >	ustedes	los / les, las	les	ustedes, sí, consigo	se

(a) Subject pronouns

(i) The polite forms of address *usted, -es* evolved from *vuestra(s) merced(es)* your worship(s), and they take third-person verbs (sg. and pl.). See section 61 for details of usage.

(ii) As with nouns and adjectives, the masculine plural of the personal pronouns is used when the reference is to both sexes:

> *Nosotros no queremos ir.*
> We don't want to go.

The *nosotros* could refer here to men or to both men and women.

(iii) *Ello* as the subject of a sentence is nowadays very rare, having a rather archaic ring. If a neuter pronoun has to be used, *esto* is preferred:

> X *Ello ocurrió en 1508.* X
> *Esto ocurrió en 1508.*
> It took place in 1508.

(iv) Personal pronouns are not normally used since verb endings are sufficient indication of the grammatical person referred to:

canto I sing

llegarás you (sg.) will arrive

The exception is the third person, where *él, ella, usted*, or *ellos, ellas, ustedes* may need to be clarified. Thus, if the context has not made it clear already, a sentence such as *Venía todos los días a las cinco* will begin with *él, ella, usted*, depending on whether 'He / She / You used to come every day at five' is meant.

It may also be necessary to remove the ambiguity in a few cases where the same verb ending may apply to the first and the third person singular. Forms like *venía*, in the previous example, *cantaría*, and the present or past subjunctive are instances of this:

Cuando yo salga será tarde.

It will be late when I go out.

but:

Dijo que no cantaría más.

He said he would not sing any more.

In the second example, no pronoun is required before *cantaría* because the *dijo* clarifies who is speaking. Notice, however, that the sentence could also mean 'He said that I would not sing any more', or 'He said that she would not sing any more', in which case, unless the context had already clarified the meaning, *yo* or *ella* would have to come before *no cantaría*.

Unless ambiguity of any form has to be avoided, personal pronouns are normally used only for contrast or for emphasis:

Yo soy sincero, pero tú nunca dices la verdad.

I am sincere, but you never tell the truth.

Esto lo digo yo. I say this.

(b) Object pronouns

The main problems arise with the third-person forms.

(i) Traditionally, the masculine forms for the direct object were *lo, los*, and the feminine forms *la, las*. This is still the case, roughly, in southern and eastern Spain (and Spanish America), but in central and northern Spain *le* is the usual masculine form for people and *lo* is kept for other masculine nouns. The issue is further complicated by the confusion in many cases between *lo/le* and *la* when the direct or indirect object is a feminine noun. The use of *lo, le, la*, technically known as *loísmo, leísmo, laísmo*, has become such a sensitive issue in Spanish grammar that these terms are very often used specifically to indicate a *wrong* use of *lo, le* or *la*.

In practice, there are few problems among educated speakers in respect of *lo* and *le* for masculine direct objects. One uses *lo* for non-human objects and *lo* or *le* for human direct objects, depending on one's preference or one's feeling for the balance of the sentence:

> *Lo vi al salir de la autopista.*
> I saw it when I was leaving the motorway. (an accident, for example)
> *Los / Les vi hace unos días.*
> I saw them a few days ago.

With *la*, however, a different problem arises. People are conscious of the fact that *laísmo* (i.e. using *la* instead of the correct indirect object form *le: la escribí una carta*, instead of the correct *le escribí una carta*) is very common among uneducated speakers and therefore they often use *le* when the form *la* is perfectly correct.

In summary:

DIRECT OBJECT
Lo vi. I saw it.
Le / Lo vi. I saw him.
La vi. I saw her.

INDIRECT OBJECT
Le escribí una carta. I wrote a letter to him / to her.
X *La escribí una carta.* X (incorrect use for 'to her')

In case of doubt, the trend is invariably towards *leísmo*.

(ii) As seen above in a(iv), in straightforward sentences the only subject pronouns usually required are third-person ones because of possible ambiguity. A similar kind of ambiguity can occur in the case of third-person object pronouns and so *a él, a ella, a usted*, etc., is often added to the sentence:

> *Le vi a usted por la calle.*
> I saw you (sg. pol.) in the street.

Les di un libro a ellas.
I gave them (f. pl.) a book.

★ In this type of sentence, the initial pronoun, although redundant, is always used.

(iii) Indirect object pronouns precede direct object pronouns in the sentence:

Me lo dio. He gave it to me.
Te las mandaré. I shall send them to you.
Nos lo traerán. They will bring it to us.

★ **(iv)** Before a third-person direct object pronoun, the indirect object forms *le, les* become *se*:

Se lo dije hace mucho tiempo. (not X *Le lo dije.* X)
I told him a long time ago.
Se las di a las secretarias. (not X *Les las di.* X)
I gave them to the secretaries.

(v) With infinitives, present participles (i.e. Spanish *gerundio*) and affirmative commands in the second person or with *Vd. / Vds.*, the object pronouns must be joined to the end of the verb form.

Está prohibido tocarlo.
It is forbidden to touch it.
'¿Qué haces?', dijo, mirándola asombrado.
'What are you doing?', he said, looking at her in astonishment.
Llámenos. Call us.

but:

No me llames temprano. Don't ring me early.

71

● However, when an infinitive is the object of another verb, it is correct either to place object pronouns before the first verb or to join them to the infinitive, following the rule in (iii) above for the order of the pronouns:

> *¿Me lo puede calentar? / ¿Puede calentármelo?*
> Can you heat it up for me?

Sometimes two infinitives are involved in this type of sentence, in which case three possibilities exist:

> *No puedo volver a explicárselo.*
> *No puedo volvérselo a explicar.*
> *No se lo puedo volver a explicar.*
> I can't explain it to him again.

(Note that, whatever the position, the pronouns are kept together; it is not possible to say, for example, **X** ~~¿Me puede calentarlo?~~ **X**)

● The same double construction is found with a present participle after *estar* and other verbs:

> *Estoy pensándomelo.*
> *Me lo estoy pensando.*
> I am thinking about it.

> *Está haciéndolo.*
> *Lo está haciendo.*
> He is doing it.

> *Siguió pintándola.*
> *La siguió pintando.*
> He went on painting it.

(vi) A peculiarity of modern Spanish, especially in the spoken language, is the widespread use of *le* in the singular, even if a plural complement follows:

> *No quiero tener que dedicarle toda la mañana a esas cosas.* (for *dedicarles*)
> I don't want to have to devote the whole morning to these things.

> *Estuvimos mucho rato dándole vueltas a todos los detalles.* (for *dándoles*)
> We spent a long time turning all the details over in our minds.

(c) Pronouns with prepositions

(i) When following a preposition, personal pronouns use the subject forms, except for the first and second persons singular, which become *mí* and *ti*. The third person, both singular and plural, also has a form *sí* used after prepositions when the meaning is reflexive, e.g. 'for himself'. When the preposition *con* precedes the forms *mí, ti, sí*, they become *conmigo, contigo, consigo*:

Este libro es para mí.
This book is for me.

¿Puedo ir contigo?
Can I go with you?

El edificio detrás de ustedes es una torre del siglo trece.
The building behind you (pol.) is a thirteenth-century tower.

Se ríe de sí mismo.
He laughs at himself.

¿Estaba Miguel con vosotros?
Was Miguel with you?

★ In a few exceptional cases, *yo* and *tú* are used instead of *mí* and *ti*. The most usual prepositions in this category are *según* and *entre*:

Según tú, todavía nos queda tiempo.
According to you, we still have time.

Entre tú y yo podemos hacerlo fácilmente.
Between you and me it can be done easily.

(ii) If the sentence begins with a prepositional pronoun (i.e. the strong or stressed form), the weak object pronoun is still required:

A ellas les será muy difícil.
It will be very difficult for them.

A nosotros nos dijeron que esperásemos.
We were told to wait.

(iii) *Sí* applies to the subject of the sentence and is often accompanied by *mismo, -a, -os, -as*:

Hablaba consigo (mismo).
He was talking to himself.

but

Hablaba con él.
He was talking to him.

In practice, apart from a few established cases, both *sí* and *consigo* tend to sound literary or formal, and it is quite usual to revert to the normal subject pronouns *él / ella / ellos / ellas*.

(d) Reflexive pronouns

For details of reflexive verbs, see section 49. The Spanish reflexive passive is explained in section 51b.

(i) In their strict reflexive use, reflexive pronouns denote forms of action which one does to or for onself:

Me lavo. I wash myself.

Me lavo la cara. I wash my face.

(For the Spanish use of the article instead of the possessive, see section 5b(iv).)

(ii) Reflexive pronouns are also used to denote reciprocal action:

Se pelearon.
They fought each other.

Los dos hermanos se ayudan mucho.
The brother and sister help each other a lot.

Because of this reciprocal idea, expressions such as *el uno al otro, los unos a los otros, mutuamente, recíprocamente, el uno con el otro,* etc., are often added:

Se pelearon los unos con los otros.
They fought one another.

Se aprecian mutuamente.
They hold each other in great esteem.

(iii) The passive voice is not as common in Spanish as in English, and the reflexive passive construction with *se* is often used instead:

Se abrió la puerta.
The door was opened.

Se is also used for impersonal statements, such as 'it is said that'. (See section 51b(v).)

(iv) The pronoun *se* is always the first pronoun in the sentence. Inversion of *se* and *me* or *te* is characteristic of uneducated or childish speech:

Se me olvidó. (not X *Me se olvidó.* X)
I forgot it.

Se te ve poco. (not X *Te se ve poco.* X)
One hardly ever sees you.

(v) Finally, note that, when added to a verb, *se* can either change its meaning or add specific connotations. In the first case, we find contrasts such as:

dormir to sleep
dormirse to fall asleep

levantar to raise, lift
levantarse to get / stand up

quitar to take away
quitarse to take off

In the second case, the reflexive form adds the notion of completeness, suddenness or speed:

Se lo comió todo en cinco minutos.
He ate everything up in five minutes.

Se lo leyó de un tirón.
He read it at one sitting.

Also, it may signal a more colloquial or emotive style than the same verb without the *se*:

Cervantes y Shakespeare murieron con pocos días de diferencia.
Cervantes and Shakespeare died within a few days of each other.

but:

Se murió la pobre, olvidada de toda la familia.
The poor old wretch died, forgotten by all her family.

31 Relative pronouns

The traditional relative pronouns in Spanish are *que, cual, quien* and *cuyo. Que* is invariable; *cual* and *quien* both have a plural form, *cuales, quienes*; and *cuyo* has normal endings marking gender and number, *cuyo, -a, -os, -as. Que* and *cual* ('who, whom, which, that') refer to people and to things; *cuyo* ('whose') may also refer to people and to things; *quien* ('who, whom') refers only to people.

★ Two things must be remembered from the start: the first is that the linking relative pronoun cannot be omitted in Spanish as it often is in English. Therefore, a clause such as 'the man we saw yesterday' must always be translated as 'the man whom we saw yesterday'. The second is that prepositions must come before the pronoun and never at the end of the sentence – thus, 'the house we went into' becomes in Spanish 'the house into which we went'.

(a) Uses of *que, quien, cual*

It has to be noted that *que* is the hardest-worked of relative pronouns and very often, in colloquial style, people use it instead of more cumbersome – though correct – combinations of relatives with prepositions and articles. The following section outlines the basic cases where *que* is correct and where another choice should be made.

(i) The most common relative pronoun for both people and things, and as either subject or object, is *que*:

el alumno que ganó el premio the student who won the prize
el tejado que se hundió the roof which collapsed
los libros que compró papá the books which dad bought

(ii) Only *que* is normally used in defining clauses:

Los platos que estaban sucios fueron retirados.
The plates which were dirty were taken away. (i.e. those which were dirty)

Los corredores que estaban cansados no pudieron llegar.
The runners who were tired could not finish the race. (i.e. the ones who were tired)

(A defining clause specifies the particular 'plates' and 'runners'; compare with the examples of non-defining clauses below.)

In non-defining clauses, *que* is also used, but *el cual, la cual, los cuales, las cuales* often appear, especially when referring to people. In this case, *quien* or *quienes* is also occasionally found:

Los platos, $\left\{ \begin{array}{l} que \\ los\ cuales \end{array} \right\}$ *estaban sucios, fueron retirados.*
The plates, which were dirty, were taken away. (i.e. all the plates)

$$Los\ corredores,\ \begin{cases} que \\ los\ cuales \\ quienes \end{cases} estaban\ cansados,\ no\ pudieron\ llegar.$$

The runners, who were tired, could not finish the race.
(i.e. all the runners)

(Note that, as in English, non-defining clauses – contrary to defining clauses – always appear between commas.)

★ English speakers often use *quien(es)* in a defining clause, instead of the correct *que*. The most practical rule to remember is that, unless there is a comma between noun and pronoun – therefore introducing a non-defining clause – *que* must be used, and that even a non-defining clause does not necessarily require *quien*. Compare:

X ~~El hombre quien dijo eso os quiere engañar.~~ X
El hombre que dijo eso os quiere engañar.
The man who said that is out to deceive you.

$$El\ hombre,\ \begin{cases} que \\ el\ cual \\ quien \end{cases} hablaba\ en\ voz\ baja,\ parecía\ asustado.$$

The man, who was speaking in a low voice, looked frightened.

(iii) When the relative pronoun refers to people and is the object of the clause, *quien, el cual, el que* are also common, especially if the personal *a* is used (see section 53):

$$el\ chico\ \begin{cases} que \\ al\ que \\ al\ cual \\ a\ quien \end{cases} mandamos\ con\ el\ recado$$

the boy (whom) we sent with the message

Note that the personal *a* is not used with *que*.

(iv) With an indirect object, *que* by itself is not possible:

$$Los\ amigos\ \begin{cases} a\ los\ que \\ a\ los\ cuales \\ a\ quienes \end{cases} escribo\ viven\ en\ París.$$

The friends I am writing to live in Paris. (i.e. 'to whom')

(v) When a preposition accompanies a relative pronoun, *quien, el cual*, etc. (for people) and *el cual*, etc. (for things) are felt to be more elegant than *(el) que*:

$$Es\ una\ chica\ con \begin{cases} quien \\ la\ cual \\ la\ que \end{cases} salgo\ los\ fines\ de\ semana.$$

She is a girl I go out with at weekends. (i.e. 'with whom I go out')

$$Es\ un\ apuro\ en \begin{cases} el\ cual \\ el\ que \\ que \end{cases} no\ quisiera\ verme.$$

It is a plight I wouldn't like to find myself in. (i.e. 'in which')

(vi) *Quien* or *el que* are used as indeterminate subjects in proverbs and similar expressions:

$$\left. \begin{matrix} Quien \\ El\ que \end{matrix} \right\} todo\ lo\ quiere,\ todo\ lo\ pierde.$$

He who wants everything, loses everything.

(vii) *Quien* or *el / la / los / las que* are used to translate 'the one(s) who / which' or 'that / those who / which':

el que compré ayer the one (which) I bought yesterday

Las que hayan terminado pueden marcharse.
Those who have finished may go.

Prefiero el que leí el mes pasado.
I prefer the one I read last month.

(viii) Since both *quien* and *el que*, etc. function as a grammatical third person, verbal agreement can vary when the subject pronoun which precedes them is a first or a second person:

$$Soy\ yo \begin{cases} quien \\ el\ que \end{cases} lo\ digo\ /\ lo\ dice.$$

I am the one who says so.

$$Eres\ tú \begin{cases} quien \\ la\ que \end{cases} debe\ /\ debes\ hacerlo.$$

You are the one who must do it.

(b) Use of *lo que* and *lo cual*

While the definite article plus *que* or *cual* refers back to a preceding noun, the neuter article *lo* plus one of these relative pronouns refers back to a whole sentence, idea or event, and it may translate an English 'what' or 'which':

No me creo lo que dices.
I don't believe what you are saying.

Empezó a llover, con lo cual no había contado.
It started to rain, which he had not reckoned on.

Note that occasionally a relative link with either the neuter *lo* or a definite article is possible, but in one case the reference is to a whole thought or event, and in the other the reference is to a specific word:

Había recibido una carta anónima, lo cual le había preocupado mucho.
He had received an anonymous letter, which (event) had worried him very much.

Había recibido una carta anónima, la cual le había preocupado mucho.
He had received an anonymous letter, which (letter) had worried him very much.

(c) Use of *cuyo, -a, -os, -as*

Cuyo is a pronoun that translates 'whose' in a relative clause. Like an adjective, it agrees in gender and number with the noun it precedes:

la casa cuyo dueño es amigo mío
the house whose owner is a friend of mine

el chico cuyo padre es maestro
the boy whose father is a teacher

el libro cuyas tapas están gastadas
the book whose covers are worn

- If two nouns follow, *cuyo* agrees with the first:

el señor cuya casa y jardín visitamos
the gentleman whose house and garden we visited

32 Interrogative pronouns

In Spanish, as in English, a number of words are used for questions and exclamations. As a complement to the preceding section on relative pronouns, this section deals with the most common types of sentences which use these pronouns in interrogative (or exclamatory) contexts and some problems which arise. For the use of the accent, see section 2.

(a) Form

(i) *Cuyo* is the only relative pronoun which is not used nowadays for questions. Instead, modern Spanish uses *de quién*:

> *¿De quién es este libro?*
> Whose book is this?

> *¿En casa de quién os alojasteis?*
> In whose house did you stay?

¿De quién? is also found in the following telephone phrase:

> *¿De parte de quién?*
> Who's calling?

(ii) *¿Quién?* presents no special difficulty as an interrogative pronoun, except that, unless the idea of plurality is very clear in the speaker's mind, the singular form is often used in contexts where several people are involved:

> *¿Quién estaba en la fiesta?* (for *quiénes estaban*)
> Who was at the party?

> *¿Quién juega en el Madrid?* (for *quiénes juegan*)
> Who's playing for Madrid?

(b) Uses of *¿Qué?* and *¿Cuál?*

★ *¿Qué?* and *¿Cuál?* are the two pronouns which tend to cause problems when used as interrogatives.

(i) *¿Qué?* meaning 'What?' before a verb usually causes no difficulty, either in direct or indirect questions, when the sense is a general one:

¿Qué quieres beber?
What would you like to drink?

No sé qué me pasa.
I don't know what the matter is with me.

¿Para qué sirve esto?
What is this used for?

(ii) Problems arise from the fact that, with an adjectival value, 'which' and 'what' tend to be used indiscriminately in English, unless a specific choice is very clearly meant: 'Which record shall I buy?', when considering two or three in front of us, as opposed to 'What record shall I buy?', thinking about records in general. In cases such as this, Spanish normally uses *¿Qué?, ¿Qué disco compro?*, rather than *¿Cuál?*, which tends to be used in constructions where it is followed by *de* or where there is no noun between it and the verb: *¿Cuál de los dos compro?* or *¿Cuál compro?*

(iii) But the real difficulty comes when one has to translate the question 'What is . . .?' – *¿Qué es?* or *¿Cuál es?*

¿Qué? implies the nature or the basic characteristics of something, while *¿Cuál?* implies one specific option out of a potential variety. Therefore to ask *¿Qué es la capital de Francia?* could invite an answer such as 'a very important city' whereas to elicit the answer 'Paris' would require the question *¿Cuál es la capital de Francia?*, implying that there were specific options.

An example taken from real life may help to clarify the point. A Spanish student was answering questions on an English passage. When he came to the question 'What are the colours of the rainbow?', his answer was 'If I understand this question correctly, I am incapable of answering it' – yet he knew all the colours of the rainbow and their names in English. Why had he answered in that way? It was because the 'What are . . .' reminded him of *¿Qué son?*, and the answer to that question could only be something like 'The colours of the rainbow are the result of light going through tiny drops of water suspended in the atmosphere'. If, on the other hand, the question had been put to him as 'Which are the colours of the rainbow?', he would automatically have understood *¿Cuáles son?*, and then his answer would have been 'Red, orange', etc.

(c) Interrogative pronouns in exclamations

(i) *¡Quién!* appears in the sort of exclamation which is a blend of question and exclamation:

> *¡Quién lo hubiese dicho!*
> Who would have said it!

With a past subjunctive in contexts where a wish is meant, *¡Quién!* translates expressions such as 'If only . . .', 'I wish . . .', or the more literary 'Would that . . .':

> *¡Quién supiera escribir!*
> If only I could write!
>
> *¡Quién fuera rey!*
> I wish I were a king!

(ii) *¡Qué!* in exclamations usually translates 'What (a) . . .', or 'How . . .'. If sentences with 'What (a) . . .' have an adjective, the corresponding Spanish adjective is preceded by either *tan* or *más*:

> *¡Qué pena!* What a shame!
>
> *¡Qué mañana tan hermosa!* What a lovely morning!
>
> *¡Qué excusas más ridículas!* What ridiculous excuses!
>
> *¡Qué difícil es convencerte!* How difficult it is to convince you!

33 Demonstrative pronouns

Demonstrative pronouns function with the same three levels of reference as their corresponding adjectives (see section 22). This section deals with a few characteristics of their use as pronouns.

(a) Form

Demonstrative adjectives and pronouns are identical in form, except in one respect. The demonstratives as pronouns – i.e. used instead of a noun – must, according to the present rules of the *Real Academia Española*, be written with an accent if any confusion is likely to arise. Thus, *Este es mi amigo* This is my friend does not need an accent, but *éste presente* this one (who is) here must take an accent to prevent ambiguity with *este presente* this present (= gift). In practice, most writers automatically use the accent when the demonstrative has the value of a pronoun.

★ Note that the neuter forms, *esto, eso, aquello*, which can only function as pronouns, never have an accent:

> *¿Qué es esto?* What is this?
>
> *Eso sí que es raro.*
> That is an odd thing.
>
> *Aquello le pasó por fiarse demasiado.*
> That happened to him for being overconfident.

(b) Use

(i) *Éste ... aquél* translates 'the former ... the latter', but it is important to bear in mind that *éste* refers to the noun near it, and *aquél* to the noun further away – i.e. the strict translation of *éste ... aquél* would be 'the latter ... the former':

> *Miguel tiene un hijo y una hija; ésta es profesora, aquél es abogado.*
> Miguel has a son and a daughter; the former is a lawyer, the latter is a teacher.

(ii) *Éste, -a, -os, -as* are often used in Spanish where English uses a personal pronoun or, sometimes, 'the latter':

> *Al tropezar Pedro y Elena, ésta se ruborizó.*
> When Pedro and Elena bumped against each other, she blushed.

★ **(iii)** Remember that *el / la / los / las que* is used to express 'that / those who / which':

> *Esta casa me gusta más que la que vimos ayer.*
> I like this house better than that which we saw yesterday.

34 Possessive pronouns

(a) Form

Possessive pronouns agree in number and gender with the noun they replace or refer to:

> *mío, -a, -os, -as* mine
> *tuyo, -a, -os, -as* yours
> *suyo, -a, -os, -as* his / hers / its / yours (pol.)
> *nuestro, -a, -os, -as* ours
> *vuestro, -a, -os, -as* yours
> *suyo, -a, -os, -as* theirs / yours (pol.)

(b) Use

(i) Used either independently or placed after a noun, possessive pronouns stand half-way between adjective and pronoun:

> *¿De quién es esto?' – (Es) mío'.*
> Whose is this? – (It is) mine.

> *un amigo nuestro* a friend of ours
> *alguna ocurrencia tuya* some bright idea of yours

(ii) With the definite article, and in a more fully pronominal function, possessive pronouns have a number of uses which range from a mere replacement of the noun to stressing the idea of possession or of contrast:

> *¿Vamos a mi casa o a la tuya?*
> Shall we go to my house or to yours?

> *Esa toalla no, que es la mía.*
> Not that towel; that's mine.

> *Tu coche va muy bien, pero el mío siempre se estropea.*
> Your car runs very well, but mine is always breaking down.

(iii) The first person is used after the noun in more or less set formulas of endearment or exclamations: *hija mía, amigos míos, padre mío.*

(iv) In a similar way to the possible connotations of *lo de* (see section 9(iii)), the combination of the neuter article and a possessive pronoun offers a whole range of meanings which only the full context can clarify:

> *Lo nuestro terminó mal.*
> Our relationship / affair / marriage / partnership had a bad ending.

> *No os olvidéis de coger lo vuestro.*
> Don't forget to take your belongings / luggage / share.

> *Lo suyo es más difícil de entender.*
> His behaviour / affairs / character / case / fixation is / are more difficult to understand.

> *Lo mío es el teatro.*
> Drama is my hobby / speciality / profession / source of income.

35 Indefinite pronouns

(i) There are several words that may function as either adjectives or pronouns, and which refer to people or things in an unspecified or indefinite way. The grammatical category of these words, in a strict sense, is determined by whether they accompany a noun – adjectives – or whether they are used without a noun – pronouns. Here are a few examples of these words used in their pronominal function.

Unos decían que sí y otros decían que no.
Some said yes and some said no.

Varias llegaron tarde.
Several arrived late.

Veinte son demasiados para este estante.
Twenty is too many for this shelf.

(ii) Apart from the indefinites that may act as both adjectives and pronouns, there are a few which never accompany a noun, and therefore can only act as pronouns. The common ones are *alguien* somebody, anybody and *nadie* nobody for people; and *algo* something, anything and *nada* nothing for things:

Tengo que preguntárselo a alguien.
I must ask somebody.

¿Hay alguien en casa?
Is anybody in?

Nadie sabe cómo hacerlo.
Nobody knows how to do it.

¿Quieres algo de la tienda?
Do you want anything from the shop?

Me contó algo que no puedo repetir.
He told me something which I can't repeat.

Aquí no hay nada que hacer.
There is nothing to do here.

¿No tiene nada mejor?
Haven't you got anything better?

For the use of the double negative in the last two examples, see section 59.

85

(iii) *Quienquiera*, pl. *quienesquiera* whoever is rather literary:

Quienquiera que seas, gracias.
Whoever you may be, thank you.

It is often replaced by *cualquiera* or by a different construction, usually a repeated subjunctive: *seas quien seas.*

VERBS

36 Agreement of subject and verb

There are three regular conjugations in Spanish, traditionally known as first, second and third. The first conjugation is that of verbs whose infinitive ends in *-ar*, the second conjugation is that of verbs whose infinitive ends in *-er*, and the third conjugation is that of verbs whose infinitive ends in *-ir*. As in other Romance languages, the various forms of a regular verb are obtained by adding to the stem of the verb – i.e. the infinitive minus the ending *-ar, -er* or *-ir* – certain endings which, with few exceptions, indicate tense, person and mood. Thus, for example, *hablo* can only be first-person singular, present indicative, of the verb *hablar*, 'to speak' while *habléis* can only be second person plural of the present subjunctive.

Appendix 1 (pp. 331–6) gives the full conjugation of *ser* and *estar*, two Spanish verbs to be, and of the auxiliary verb *haber* to have; Appendix 2 gives the full conjugation of three regular verbs, *hablar* to speak, *comer* to eat and *vivir* to live; Appendix 3 gives the full conjugation of the reflexive verb *lavarse* to wash oneself; and Appendix 4 is a list of the most common irregular verbs.

37 *Ser* and *estar*

Ser and *estar*, the two verbs that translate 'to be', are one of the traditional difficulties of Spanish as a foreign language. See Appendix 1 for their full conjugations.

(i) One of the most usual starting-points for any attempt at categorizing their differences is to say that *ser* expresses permanent characteristics, while *estar* expresses temporary ones. This difference helps but cannot be taken as a safe guiding principle – not because the borderline between permanent and temporary may be subjective, but simply because usage has developed specific nuances. Thus, one says *estar vivo* and *estar muerto*, contrary to logic since both – certainly *estar muerto* – state a permanent condition.

Another example is that one would usually say of a bald man *es calvo*, not because he has always been bald, but because *está calvo* suggests that he is balder than you might have expected, or perhaps that he has become rather bald since you last saw him. In other words, *ser* is the purely impersonal or objective statement, whereas *estar* tends to add some form of emotional or subjective note. The same would apply to cases such as *es alto* and *está alto*, or *es viejo* and *está viejo*, where *ser* is purely descriptive and *estar* implies a certain amount of surprise or admiration.

(ii) Related to the question of permanent versus temporary are cases where the choice of *ser* or *estar* will depend on whether we are talking about something in general or referring to one specific case or example, or whether the same adjective has a different meaning depending on the use of *ser* or *estar*. In these cases the underlying idea of *ser* = permanent or intrinsic and *estar* = temporary or accidental still applies. Compare the following examples:

¡Qué bonita eres!	*¡Qué bonita estás!*
How pretty you are!	How pretty you look!
Es muy triste.	*Está muy triste.*
He has a sad temperament.	He is feeling very sad.
La paella es un plato muy bueno.	*Esta paella está muy buena.*
Paella is a very nice dish.	This paella is very good.
Es muy malo.	*Está muy malo.*
He is very wicked.	He is very ill.
Juan es bueno.	*Juan está bueno.*
Juan is good.	Juan is well. (= healthy)
Es muy aburrido.	*Está muy aburrido.*
He is very boring.	He is very bored.
Aurora es lista.	*Aurora está lista.*
Aurora is clever.	Aurora is ready.

(iii) One simple difference in meaning is that *ser* is used for the passive voice (and thus means that something is, was or will be taking place), whereas *estar* states the result of something which has been completed at some earlier point:

Fue construido en el siglo diecinueve.
It was built in the nineteenth century.

Está hecho de mármol.
It's made of marble.

(iv) After these general considerations, the basic uses of *ser* and *estar* can be summarized as follows:

ser

* With adjectives or adjectival phrases which refer to something permanent:

    El caballo es un animal veloz.
    The horse is a swift animal.

    La miel es dulce.
    Honey is sweet.

    Estas monedas son de oro.
    These coins are gold.

    Estas chicas son inglesas.
    These girls are English.

* In questions where a definition or clarification is being sought:

    ¿Qué es esto?
    What is this?

    ¿Quién es ese hombre?
    Who is that man?

    ¿Cuál es el mejor?
    Which is the best?

* To state the time, part of the day, day of the week or month, and seasons of the year:

    Son las cinco y media. It is half past five.

    Es de noche. It is night.

    Hoy es lunes. Today is Monday.

    Mañana es día 30. Tomorrow is the 30th.

    Aquí es verano, pero en Buenos Aires es invierno.
    It is summer here, but it is winter in Buenos Aires.

★ Note, however:

    Estamos a 30. It is the 30th.

and

    Estamos en verano. It is summer.

89

- With the past participle of verbs for the passive voice:

  El discurso será pronunciado por el presidente.
  The speech will be given by the chairman.

  El edificio fue destruido por un incendio.
  The building was destroyed by a fire.

- To state where something takes place or happens (past, present or future):

  El atraco fue en el Banco de Valencia.
  The hold-up was at the Bank of Valencia.

  La fiesta será en casa de Juan.
  The party will be at Juan's.

★ This use is not to be confused with mere **location**, for which *estar* is used:

  El Banco de Valencia está en la calle Aguadores.
  The Bank of Valencia is in Aguadores Street.

- Identification:

  María es mi hermana.
  María is my sister.

  Madrid es la capital de España.
  Madrid is the capital of Spain.

estar

- With adjectives or adjectival forms which refer to something impermanent:

  Este café está demasiado dulce.
  This coffee is too sweet.

  Hace tres días que está enfermo.
  He has been ill for three days.

  ¿A cuánto está hoy la libra?
  What is the exchange rate for the pound today?

  ¿Están llenas las botellas?
  Are the bottles full?

- To state position or location:

  Madrid está en el centro de España.
  Madrid is in the centre of Spain.

¿Dónde está mi libro?
Where is my book?

Ayer estuvimos en el teatro.
Yesterday we were at the theatre.

- To form the present and past continuous tenses:
  Estoy escribiendo. I'm writing.
  Estaban cantando. They were singing.

- For *estar por / estar para*, see section 53.

(v) Finally, note that there are a few borderline cases where *ser* and *estar* are practically interchangeable, even if some semantic or stylistic nuance can be established. Examples are words relating to marital status, where *ser* tends to be a little more formal than *estar*:

  Es soltero. / Está soltero. He is a bachelor.

38 *Haber*

For the full conjugation of *haber*, see Appendix 1 (pages 331–6).

(i) In modern Spanish, *haber* is used as an auxiliary verb to form all compound tenses of verbs.

  Hemos cantado.
  We have sung.
  Habían llegado tarde.
  They had arrived late.

(ii) In the third singular forms, it is also used as an impersonal verb that translates the English 'there + to be' ('there is', 'there were', etc.):

  En esta clase hay diez alumnos.
  There are ten students in this class.
  No habrá bastante tiempo.
  There will not be enough time.

★ In its impersonal sense, the present indicative form is *hay*. Note, also, that only the third-person **singular** is used in **all** cases; thus *hay* there is / are, *había* there was / were, etc.

(iii) Note the idiomatic use of *haber de* and *haber que* plus infinitive to express the idea of obligation or necessity. The construction with *de* is personal, and the construction with *que* is impersonal:

> *Has de tener más paciencia.*
> You have to be more patient. (i.e. 'you', the person I am speaking to)
>
> *Hay que tener más paciencia.*
> One has to be more patient.

39 The indicative

The indicative mood has the fullest system of tenses and allows the speaker to make specific reference to the past, present or future. Much the same as in English, the strictly temporal value of 'past', 'present' and 'future' tenses in Spanish is relative in the sense that only the full context in which a verbal form appears can determine its precise value. For example, 'I am going to Paris tomorrow' immediately refers to the future because of the temporal adverb 'tomorrow'. The same occurs in Spanish with *Mañana voy a París*. There are, however, many cases where usage of a specific tense is not the same in both languages, as will be seen in sections 40–45. Remember too that there is no equivalent in Spanish of the English 'do / does', etc., in negative and interrogative structures:

> I don't like that.
> Do you enjoy sailing?

40 Present indicative

(a) Form

(i) The conjugation of regular and irregular verbs in the present tense is given in Appendixes 2 and 4. Note particularly the verbs that have a stem vowel change in all but the first and second persons plural (e.g. *cerrar*, *contar*, *divertirse*). There are also a number of verbs with irregular first-person singular forms (e.g. *conozco* from *conocer*, *pongo* from *poner*). Any irregularity in the present indicative will also affect the present subjunctive and the imperative.

(ii) The continuous form is constructed with the verb *estar* and the present participle:

> *Está jugando en el jardín.*
> He's playing in the garden.

(b) Uses of the present indicative

(i) As in English, the present simple is used for general truths or habitual actions:

> *La Tierra es el planeta que habitamos.*
> The Earth is the planet on which we live.
>
> *Se levanta a las siete y sale de casa a las ocho.*
> He gets up at seven and leaves home at eight.

(ii) The continuous form may refer to a strict 'now' or, in a wider context, it may be interchangeable with the present simple:

> *Estoy viendo la televisión.*
> I'm watching television.
>
> *Trabaja / Está trabajando en un banco muy importante.*
> He works / He is working in a very important bank.

(iii) The present simple may be used for the future in the same way as the continuous form is used in English:

> *Mañana salgo para Madrid.*
> Tomorrow I'm leaving for Madrid.

(iv) The present is used in Spanish in the type of question where English uses 'shall' to ask somebody's opinion or to make a suggestion:

> *¿Vamos al cine?*
> Shall we go to the pictures?
>
> *¿Abro la ventana?*
> Shall I open the window?

(v) In colloquial registers, it is often used instead of an imperative form and in contexts where the implications may range from downright command to polite request:

> *Te sientas aquí y lo haces ahora mismo.*
> Sit down and do it at once.

¿Me das el periódico?
Could you give me the paper?

(vi) The so-called historic present (i.e. instead of a past form) is used both in literary and colloquial registers to add vividness to a narrative:

En 1558 muere el Emperador en el monasterio de Yuste.
In 1558 the Emperor died at the monastery of Yuste.

Entonces, sin poder aguantar más, lo cojo por el cuello y lo saco de la habitación.
Then, not being able to stand it any more, I got hold of him by the scruff of the neck and took him out of the room.

★ **(vii)** Special attention must be paid to the use of the present simple in Spanish in sentences where English uses a present perfect (continuous) with 'for' or 'since':

Vivo aquí desde hace cinco años.
I have lived / have been living here (for) five years.

Está enfermo desde mayo.
He has been ill since May.

Hace dos meses que está enfermo.
He has been ill for two months.

41 Perfect indicative

This tense is formed with the present indicative of *haber* plus the past participle of the main verb. (See Appendix 1, pages 334–6, for the full conjugation of *haber*.)

(i) The perfect basically coincides with the present perfect in English when referring to something that happened in the more or less recent past, but the consequences or effects of which are still felt in the present:

Hoy he escrito un capítulo de mi novela.
Today I have written one chapter of my novel.

Ha viajado mucho por Italia.
She has travelled in Italy a lot.

(ii) Because the overlap between past and present tends to be nebulous, usage sometimes varies between the perfect and the past simple:

> *Ayer llovió mucho. / Ayer ha llovido mucho.*
> It rained a lot yesterday.
>
> *Esta mañana ha llovido mucho. / Esta mañana llovió mucho.*
> It rained a lot this morning.

In this type of sentence, educated speakers usually prefer the preterite *llovió* for 'yesterday' and *ha llovido* while it is still 'today'. There are regional differences, even in standard Spanish, but if in doubt stick to the perfect for anything that applies to 'today' and to the preterite for anything that applies to 'yesterday'.

(iii) Related to the previous point, note that in questions of the type 'What did you (just) say?' standard Spanish always uses the perfect, *¿Qué has dicho?* In standard registers – as opposed to regional – a preterite used in this type of question cannot refer to 'just now':

> *¿Puedes repetir lo que has dicho?*
> Can you repeat what you said (just now)?
>
> *¿Puedes repetir lo que dijiste?*
> Can you repeat what you said (on that occasion)?

(iv) See section 40b(vii) for the English present perfect in expressions of time with 'for' and 'since'.

42 Imperfect and preterite indicative

(a) Form

(i) The regular endings for these two tenses are:

-AR VERBS		-ER AND -IR VERBS	
IMPERFECT	PRETERITE	IMPERFECT	PRETERITE
-aba	-é	-ía	-í
-abas	-aste	-ías	-iste
-aba	-ó	-ía	-ió
-ábamos	-amos	-íamos	-imos
-abais	-asteis	-íais	-isteis
-aban	-aron	-ían	-ieron

(ii) There is also a group of verbs with irregular preterite stems which have their own set of endings. These are sometimes referred to as 'strong preterites' or *pretéritos graves*. The endings for these verbs are:

-e, -iste, -o, -imos, -isteis, -(i)eron

(See Appendix 4, pages 345–61, for these and other irregular verbs.)

★ **(iii)** Note that the second-person singular of the preterite is the only second-person singular of any conjugation that **does not** end in *-s*. Because of this, an incorrect *-s* is sometimes heard in non-standard speech: X ~~comistes~~ X

★ **(iv)** Irregular preterites will provide the stem for the imperfect subjunctive.

(v) The continuous form of the past is constructed with the verb *estar* in the imperfect with the present participle (Spanish *gerundio*):

Estaban cenando cuando llegué.
They were having supper when I arrived.

(b) Uses of the imperfect and the preterite

The Spanish imperfect and preterite often pose problems for English speakers. The starting-point for a consideration of the two past simples in Spanish is to remember that:

● The imperfect is used for a past event in its duration, while it was happening, and is not concerned with the beginning or the end.

● The preterite, on the other hand, sees the past event as a completed action, something that came to an end.

The following is a summary of the ways in which imperfect and preterite are used.

(i) The imperfect and the preterite often occur in the same sentence in order to state that something *happened* while something else *was going on*. As in English, the action that was going on may appear in a continuous form:

Dormíamos
Estábamos durmiendo } *cuando sonó el teléfono.*
We were asleep when the telephone rang.

★ Note that the continuous form would normally only be found in cases similar to this, where there is an interrupted action. The imperfect tense is the correct form for a description such as 'The sun was shining'. See (ii) below.

(ii) The imperfect is found in descriptions or narrative in the past, since it records something in its duration or development:

> *Era un día lluvioso, hacía viento y hasta los árboles parecían tristes.*
> It was a rainy and windy day, and even the trees looked sad.

(iii) The imperfect is also used in sentences where the idea of repetition is clearly stated or implied. In this type of sentence, English often uses 'used to' or 'would':

> *Iba a la playa todas las mañanas.*
> He used to go to the beach every morning.

> *De pequeña, nunca hacía lo que le decían.*
> As a child, she would never do as she was told.

> *Se levantaba siempre a la misma hora.*
> He always got up at the same time.

(iv) The preterite implies that something came to an end:

> *Tuvimos dos horas para hacerlo.*
> We had two hours in which to do it. (i.e. We did it within two hours and that was all the time we had available.)

Compare:

> *Teníamos dos horas para hacerlo.*
> We had two hours in which to do it. (i.e. That was the prospect in front of us at the time.)

(v) The preterite indicates that something happened at a precise time, whereas the imperfect would indicate that the action had been going on for some time:

> *Lo supe cuando hablé con él por teléfono.*
> I knew (i.e. I found out) when I spoke to him on the telephone.

> *Lo sabía cuando hablé con él por teléfono.*
> I (already) knew when I spoke to him on the telephone.

(vi) The imperfect is used in requests, as a polite way of avoiding the abruptness of a direct present:

> *¿Qué querían ustedes?*
> What would you like? / What can I do for you?
>
> *Quería ver al señor Domínguez.*
> I would like to see Mr Domínguez.

Both the conditional and the imperfect subjunctive might be used in these instances. See sections 45b(iv) and 46a(iii).

43 Pluperfect and past anterior indicative

The pluperfect and the past anterior are formed with the imperfect indicative and the preterite of the auxiliary *haber* (respectively), and the past participle of the main verb.

(i) The pluperfect basically corresponds to the same tense in English; that is, it indicates that something had taken place before something else happened:

> *Cuando llegaron, habíamos terminado de comer.*
> When they arrived, we had finished lunch.

(ii) The past anterior is literary and now rarely used. It also refers to two actions that took place in the past, but refers more precisely to the ending of the one that took place first:

> *Cuando hubimos terminado, nos levantamos de la mesa.*
> < literary >
> When we had finished, we got up from the table.

Although the past anterior is occasionally used by writers who are very sensitive to the nuances of tenses, in contemporary Spanish the pluperfect or even the preterite is used instead. The sentence above would be expressed in either of these two ways:

> *Cuando habíamos terminado, nos levantamos de la mesa.*
> *Cuando terminamos, nos levantamos de la mesa.*

44 Future simple and future perfect indicative

(a) Form

(i) The endings of the future simple are added to the infinitive (in most cases) as follows:

-*AR* VERBS	-*ER* VERBS	-*IR* VERBS
-aré	*-eré*	*-iré*
-arás	*-erás*	*-irás*
-ará	*-erá*	*-irá*
-aremos	*-eremos*	*-iremos*
-aréis	*-eréis*	*-iréis*
-arán	*-erán*	*-irán*

For verbs with irregular stems in the future, see Appendix 4 (page 347). Any irregularity in the future will affect the conditional, too.

(ii) The future perfect is formed with the future simple of *haber* (see Appendix 1, page 335) plus the past participle of the main verb.

(iii) For the use of *ir* plus infinitive to express the English 'going to', see section 48a(ii).

(b) Uses of the future and future perfect

(i) Both of these tenses refer, as their name implies, to future actions or events.

- The future simple tells us that something will take place:

  El parte meteorológico dice que mañana lloverá.
  The weather forecast says that it will rain tomorrow.

  Jaime llegará a las cinco.
  Jaime will arrive at five.

- The future perfect tells us that something will have taken place:

  A las dos y media habré terminado esto.
  At half past two I will have finished this.

  Cuando tú te levantes, yo ya habré salido.
  When you get up, I will already have left.

(ii) The future, especially the simple form, can be used in Spanish to express hypothesis or probability. In this type of sentence, it means the same as the hypothetical 'must' in English:

¿Qué hora es? – Serán alrededor de las cinco.
What's the time? – It must be about five.

Su hija tendrá ahora unos veinte años.
Her daughter must be about twenty now.

(iii) The future is also used to express commands and prohibitions:

El importe se pagará en efectivo.
The amount must be paid in cash.

No me volverás a hablar del tema.
You are not to speak to me about that again.

45 Conditional and conditional perfect

(a) Form

(i) The endings of the conditional are added to the infinitive (in most cases) as follows:

-AR VERBS	-ER VERBS	-IR VERBS
-aría	-ería	-iría
-arías	-erías	-irías
-aría	-ería	-iría
-aríamos	-eríamos	-iríamos
-aríais	-eríais	-iríais
-arían	-erían	-irían

Verbs with irregular future stems have the same irregularity in the conditional. (See Appendix 4, page 347.)

(ii) The conditional perfect form is made with the present conditional of *haber* (see Appendix 1, page 335) plus the past participle of the main verb.

(b) Uses of the conditional and conditional perfect

(i) The conditional expresses the main clause of a hypothesis such as 'If *x* happened, I would . . .'.

Si tuviera mucho dinero, me compraría una villa en el campo.
If I had a lot of money, I would buy myself a house in the country.

★ The imperfect subjunctive, not the conditional perfect, is used in a hypothesis such as 'If *x* had happened, I would have . . .'. See section 46b(v).

(ii) Both the conditional and conditional perfect are used in indirect speech or thought, as in English:

Dijo que iría más tarde.
He said he would go later.

Creí que a estas horas ya lo habría terminado.
I thought that he would have finished it by now.

(iii) In the same way as the future tenses, the conditional is used for hypothesis or probability, but with reference to the past:

Serían las doce cuando empezó el incendio.
It must have been twelve when the fire started.

La última vez que la vi tendría unos diez años.
Last time I saw her she must have been about ten.

(iv) The present conditional is also used in requests as a polite way of avoiding the abruptness of the present:

Querría ver la corbata del escaparate.
I would like to see the tie in the window.

See also sections 42b(vi) and 46a(iii).

(v) An increasing use of the conditional, not accepted as correct Spanish, but common in journalistic reports, is to convey information which is not given as factual but as something that may happen or may have happened:

El Primer Ministro viajaría a los E.E.U.U. en mayo.
The Prime Minister might go to the USA in May.

Durante la reunión se habría decidido el futuro del club.
In the course of the meeting the future of the club may have been decided.

46 The subjunctive

Contrary to English, where the subjunctive is found only in a few set phrases, mainly with the verb 'to be' ('If I were you', 'the powers that be', 'so be it') or in some formal registers ('I demand that he withdraw his claim'), in Spanish the subjunctive is constantly needed in both the written and the spoken language. Although mainly found in subordinate clauses where it signals hypothesis or something that is not yet a real fact, it is also found in a number of contexts where the subjective standpoint of the speaker matters more than the objective reality – and this is the use of the subjunctive that English speakers find most difficult to grasp.

In the sections that follow, the forms and the basic meaning of the various tenses of the subjunctive mood are explained, and the general rules of subjunctive use are summarized. No set of rules or explanations, however, could be sufficiently detailed to cover all possibilities, and it is essential to pay special attention to the nuances of each individual sentence.

(a) Tenses of the subjunctive

(i) Present

(See Appendixes 1 and 4 for the subjunctive forms of *ser*, *estar*, *haber* and *saber*.)

The regular endings of the present subjunctive are:

-AR VERBS	-ER AND -IR VERBS
-e	-a
-es	-as
-e	-a
-emos	-amos
-éis	-áis
-en	-an

★ Remember that irregularities in the present simple will apply here, too.

• The present subjunctive in a subordinate clause usually refers to something in the present or in the future that is regarded as uncertain or which has yet to become a fact:

Espero que llegue antes de las seis.
I hope he comes before six.

No creo que sepa lo ocurrido.
I don't think she knows what has happened.

Cuando te levantes, pon el calentador.
When you get up, switch the heater on.

- It is found in main clauses which express a wish or hesitation:

  ¡Dios salve al Rey!
  God save the King!

  Acaso salga más tarde.
  Perhaps I'll go out later.

- It supplies first- and third-person forms for the imperative (see section 47).

(ii) Perfect

The perfect subjunctive is formed with the present subjunctive of the auxiliary *haber* (see Appendix 1) plus the past participle of the main verb.

Its main use is in subordinate clauses which refer to the possibility that something may or may not have happened, either at some point in the past or at some time in the future:

Confiamos en que haya aprobado los exámenes.
We trust that she will have passed her examinations.

Cuando haya terminado te avisaré.
When I have finished I shall let you know.

(iii) Imperfect

The regular endings of the imperfect subjunctive are added to the stem of the verb.

-AR VERBS	-ER AND -IR VERBS
-ara / -ase	-iera / -iese
-aras / -ases	-ieras / -ieses
-ara / -ase	-iera / -iese
-áramos / -ásemos	-iéramos / -iésemos
-arais / -aseis	-ierais / -ieseis
-aran / -asen	-ieran / -iesen

103

★ Remember that irregularities in the preterite will apply here, too.

• The imperfect subjunctive has two forms. In their strict subjunctive function, these two forms are practically interchangeable, although the -ra form is more common.

• The -ra form is also used as a polite alternative to the present of the verb *querer* when requesting something (see also sections 42b(vi) and 45b(iv)).

> *Quisiera ver blusas de verano.*
> I would like to see some summer blouses.

(iv) Pluperfect

The pluperfect is formed with the imperfect subjunctive of the auxiliary *haber* (see Appendix 1) and the past participle of the main verb.

• The pluperfect is used in subordinate clauses which refer to a past action that took place before another action also in the past. Usually there is an element of doubt, shown here by *No sabía*:

> *No sabía que tu hijo hubiera / hubiese llegado.*
> I did not know that your son had arrived.

(Note that, although in this example the son's arrival is a fact, the subjunctive is more usual than the indicative. This is particularly the case with verbs of saying, thinking or believing used in the negative.)

• The pluperfect subjunctive is sometimes used instead of the conditional perfect, in which case the -ra form is more usual:

> *Hubiera / Habría preferido algo más barato.*
> I would have preferred something cheaper.

(v) Future and future perfect

The forms for both these tenses can be found in Appendix 2, but it is not important to learn them as the future and future perfect subjunctive have disappeared from modern Spanish, except in a few set phrases and some kinds of formal language, especially legal:

> *Sea lo que fuere . . .*
> Be that as it may . . .

Viniere lo que viniere . . .
Come what might . . .

Si hubiere expirado el plazo . . .
Should the deadline have expired . . .

Other tenses of the subjunctive (present for future simple; imperfect for future perfect) are used instead: *Sea lo que sea* . . ., *Venga lo que venga* . . ., *Si hubiera expirado* . . ., etc.

(b) Main uses of the subjunctive

(i) The subjunctive is used in subordinate clauses after verbs that express commands, requests, permission, desires, wishes, etc. These are typical clauses where the subordinate clause indicates something that is not a reality at the time of expression:

Quiero que venga Jaime.
I want Jaime to come.

Le pedimos que lo hiciera.
We asked her to do it.

Diles que no se marchen.
Tell them not to go away.

Prefiero que te quedes conmigo.
I prefer you to stay with me.

Quisiera que no lo mencionaras más.
I would like you not to mention it again.

¿Me permite que fume?
Will you allow me to smoke?

(ii) It is also used with verbs of saying, thinking or believing used in the negative, as well as in any clause which expresses doubt, possibility or uncertainty:

No creo que venga.
I don't think he will come.

Jamás pensaron que pudiera ser cierto.
They never thought that it might be true.

No digo que no me lo crea.
I am not saying that I don't believe it.

Dudo que tenga tanto dinero.
I doubt that he has so much money.

No está claro que se haya recuperado.
It is not clear that she has recovered.

Es posible que vaya el mes próximo.
It is possible that I may go next month.

(iii) The subjunctive is required in a relative clause, when the antecedent is hypothetical or unknown:

Necesitamos un traductor que sepa hebreo.
We need a translator who knows Hebrew.

Los que estén cansados pueden retirarse.
Those who are tired may leave.

Aquí no hay nada que me sirva.
There is nothing here I can use.

(iv) The subjunctive is used after any subordinating word introducing a hypothetical or future event:

Cuando tenga dinero, iré al cine.
When I have some money, I'll go to the cinema.

Note an important contrast between the temporal clause and this conditional clause:

Si tengo dinero, iré al cine.
If I have some money, I'll go to the cinema.

★ Note that *si* never takes a present subjunctive.

(v) The subordinate clause in the construction 'If I had . . ., I would . . .' uses the imperfect subjunctive:

Si tuviera / tuviese dinero, iría al cine.
If I had some money, I would go to the cinema.

• 'If I had . . ., then I would have . . .' is expressed by the pluperfect subjunctive:

$$\textit{Si lo} \left\{ \begin{array}{c} \textit{hubiera} \\ \textit{hubiese} \end{array} \right\} \textit{sabido, no} \left\{ \begin{array}{c} \textit{hubiera} \\ \textit{hubiese} \end{array} \right\} \textit{ido.}$$

If I had known, I would not have gone.

However, colloquial registers often avoid these by substituting the present indicative in both clauses:

Si lo sé, no voy. < coll. >

(vi) The subjunctive is normally used after impersonal expressions, except in those cases where the reality of a fact is categorically asserted:

El hecho de que sea rico no es ninguna excusa.
The fact that he is rich is no excuse.

Fue una lástima que se rompiera la pierna.
It was a shame that she broke her leg.

Es importante que hables con él.
It is important that you talk to him.

No era necesario que os molestarais.
It wasn't necessary for you to have bothered.

Hace falta que te vayas.
You should go.

- Compare the uncertainty of a sentence such as:

No era cierto que hubiesen fracasado.
It was not definite that they had failed.

with the certainty of:

Lo cierto es que habían fracasado.
The fact is that they had failed.

(vii) A number of conjunctions and conjunctive phrases always take the subjunctive. Whatever the precise meaning of these conjunctions, what they have in common is that they express something that is not a reality:

Lo hice para que estés contenta.
I did it so that you would be happy.

Se enfadó sin que nadie le hubiera dicho nada.
He got angry without anyone having said anything to him.

Con tal de que todo acabe bien, no importa.
Provided that all's well in the end, it doesn't matter.

Era como si hubiese vuelto a la niñez.
It was as if he had gone back to his childhood.

Me voy antes de que llueva.
I'm leaving before it rains.

No es justo que todavía estés sin trabajo.
It is not fair that you are still without a job.

Aunque lo ame, lo trata muy mal.
Although she loves him, she treats him very badly.

Note that conjunctive forms that refer to statements of fact still tend to use the subjunctive.

(viii) Finally, although the subjunctive appears mainly in subordinate clauses, it also occurs in main clauses expressing wishes, doubt or amazement:

¡(Que) Dios nos bendiga! God bless us!

¡Viva España! Long live Spain!

Acaso llueva. Perhaps it will rain.

¡Quién lo hubiera pensado! Who would have thought it!

47 The imperative

(i) There are distinct imperative forms for the second person singular and plural. These are added to the stem, e.g. *canta, comed,* and are as follows:

-AR VERBS	-ER VERBS	-IR VERBS
-a	*-e*	*-e*
-ad	*-ed*	*-id*

There are also some irregular forms. (See the Appendixes.)

(ii) The second-person plural form loses its final *-d* when the reflexive pronoun *-os* is added to it, and similarly the first-person plural loses its final *-s* when *nos* is added to it:

Sentaos aquí.
Sit down here.

Sentémonos aquí.
Let's sit down here.

(iii) However, to address a first or a third person (including *Vd. / Vds.*) for some form of command, request or exhortation, the forms of the present subjunctive are used:

Hablemos con propiedad.
Let us speak with propriety.

Vaya usted ahora mismo.
Go at once.

This is the usual form in public notices (i.e. addressing *Vd. / Vds.*).

- Third-person forms, other than *Vd. / Vds.*, are normally preceded by an introductory *que*:

  Que se marche.
  Let him go away. (i.e. 'He is to go away.')

  Que hagan lo que quieran.
  Let them do whatever they like. (i.e. 'They may do as they please.')

(iv) For the negative imperative, or prohibition, the present subjunctive forms are used for all persons:

  No contestes. Do not answer.

  No habléis tanto. Don't talk so much.

(v) In colloquial registers, the *-d* of the second-person plural is replaced by *-r* with the result that the infinitive of the verb seems to be used instead of the imperative form:

  Venir aquí < coll. > (for *Venid*) Come here.

NO ACERCARSE
AL   BARCO
PELIGRO

Comeros esto. < coll. > (for *Comeos*) Eat this up.

This infinitive for the imperative is very frequent in public notices of the type 'Pull', 'Push', 'Ring the bell' or prohibitions.

It is increasingly found in written instructions such as recipes.

COCINA PRACTICA • VERANO 92
Viernes, 7 de agosto
Gazpachuelo

Ingredientes: 1,5 kg. de tomates maduros; 1 cebolla; 4 cucharadas de aceite; 2 cucharadas de vinagre; orégano; tomillo; sal.

Elaboración: Poner en un recipiente de cristal los tomates partidos en trozos pequeños, añadir la cebolla picada, el tomillo, el orégano, el aceite, el vinagre y la sal. Dejar enfriar en el frigorífico por lo menos 2 horas. Sacar y pasar por el pasapurés o chino. Si quedara algo espeso, añadir agua o hielo.

Presentación: Servir muy frío en tazas de consomé o en cuencos.

Un truco útil: Puede tritutarse con la batidora.

Preparado para: Seis personas.

Grado de dificultad: Sencillo *

48 Non-finite forms of the verb

A defining characteristic of the non-personal forms of the verb is that they function both as a verb and as another part of speech. Thus, the infinitive can work as a noun, the gerund as an adverb (and, controversially, as an adjective), and the past participle as an adjective.

(a) The infinitive

The infinitive, in its simple form, is the name of the verb. As we have seen, there are three conjugations in Spanish, characterized by the endings *-ar, -er* and *-ir*. There is also a perfect infinitive, formed with the infinitive *haber* and the past participle of the main verb, which expresses the idea of the verb as completed: *haber comido* to have eaten. The infinitive can function as either a verb or a noun.

(i) Its value as a verb can be seen in certain constructions, for example, when it is preceded by a preposition or when it is governed by another verb:

> *Queremos dormir.*
> We want to sleep.

> *Vinieron a comer.*
> They came to lunch.

> *papel de / para escribir* writing paper

★ Remember that, in Spanish, prepositions always take an infinitive, whereas in English they are followed by a present participle:

> *Al cruzar la calle, se me cayó un guante.*
> In crossing the street, I dropped a glove.

> *Esto es por haber sido tan amable.*
> This is for having been so kind.

(ii) English 'going to' is expressed by the verb *ir a* plus infinitive:

> *Van a llamar mañana.*
> They are going to call tomorrow.

> *Voy a decírselo.*
> I'm going to tell her.

111

(iii) As a noun, the infinitive has the same syntactical value as any other noun and it corresponds to the English gerund:

Nadar es muy sano.
Swimming is very healthy.

Correr no servirá de nada.
Running will be no good.

The infinitive as a noun is always masculine. (For the use of the article with the infinitive see section 5g(ii). See section 30b(v) for the position of accompanying object pronouns.)

(b) The gerund

The gerund (Spanish *gerundio*) is the non-finite form of the verb that can either have a verbal function or act as a modifier of another verb. Its endings are *-ando*, for the first conjugation, and *-iendo* for the other two. There is also a compound form made with *habiendo* and the past participle of the main verb: *habiendo comido* having eaten. Remember that, whereas English prepositions govern a present participle, in Spanish, prepositions govern an infinitive (see section a(i) above).

(i) As a verb, the gerund is used with *estar* in continuous forms, the same as the present participle in English:

Estuvimos nadando durante dos horas.
We were swimming for two hours.

★ **(ii)** Pay special attention to the verbs *seguir* and *continuar*, which are followed by a gerund:

Continué durmiendo un poco más.
I went on sleeping a little more.

Me dijo que siguiera escribiendo.
He told me to go on writing.

★ **(iii)** The Spanish gerund can be a useful translation of English verbs of movement used with a preposition. In this case, the English preposition is translated by an equivalent Spanish verb and the English verb by a Spanish gerund:

Cruzó el río nadando.
He swam across the river.

Salieron corriendo de la casa.
They ran out of the house.

(iv) The Spanish gerund is often found modifying or complementing another verb – which is another way of saying that it works as an adverb (*salió corriendo, llegó fumando,* etc.). In practice, this use of the gerund poses a number of problems, which we shall summarize by referring to its function as an adverb and to its possible adjectival values.

As a modifier of another verb, the traditional view is that both actions must be simultaneous:

Se levantó bostezando.
He got up yawning.

While some people would see that view as too narrow, it is generally agreed that the gerund is incorrect when there is a marked interval between both actions. Thus this sentence is an incorrect use of the gerund for *y murió* or *donde murió*:

~~**X** Fue llevado al hospital, muriendo pocos días después.~~ **X**
He was taken to hospital, dying a few days later.

Even more complicated problems arise with the increasing use of the gerund as an adjective – i.e. qualifying a noun. This use is rejected by careful speakers, although the odd case does exist where it is acceptable. The standard example is the title of a picture:

Napoleón hablando con sus generales
Napoleon talking to his generals

The problem seems to be that some combinations of noun and gerund sound unacceptable to practically all speakers, some are more or less controversial, and some do not sound particularly incorrect. The subject is too complex to develop at length here, but in case of doubt it is better to use a relative clause with *que*:

cajas que contenían naranjas
~~**X** cajas conteniendo naranjas.~~ **X**
boxes containing oranges

However, languages evolve and constant pressure from other languages – mainly English – may ultimately prove more effective than the recommendations of any grammar book!

(c) The past participle

The regular endings of the past participle in Spanish are *-ado*, for the first conjugation, and *-ido* for the other two: *hablado, comido, vivido*. The functions of the past participle can be verbal and adjectival.

(i) In its verbal function, it is invariable and, with the simple tenses of the auxiliary *haber*, it is used to form compound tenses (see sections 41 and 43–5): *he hablado, habían comido, habremos vivido*, etc.

(ii) As an adjective it is used with nouns like any normal adjective:

Llegaron muy cansadas.
They arrived very tired.

paquetes pesados heavy parcels
precios elevados high prices

(iii) Note that Spanish uses past participles to refer to a person's position in cases where English uses present participles:

Estaba sentada.
She was sitting.

Permanecieron arrodillados.
They remained kneeling.

Estaba apoyado contra la pared.
He was leaning against the wall.

(iv) With the verb *ser*, it is used for passive constructions (see section 51a).

(v) Instead of the regular endings *-ado* and *-ido*, some verbs have an irregular past participle in *-cho*, *-to* or *-so*, such as *hecho* (from *hacer* to make, to do), *escrito* (from *escribir* to write), *impreso* (from *imprimir* to print). A fairly large number have two participles, one regular and one irregular, in which case the regular form is used for the compound tenses of the verb and the irregular form is used as an adjective. Here are some examples:

Los niños se han despertado a las siete.
The children woke up at seven (this morning).

Los niños están despiertos desde las siete.
The children have been awake since seven.

El sacerdote ha bendecido a los fieles.
The priest has blessed the faithful.

El sacerdote les echó agua bendita.
The priest sprinkled them with holy water (literally: blessed water).

These participles are a rather complex area. In some cases, the regular form is giving way to the irregular, even in compound tenses; thus, the regular *freído* and *imprimido*, for example, are still correct but seldom used:

He frito (freído) los dos huevos que quedaban.
I have fried the two eggs that were left.

Se han impreso (imprimido) mil ejemplares.
A thousand copies have been printed.

(d) The historic present participle

Originating from the historical present participle, which had a verbal value much the same as the English '-ing' in cases like 'a film lasting two hours', there are a number of words ending in *-ante, -ente* or *-iente* that act mainly as nouns or adjectives, but also as adverbs, prepositions or conjunctions. Here are a few examples of the different grammatical categories:

Todavía existen casas que no tienen agua corriente.
There are houses which still haven't got running water.

No nos bañamos porque había una corriente muy fuerte.
We didn't go for a swim because there was a strong current.

Durmió durante dos horas.
He slept for two hours.

Hablaba con voz doliente.
She was speaking in a plaintive voice.

Se sentía mal; no obstante, se levantó.
He felt ill; nevertheless, he got up.

(See also section 13a(iii) on the question of the feminine of nouns ending in *-ante, -(i)ente.*)

49 Reflexive verbs

A reflexive verb shows that the subject does something to himself or herself. In English, this is usually shown by means of the pronouns 'myself', 'yourself', etc. In Spanish, a reflexive verb always has the pronouns *me, te, se, nos, os, se*. See section 30d for the use of these pronouns, and Appendix 3 for the full conjugation of *lavarse* to wash oneself, as a model of a reflexive verb.

(i) See section 30b(v) for object pronouns placed after the verb. Any reflexive pronouns attached to an infinitive or a gerund will of course vary depending on the subject:

Tenéis que lavaros.
You must wash yourselves.

(ii) Note that a reflexive verb in Spanish is not necessarily reflexive in English:

Me levanto a las siete.
I get up at seven.

Se quitó la chaqueta.
He took his coat off.

Se fugaron a medianoche.
They ran away at midnight.

arrepentirse de los pecados to repent of one's sins

(iii) See section 51b for the use of the reflexive passive:

Se habla inglés. English spoken here.

(iv) Finally, remember that a verb in the reflexive form may acquire different connotations or even have a different meaning from the non-reflexive form (see section 30d(v)).

50 Impersonal and defective verbs

(a) Impersonal verbs

(i) Spanish grammar books usually differentiate between *verbos impersonales* and *verbos unipersonales*. Any verb used in the third-person plural when the subject is unknown or irrelevant belongs to the first category:

> *Llaman a la puerta.*
> There is somebody at the door.
>
> *No dejan entrar a nadie.*
> Nobody is allowed in.

(ii) 'Unipersonal' verbs are usually those which express natural phenomena and are therefore used only in the third-person singular:

> *amanecer* to dawn
> *anochecer* to grow dark
> *llover* to rain
> *nevar* to snow
> *tronar* to thunder

• If they are used figuratively, they become personal verbs:

> *Su voz tronaba por los pasillos.*
> His voice thundered along the corridors.

(iii) For the use of *se* in impersonal statements, see section 51b on the reflexive passive.

(b) Defective verbs

(i) Defective verbs are those which, for a number of reasons – usually because of their meaning, or because of phonetic complexities – are used only in some persons or tenses. Nearly all of them belong to the literary register. Examples are:

> *abolir* to abolish < literary >
> *atañer* to behove < literary >
> *compungir* to cause or feel compunction < literary >
> *placer* to please < literary >

117

(ii) An important example is *soler* used to or to ... usually. It can be used in all persons, but because of its meaning is generally found only in the present or the imperfect:

Solemos ir con ellos al colegio.
We usually go to school with them.

Solían irse de vacaciones en agosto.
They used to go on holiday in August.

(iii) See section 78 for the use of *gustar* to please, used in Spanish for the English 'I like', etc.

51 The passive voice

(a) Passive form of verbs

As in English, the passive form is made with the verb *ser* to be and the past participle of the main verb, which in Spanish will agree in gender and number with the passive subject:

El fugitivo fue visto por última vez cerca del río.
The runaway was last seen near the river.

Las facturas serán pagadas a su debido tiempo.
The invoices will be paid in due course.

While it is true that the passive form is less used in Spanish than in English, it is nevertheless far from rare, especially in the written language, and, if anything, all evidence seems to indicate that this is another grammatical area where the pressure from English is on the increase. The most serious grammatical problem is that some Spanish verbs cannot take a passive construction in any register, and therefore you should avoid this construction unless absolutely sure that it is correct.

(b) Reflexive passive

(i) The passive form is less used in Spanish than in English, and an impersonal construction with *se*, traditionally known as *pasiva refleja* ('reflexive passive') is very common:

Se abrieron las puertas.
The doors were opened.

Se repartieron muchos premios.
Many prizes were given out.

Se habla inglés. English spoken (i.e. English is spoken here).

(ii) The general rule of verb agreement is that, if the passive subject does not refer to human beings, the verb agrees in number with it:

Se vende vino. Wine sold.

Se venden libros. Books sold.

But, if the passive subject does refer to human beings, the verb is used in the singular followed by the personal preposition *a*:

Se llamó a Pedro. Pedro was called.

Se llamó a los soldados. The soldiers were called in.

(iii) There is a strong tendency, however, to use the verb in the singular even with a plural subject (e.g. *Se vende libros*). In cases like this, when the passive subject comes immediately after the verb, the form is not considered correct Spanish, but is very common indeed. The question of agreement becomes more delicate when there are other words between the verb and the subject, or when the verb may be considered impersonal; it seems safe to say that, on the whole, the greater the distance between the verb and the subject, the less likely it is that the lack of agreement will be noticed:

Se tiene(n) que vender estos libros más baratos.
These books have to be sold cheaper.

Se necesita(n), con la mayor urgencia posible y para empezar en seguida, carpinteros, yeseros y pintores.
Wanted as soon as possible, to start at once, joiners, plasterers and decorators.

119

(iv) In the reflexive for passive construction, pronouns instead of nouns are also used:

> *¿Por qué no se le avisó?*
> Why wasn't he told?
>
> *Se os vio de madrugada.*
> You were seen in the early hours.

• In this type of sentence, contemporary Spanish is almost invariably *leísta, le* and *les* being used for the accusative masculine of both people and things:

> *Se le encuentra mucho en el sur de España.*
> It is found abundantly in the south of Spain.

(v) This reflexive passive construction is also used for impersonal statements. In these sentences, it has the same value as a third person plural and translates English forms like 'they', 'one', 'you' or a passive construction:

> *Se dice* ⎫
> *Dicen* ⎭ *que habrá una guerra.*
>
> It is said ⎫
> They say ⎭ that there will be a war.
>
> *¿Se puede tocar?* Can one touch it?
>
> *Nunca se sabe lo que puede pasar.*
> One never knows ⎫
> You never know ⎭ what may happen.

• In the imperative form, it is also the traditional way of stating commands or instructions where English uses a personal form:

> *Coméntese este tema.*
> Discuss this subject.
>
> *Para más detalles, véase el capítulo XII.*
> For further details, see chapter XII.

The infinitive (see section 48a) is often used in these constructions, especially in contexts where a whole set of instructions is given, but it is not considered correct in speech.

★ **(vi)** Care must be taken not to leave an impersonal sentence without an impersonal subject (a mistake often made by English speakers of Spanish when they try to use a reflexive verb impersonally). The point to remember is that, if the verb is reflexive, the *se* is an intrinsic part of it and the impersonal subject has to be expressed by some other means – usually by *uno*:

> X Para hacer bien las cosas, se tiene que informar con antelación. X
> Para hacer bien las cosas, uno se tiene que informar con antelación.
> In order to do things well, one should be well informed
> beforehand. (i.e. *one* has to inform *oneself*)

With other verbs, where *se* is not an intrinsic part of the infinitive, the choice between *se* and *uno* in an impersonal sentence is possible and correct:

> A la vista de tanta miseria, $\left\{ \begin{array}{l} se \\ uno \end{array} \right\}$ comprende que a veces la
> gente robe.
> Seeing such poverty, you can understand that people sometimes
> steal.

PREPOSITIONS

52 Function of prepositions

Prepositions are link words joining nouns, adjectives or verbs to another word. From a syntactical point of view, their function is very similar in English and Spanish, the most obvious difference being that in Spanish – as mentioned in section 31 – it is not possible to end a relative clause with a preposition. Thus, sentences like 'Where are you from?' or the clause 'the village they live in' have to be expressed in Spanish as 'From where are you?' and 'the village in which they live'. The main problem, however, is that prepositions in any language are often seen as very idiosyncratic, if not totally illogical, when looked at from the point of view of another language.

Many prepositions are very common and, through constant wear and tear, they have come to cover a wide range of syntactic / semantic relationships between words. It is therefore impossible to give the 'translation' into Spanish of prepositions such as 'to', 'on', 'with', etc., or into English of prepositions such as *a, de, por*, etc., unless they are given within a specific context. The following section lists the main Spanish prepositions in alphabetical order, with some examples of their use. Sections 54–6 look at expressions of time and place, prepositional phrases and prepositions governing adjectives and verbs.

53 Main Spanish prepositions before nouns

a at / to

(i) It expresses the idea of motion, beginning or purpose:

Vamos a Sevilla. We are going to Seville.

Se puso a llover. It started to rain.

He venido a verte. I have come to see you.

(ii) Time, distance, price or rate:

a las cinco at five o'clock

a diez kilómetros de Madrid (at) ten kilometres from Madrid

a sesenta pesetas el kilo at sixty pesetas a kilo

a cien kilómetros por hora at a hundred kilometres an hour

(iii) With the masculine singular of the definite article and an infinitive following, it translates the English 'on -ing':

al cruzar la calle on crossing the road

al salir del restaurante on coming out of the restaurant

(iv) It is used in many adverbial phrases of manner:

Lo haré a tu gusto.

I shall do it as you like it.

A lo lejos se veía brillar el río.

In the distance the river could be seen glistening.

★ **(v)** An important feature of Spanish syntax is the 'personal *a*', the use of this preposition before a personal direct object:

Vimos a mi primo Juan.

We saw my cousin Juan.

No asustes a los niños.

Don't frighten the children.

• Grammarians usually explain that the presence or the absence of this personal *a* establishes the difference between referring to specific individuals or speaking in general. Thus:

Busco un cocinero.

I am looking for a cook. (implying that I haven't got one)

while *Busco a un cocinero* implies that I am looking for one already known to me. This is a controversial issue since in practice the rule may or may not apply, especially if the sentence makes the meaning clear by other means.

• Apart from the occasional verb which does not usually take a personal *a* (*tienen un hijo* they have a son), or where a semantic

123

difference may exist (*quiere un camarero / quiere a un camarero* she wants a waiter / she loves a waiter), it is generally true that a personal direct object is usually preceded by the personal *a*. This preposition is also often used when the object is not a person. It applies particularly with animals and with more or less personified objects, but it also happens in many cases where the only possible explanation is an instinctive desire, on the part of the speaker, to leave no doubt as to which is the subject and which is the object of the sentence – an instinct undoubtedly having its roots in the flexibility of word order in Spanish. The following are a few examples of sentences where a 'personal *a*' is likely to be found, although it is superfluous according to strict grammar:

> *Los tiburones atacaron a las débiles embarcaciones.*
> The sharks attacked the fragile vessels.

> *Se trata de un estilo que individualiza a toda una época.*
> This is a style which characterizes a whole age.

> *Nuestra civilización está destruyendo al medio ambiente.*
> Our civilization is destroying the environment.

• On the other hand, it is also possible to omit the personal *a* deliberately, to avoid ambiguity. A typical example is the verb *presentar* to introduce, since a sentence such as *Juan presentó a Miguel a María* does not tell us who is introduced to whom. By saying *Juan presentó Miguel a María*, there is no doubt that the person introduced is *Miguel.*

ante before

This is a fairly literary preposition which means 'before' in the sense of 'in front of', and it can be used in a literal or in a figurative sense:

> *Compareció ante el juez.*
> He appeared before the judge.

> *Ante tal disparate, no supo qué decir.*
> Faced with such nonsense, he didn't know what to say.

• Note:

> *ante todo* above all

bajo under / below

This refers to position and, although it can be used in the physical sense, its most frequent use is figuratively to refer to temperature or to subordination:

Anduvieron bajo la noche estrellada.
They walked under the starry sky.

cinco grados bajo cero five degrees below zero
España bajo el régimen franquista Spain under the Franco regime

con with

(i) In general terms, this is the English 'with':

Vino con su hermano.
She came with her brother.

¿Con qué abro esto?
What can I open this with?

(ii) Followed by an infinitive, or by *que* and the finite form of a verb, it expresses condition or requirement:

Con llegar antes de la una, hay tiempo de sobras.
Provided we arrive before one o'clock, there is plenty of time.

Con que me des (subj.) un poco de fruta, no quiero nada más.
If you give me a little fruit, I don't want anything else.

(iii) In some cases it is used to convey the idea of attitude towards people or things:

Es muy amable con sus vecinos.
He is very kind towards his neighbours.

Con la limpieza es muy estricto.
He is very strict when it comes to cleanliness.

(iv) With some verbs or adjectives it indicates state or condition:

Anda muy preocupado con los exámenes.
He is very worried about his examinations.

Está con fiebre. She has got a temperature.

contra against

> *El domingo que viene juegan contra el Atlético Madrid.*
> Next Sunday they are playing against Atlético Madrid.
>
> *Apoyó la bicicleta contra la pared.*
> She leaned her bicycle against the wall.

de of / about

(i) This expresses the idea of possession given in English by 'of' or the apostrophe 's / s':

> *los libros del profesor* the teacher's books
> *la fuerza del viento* the force of the wind

(ii) Spanish uses *de* in adjectival phrases which express 'matter', 'content' or 'origin', and which English tends to express by an adjectival noun. This construction also marks category:

> *un reloj de oro* a gold watch
> *un vaso de leche* a glass of milk
> *vino de La Rioja* Rioja wine
> *el agente de seguros* the insurance broker

(iii) *De* also appears with some verbs, in the sense of 'about', 'concerning':

> *Habló de sus últimos viajes.*
> He talked about his last trips.
>
> *Vengo a quejarme de lo ocurrido.*
> I have come to complain about what has happened.

★ **(iv)** *De* is sometimes **omitted** in colloquial speech after verbs such as *olvidarse de*, 'to forget', or *acordarse de*, 'to remember', when followed by *que*:

> *No te olvides (de) que tienes que madrugar.*
> Don't forget (that) you have to get up early.

> *Acuérdate (de) que hoy llega tu tío.*
> Remember (that) your uncle is coming today.

● Occasionally this is found even when a noun, not a clause, follows:

> *Me he olvidado (de) las llaves.*
> I have forgotten my keys.

(v) Followed by an infinitive, *de* expresses condition:

> *De venir Juan, avíseme.*
> If Juan comes, let me know.

(vi) *De* is used in comparisons before numerals and instead of *que* if a clause follows:

> *Había más de cien personas.*
> More than a hundred people were there.

> *Ganamos más de lo que habíamos esperado.*
> We earned more than we had expected.

(vii) *De* is used in superlative sentences that use 'in' in English:

> *el mejor del mundo* the best in the world

(viii) To refer to the colour or the 'meaning' of the clothes someone is wearing:

> *La novia iba vestida de blanco.*
> The bride was dressed in white.

> *Apareció vestido de bombero.*
> He turned up dressed as a fireman.

(ix) *De* is also found between some adjectives and infinitives:

> *Esto es difícil de creer.*
> This is difficult to believe.

> *una medicina agradable de tomar* a medicine pleasant to take
> *fácil de contentar* easy to please

★ • Note that *de* is not used if the infinitive governs another word:

> *Este problema es difícil de resolver.*
> This problem is difficult to solve.

but:

> *Es difícil resolver este problema.*
> It is difficult to solve this problem.

(x) In literary style, *de* is sometimes found, instead of the usual *por*, before the passive agent:

> *querido de todos* < literary > loved by everybody
> *conocido de todo el mundo* < literary > known by everybody

desde from / since

This is basically a more emphatic form of *de* to express distance or motion and it is also used in time contexts to mean 'from' or 'since':

> *Desde su punto de vista todo es fácil.*
> From his point of view everything is easy.

> *Desde Valencia viajamos en coche.*
> From Valencia we travelled by car.

> *Desde 1492 las cosas han cambiado mucho.*
> Since 1492 things have changed a lot.

• *Desde . . . hasta* is a little more emphatic than *de . . . a*:

> *Estuvieron en Roma* $\begin{Bmatrix} desde\ el \\ del \end{Bmatrix}$ 6 $\begin{Bmatrix} hasta\ el \\ al \end{Bmatrix}$ 11.
> They were in Rome from the 6th to the 11th.

(The usual combinations are either *desde . . . hasta*, or *de . . . a*, but both *desde . . . a* and *de . . . hasta* also occur.)

después after

> *Después de él, voy yo.* I'm after him.

durante for / during

This refers to a specified period of time seen in its duration – 'while it lasts' – and, in this context, it is usually preferred to *por*, which can also be used when the chronological reference is more vague (cf. *por* below):

> *durante la guerra* during the war (i.e. 'while it lasted')

Habló durante quince minutos.
He spoke for fifteen minutes.

en in / on / at

(i) The exact translation of *en* depends on the context. Here are some examples:

con las manos en los bolsillos with his hands in his pockets

Entró en el dormitorio.
He went into the bedroom.

Se pasa horas en la playa.
She spends hours on the beach.

En aquella ocasión tuvo suerte.
On that occasion he was lucky.

Estará en el colegio hasta las doce.
He will be at school until twelve.

(ii) In expressions of time, note the difference between sentences such as *Lo haré en tres días* and *Lo haré dentro de tres días*, where the former tells us *how long* it will take me to do it, but not *when* I shall do it, while the latter tells us *when* I shall do it, but not *how long* it will take me to get it done. Note, also, that *al cabo de* or *después de* is used in the past instead of *dentro de*:

Dentro de tres días iremos a Barcelona.
In three days we shall go to Barcelona.

Primero estuvimos en Barcelona y $\left\{ \begin{array}{l} \textit{después de} \\ \textit{al cabo de} \end{array} \right\}$ *dos días*
fuimos a Mallorca.
First we went to Barcelona and two days later we went to Majorca.

entre between / among

The uses of *entre* can be divided between those cases where it translates 'between' or 'among', and cases where a different translation is required:

(i) 'between / among':

La niña estaba sentada entre su padre y su madre.
The little girl was sitting between her mother and father.

Entre los dos, podéis hacerlo en una hora.
Between the two of you, you can get it done in an hour.

129

Entre los pueblos primitivos no se conocía esta enfermedad.
Among primitive people, this disease was unknown.

Vamos a dividirlo entre todos nosotros.
Let us share it among all of us.

(ii) Other possibilities:

'¿Habrá otro – entre sí decia – más pobre y triste que yo?'
(Calderón)
'Can there be anyone else', he said to himself, 'poorer and more wretched than me?'

El ejército avanzaba entre las sombras.
The army was moving forward in the dark.

Estos dos colores se combinan muy bien entre sí.
These two colours go very well together.

Entre el calor y las moscas, estoy harto.
What with the heat and the flies, I'm fed up.

hacia   towards / about / around

(i) 'Towards', meaning direction:

Cuando lo vimos, iba hacia el parque.
When we saw him, he was going towards the park.

Esto queda hacia Almería.
This place is in the Almería region. (i.e. 'going towards Almería')

(ii) 'About' or 'around', in time phrases:

Serían hacia las tres de la tarde.
It must have been around three in the afternoon.

hasta   as far as / including

(i) 'As far as', for distance:

Vamos hasta la piscina.
Let's go as far as the swimming pool.

(ii) 'Until', for time:

Nos quedaremos hasta el domingo.
We shall stay until Sunday.

(iii) 'Up to', for quantity:

Este puede contener hasta veinticinco.
This one can take up to twenty-five.

(iv) 'Even', 'including':

Hasta los niños lo saben.
Even little children know it.

Se baña hasta en invierno.
He goes for a swim even in winter.

para and *por* for

★ These two prepositions are dealt with together because they are one of the traditional stumbling blocks in Spanish. In general terms, *para* indicates purpose or destination, while *por* indicates case or reason – which accounts for the fact that both may translate 'for' – but the difference often becomes tenuous or may practically disappear. Another difficulty is that there are cases where an English speaker feels that something is done 'for the benefit of' somebody else (*para*), whereas a Spanish speaker feels, rather, that it is done 'because of' (*por*) somebody else. However, in any given case, there is only one possible choice of prepositions.

para

(i) Purpose, destination:

Esto es para ti.
This is for you.

He venido para verte.
I have come (in order) to see you.

¿Para qué es esto?
What is this for?

El alcohol es malo para el hígado.
Alcohol is bad for your liver.

(ii) In the following expressions of time:

¿Podría hacerlo para el lunes?
Could you do it for Monday?

Para las seis, ya estaremos en casa.
We'll be home by six o'clock.

Quisiera una habitación para tres noches.
I would like a room for three nights.

Lo dejaremos para el año que viene.
We shall leave it for / until next year.

(iii) To translate 'for' when it means 'taking into account':

Hace mucho calor para diciembre.
For December it is very hot.

(iv) With *estar*, to mean that something is about to happen:

El tren está para salir. The train is about to leave.

See also below, for *estar por / estar para.*

por

(i) To refer to time and place, usually in a more general or vague manner than other prepositions:

Te veré por la mañana.
I shall see you in the morning.

Por aquella época ya había terminado sus estudios.
By then she had finished her studies.

Viajaron por Italia y Francia.
They travelled through Italy and France.

Paseaban por el jardín.
They were strolling in the garden.

Tendremos que entrar por la ventana.
We shall have to get in through the window.

El hotel queda por el centro.
The hotel is somewhere in the centre.

(ii) With the idea of exchange or equivalence:

Le doy mil pesetas por ese libro.
I'll give you a thousand pesetas for that book.

Gracias por el regalo.
Thank you for the present.

Preséntate tú por mí.
You go instead of me.

por ejemplo for example

(iii) With prices, measures and rates in general:

Consiguió un contrato por diez millones de pesetas.
He managed to get a contract worth ten million pesetas.

Esto se vende por litros.
This is sold by the litre.

El coche iba a 180 km por hora.
The car was travelling at 180 km per hour.

dos veces por semana twice a week
diez por ciento ten per cent

(iv) To show the means by which something is done:

por escrito in writing

Le avisaron por teléfono.
He was told over the telephone.

(v) To translate 'by' in passive constructions:

El cuadro había sido pintado por su abuelo.
The picture had been painted by his grandfather.

(vi) To indicate that something is still pending or has not taken place:

¿Les queda algún piso por alquilar?
Have you got any flats to let?

Eso está aún por descubrir.
That hasn't been discovered yet.

(vii) Cause:

cerrado por vacaciones closed on account of holidays

No podía dormir por el ruido.
She could not sleep for (because of) the noise.

Por eso te lo dije.
That's why I told you.

(viii) Purpose:

Lo he hecho por ti.
I have done it for you.

Hay un señor que pregunta por usted.
There is a gentleman asking to see you.

Ha ido (a) por vino.
He has gone to get some wine.

• The construction *a por*, instead of the simple *por*, is an old bone of contention in Spanish. The traditional view has been that it is incorrect, but many reliable linguists and good writers now defend it as a correct construction. Moreover, in some cases the presence or the absence of the *a* may, in fact, alter the meaning:

> *Vine a por ti.* I came to fetch you.
>
> *Vine por ti.* I came because of you.

• On the question of *para / por* expressing 'cause' and 'purpose', see also below, 'Some contrasts between *para* and *por*'.

(ix) Followed by an adjective or adverb plus *que*, *por* is used in concessive sentences:

> *Por mucho que estudies, no aprobarás.*
> However much you (may) study, you will not pass.

Some contrasts between *para* and *por*

• *Estar para / estar por*

Care is needed with *estar* and these two prepositions. First of all, as has been seen, *estar por* means that something still hasn't happened or been done, and *estar para* means that something is about to take place:

> *Este problema aún está por resolver.*
> This problem is still to be solved.
>
> *Ya estaba para irme, cuando sonó el teléfono.*
> I was about to leave, when the telephone rang.

On the other hand, these combinations may be found with a different meaning. When *estar por* has a personal subject and a personal object, the meaning is 'in favour of':

> *Yo estoy por Jaime.* I am for Jaime.

The meaning 'in favour of' also applies when the object is not personal:

> *Yo estoy por la subida.* I am for the increase.

If the subject is a person and an infinitive follows, the meaning may be rather like the English 'to have a mind to' or 'to have all but done something':

> *Estuve por darle con la puerta en las narices.*
> I had a mind to slam the door in his face.

In the case of *estar para*, very often the expression *estar a punto de* is used instead, probably because *estar para* is often used in two colloquial expressions:

Está para que lo aten / para que lo encierren.
He's as mad as a hatter.

Está para que lo maten / para matarlo.
(This is said of an actor whose performance was abysmal.)

- Cause and purpose

These two aspects cause the greatest confusion for English speakers. As was said at the beginning, *por* basically indicates cause or reason – i.e. looks backwards – while *para* indicates purpose or destination – i.e. looks forwards. This is usually clear when *por* can be seen to mean 'because of' and *para* can be seen to point towards the recipient of something or to mean 'in order to'. In some cases that seem to contradict the rule, Spanish interprets an action as being motived *by somebody*, rather than being directed *towards somebody*, and hence the use of *por*. The most obvious cases occur with verbs of 'doing' something for the sake of somebody else, or on somebody else's behalf:

Lo he hecho por ti.
I have done / I did it for you.

Murieron por la patria.
They died for their country.

★ Note the difference in meaning with the verb *hacer*:

> *Esto lo he hecho **por** ti.*
> I have done this for you. (i.e. 'because of')
>
> *Esto lo he hecho **para** ti.*
> I have made this for you.

The guiding rule in all this is that when the meaning is 'to do something for the sake of somebody', the only option is *por*.

según according to

> *Según me han dicho, está en París.*
> According to what I have been told, he is in Paris.
>
> *Mañana nevará, según la radio.*
> Tomorrow it will snow, according to the radio.
>
> *Me levantaré más o menos temprano, según cómo me sienta.*
> I shall get up more or less early, depending on how I feel.

sin without

> *Entró sin llamar a la puerta.*
> He came in without knocking on the door.
>
> *sin duda alguna* without any doubt

● Note that *sin* often occurs in Spanish in cases where English uses other means of exclusion:

> *gasolina sin plomo* unleaded petrol
> *régimen sin sal* salt-free diet

sobre on / over / above / about (= concerning)

veinte grados sobre cero twenty degrees above zero

Lo he dejado sobre la silla.
I left it on the chair.

El avión voló sobre París.
The aeroplane flew over Paris.

Sobre todo, no lleguéis tarde.
Above all, don't be late.

Dio una conferencia sobre Galdós.
He gave a lecture on Galdós.

tras after / behind

This is a somewhat literary way of translating 'after' or 'behind':

día tras día day after day

Tras el coche del alcalde iba el de los concejales.
Behind the mayor's car there was the councillors'.

54 Prepositions in expressions of time and place

The previous section includes many of the rules for the use of prepositions in expressions of time and place. However, as these are areas that cause particular problems, the most important points are summarized below.

(a) Expressions of time

(i) To translate the English preposition 'in', Spanish uses *en* and *dentro de*.

● *En* refers to the length of time taken to complete an action:

Lo hice en una semana. I did it in a week.

● *Dentro de* refers to the time in the future, 'from now', at which the action will be performed:

Lo haré dentro de dos semanas.
I'll do it in two weeks' time / within two weeks.

- *Por* is used with parts of the day:

  Van a venir por la tarde.
  They are going to come in the afternoon.

(ii) To translate the English preposition 'for', Spanish uses *para*:

  Voy a Francia para una semana.
  I'm going to France for a week.

Durante is used to show duration:

  Cerró la tienda durante un mes.
  He closed the shop for a month.

★ Remember that the English 'have done' / been doing ... for *x'* is expressed by the present simple plus *desde hace* (and similar constructions):

  Vivo aquí desde hace dos años.
  I've lived / been living here for two years.

(See section 40b(vii).)

(iii) 'From' is usually translated by *de* or *desde* and 'from ... to ...' is expressed by *de ... a* or *desde ... hasta*:

  abierto de 8 a 3 open from 8 till 3

  Desde el 23 hasta el 26 estuve en Sevilla.
  I was in Seville from the 23rd to the 26th.

(b) Expressions of place

The main cause of confusion here is that the Spanish preposition *en* can be translated in many ways, including 'in', 'into' and 'on'.

(i) 'Into' is no problem – *en* is used for this. Note that the verb *entrar* always takes *en* before a noun:

  Entraron en el palacio.
  They entered / went into the palace.

(ii) *En* meaning 'in' causes no problems either, but note the difference between *en* on and *sobre* on.

- *En* is used in a general sense for 'on':

   Estaba en la playa cuando me llamó.
   I was on the beach when he called me.

- *Sobre* can only be used when something has been 'placed' somewhere:

   El libro está sobre la mesa. (*en* is also possible)
   The book is on the table.

   hockey sobre hielo ice-hockey

55 Prepositional phrases

Apart from the simple, or one-word, prepositions, there are also many compound prepositions, or prepositional phrases, usually combining simple prepositions or prepositions and adverbs. Many of these have *de* at the end:

   Saltó por encima de la cerca.
   He jumped over the fence.

   El autocar paró delante de la catedral.
   The coach stopped opposite the cathedral.

   Viven en el piso de al lado.
   They live in the flat next door.

   Los niños corrían a lo largo de la playa.
   The children were running along the beach.

   Desapareció por entre la multitud.
   He disappeared among the crowd.

   El río pasa por debajo de la ventana.
   The river flows under the window.

   Iremos a través del bosque.
   We shall go through the forest.

   Lo ha dejado al lado de la mesa.
   She has left it beside the table.

56 Prepositions governing adjectives and verbs

Finally, remember that prepositions are a very idiosyncratic component of any language, and therefore it is always a good idea to try to learn words such as adjectives and verbs together with the preposition they govern.

(i) Sample Adjectives

> *difícil / fácil de . . .* difficult / easy to . . .
> *inherente a* inherent in
> *sensible a* sensitive to

(ii) Sample Verbs

> *abstenerse de* to abstain from
> *casarse con* to marry
> *confiar en* to trust, to rely on
> *consistir en* to consist of / in
> *depender de* to depend on
> *escuchar* to listen to
> *mirar* to look at
> *pensar en* to think of
> *reírse de* to laugh at
> *arrepentirse de* to regret, to repent
> *traducir a(l)* to translate into

★ Note the two verbs that are a common source of error:

> *Escucho la radio.* **X** ~~*Escucho a la radio.*~~ **X**
> I listen to the radio.

> *Estaba mirando el cuadro.* **X** ~~*Estaba mirando al cuadro.*~~ **X**
> She was looking at the picture.

SENTENCE STRUCTURE

57 Simple and complex sentences

(a) Simple sentences

(i) A simple sentence consists of one main clause which has full independent meaning. Its basic components are a noun or pronoun (the subject) and a verb, with or without an object (the predicate). Each of these two components may be accompanied by qualifying words or other forms of complement:

Juan duerme. Juan sleeps.

Yo leo una novela. I read a novel.

Antonio quiere mucho a su madre.
Antonio loves his mother very much.

Mis amigos viven en Madrid.
My friends live in Madrid.

¿Quién viene? – Miguel.
Who is coming? – Miguel.

¿Qué está haciendo tu hermana? – Cosiendo.
What is your sister doing? – Sewing.

¿Dónde dejaste el libro? – En el comedor.
Where did you leave the book? – In the dining-room.

Note that either the subject or the predicate may be understood, especially in answers.

(ii) Two or more independent clauses may be linked by means of a co-ordinating conjunction and keep their independent meaning. The most usual co-ordinating conjunctions are *y* and (*e* before a word beginning *i-* or *hi-*); *o* or (*u* before a word beginning *o-* or *ho-*); *pero* but; *sino* but; *aunque* although; *por (lo) tanto* therefore:

Jaime viene hoy y Miguel llegará mañana.
Jaime is coming today and Miguel will arrive tomorrow.

Podemos ir al cine o podemos quedarnos en casa.
We can go to the cinema or we can stay at home.

Although the clauses form a single sentence, the word order of each clause is not affected by the co-ordinating conjunction.

(b) Complex sentences

Complex sentences consist of one or more main clauses and one or more subordinate clauses. The link between a main and a subordinate clause is a conjunction or a relative pronoun:

> *El hombre con quien me viste es carpintero.*
> The man you saw me with is a joiner.

> *Volveré cuando tengas más tiempo.*
> I shall come back when you have more time.

The conjunctions linking main and dependent clauses often affect not only the structure of the sentence but also the mood of the verb to be used. For the uses of the Spanish subjunctive, see section 46b.

58 Statements and questions

(a) Statements

The word order of statements in Spanish is generally the same as in English:

> *Julián escribió una carta.*
> Julián wrote a letter.

There are, however, many cases where this regular order is altered, and the following sections show the most common cases.

(i) In dependent clauses, the subject usually comes at the end after the verb:

> *No sé cuánto dinero gana Juan.*
> I do not know how much money Juan earns.

(ii) If an adverbial phrase opens the sentence, the subject comes after the verb:

> *Enrique llegó a las ocho en punto.*
> Enrique arrived at eight sharp.

but:

> *A las ocho en punto, llegó Enrique.*

(iii) Adverbs and adverbial phrases often come between the verb and its object in a way that would be odd in English:

> *Me gustan mucho los helados.*
> I like ice-cream very much.

Habla muy bien el francés.
She speaks French very well.

(iv) The subject also follows the verb after direct speech:

– *¿Tienes frío? – preguntó él.*
'Are you cold?', he asked.

(v) In short sentences with one subject and one verb, the order may be determined by considerations of style or emphasis, but the verb tends to come first when it is not modified by an adverb or adverbial phrase:

Soplaba el viento. The wind was blowing.

Se veía el pueblo. The village could be seen.

(b) Questions

(i) In spoken Spanish, raising the voice at the end of any sentence is generally enough to turn a statement into a question. However, note that the usual order is verb – subject, or verb – subject – object.

¿Vendrá Miguel?
Will Miguel come?

¿Dónde vive tu amigo?
Where does your friend live?

However, unlike English, note that no words may come between auxiliary verbs and past participles:

¿Han hecho todos lo que les dije?
Have they all done what I told them?

¿Fue visto por alguien el ladrón?
Was the thief seen by anyone?

(ii) The English question tags ('isn't it', 'don't they', etc.) added at the end of a sentence are expressed in Spanish by the words *verdad* or *no*:

Es muy rico, ¿verdad?
He is very rich, isn't he?

Te lo comerás todo, ¿no?
You'll eat everything, won't you?

59 Negation

(i) The Spanish negative *no* is placed before the verb in simple and compound tenses:

> *¿Quieres beber algo? – No, gracias.*
> Would you like to have a drink? – No, thank you.

> *La secretaria no llegará hasta más tarde.*
> The secretary will not arrive until later.

> *A las cuatro todavía no habían terminado de comer.*
> At four o'clock they still hadn't finished their lunch.

If the verb has any preceding object pronouns, *no* is placed before them:

> *No lo tengo aquí.* I haven't got it here.

> *¿No se lo habíais dicho?* Had you not told him?

(ii) In those cases where the English 'not' is governed by a verb of thinking, hoping, saying, etc., Spanish has *que no* (*que sí*, in the affirmative):

> *Espero que no.* I hope not.

> *Creo que no.* I don't think so.

Note that *que no* and *que sí* may also be used where an auxiliary is used in English:

> *Le pregunté si iba a llegar a tiempo, pero dijo que no.*
> I asked him if he was going to arrive on time, but he said he wouldn't.

★ (iii) When words such as *nadie* nobody, *nada* nothing, *nunca / jamás* never, *ningún / ninguno* no / none, etc., follow the verb, *no* must precede it. Once a negative word has been used in Spanish, the negation has to be repeated as many times as necessary in the rest of the sentence:

> *Nadie le contestó. / No le contestó nadie.*
> Nobody answered him.

> *No se oía ningún ruido.* No noise could be heard.

> *Nunca da*
> *No da nunca* } *nada a nadie.*
> He never gives anything to anyone.

(iv) A redundant *no* is often used in sentences involving *más que, mejor que, hasta que,* or to avoid starting a dependent clause with *que* immediately after another *que*:

No te lo digo hasta que (no) me digas tú qué ha pasado.
I am not telling you until you tell me what has happened.

Más vale estar preparados que (no) que nos coja por sorpresa.
Better be ready than be taken by surprise.

(v) The redundant *no* is also fairly common in exclamatory sentences:

¡Cuántos países (no) habrá visitado!
How many countries he must have visited!

¡Las veces que (no) se lo advertí!
I told her so many times!

(vi) *Ni . . . ni* translates 'neither . . . nor', and follows the general rule of requiring *no* if the verb comes first. When the verb comes first, a single *ni* is also used:

Ni Juan ni Pedro estaban allí / No estaban allí (ni) Juan ni Pedro.
Neither Juan nor Pedro was there.

No me gusta (ni) el fútbol ni el rugby.
I don't like either football or rugby.

No sabían nada (ni) el padre ni el hijo.
Neither the father nor the son knew anything.

- Although *no* before the verb is not standard in modern Spanish if *ni . . . ni* comes first, constructions of the type *ni Juan ni Pedro no estaban allí* occasionally occur in colloquial Spanish.

(vii) *Sino* translates 'but' when a positive statement is in direct contradiction to a preceding negation:

> *No fuimos al cine, sino al teatro.*
> We didn't go to the cinema but to the theatre.

If a verb is used in the affirmative clause, *sino que* is the usual form:

> *No fuimos al cine, sino que fuimos al teatro.*
> We didn't go to the cinema but to the theatre.

★ Since both *pero* and *sino* translate 'but', English speakers have some difficulty with these two conjunctions. Their difference is that *sino* expresses a straightforward contradiction of the type 'not A but B', while *pero* – which always needs a verb – covers a wider range of possibilities. Compare the previous example with this sentence:

> *No fuimos al cine, pero lo pasamos muy bien.*
> We didn't go to the cinema, but we had a very good time.

● Note *no sólo . . . sino* not only . . . but:

> *No sólo es presumido sino ignorante.*
> He is not only conceited but ignorant.

No sólo . . . sino is often used with *también* or *además*, and also takes *que* when a verb follows:

> *No sólo había cucarachas, sino también ratones.*
> There were not only cockroaches, but also mice.

> *No sólo trajeron a los niños sino que, además, se quedaron hasta muy tarde.*
> Not only did they bring the children but, on top of that, they stayed until very late.

(viii) *Tampoco*, often preceded by *ni*, translates 'neither', 'not . . . either':

> *Juan tampoco llega.* Juan can't reach either.

> *No estaba Pedro ni tampoco Miguel.*
> Pedro wasn't there and neither was Miguel.

★ Note that *tampoco* is the opposite of *también* also and must be used in any combination of the type 'also . . . not', since *también no* is not used in Spanish:

> *El tampoco vino.* He didn't come either.

PART 2

Contemporary functional language

Manuel Santamarina

COURTESY

Speaking good idiomatic Spanish requires not only a sound grasp of grammar and vocabulary, but also a sensitivity to the different registers appropriate to situations. How speakers suit the form of expression to the social context has given rise to the branch of study known as sociolinguistics. You will notice in Part 2 of this book a particular emphasis on differing styles and registers. As an introduction, here are some guidelines on courtesy in common situations, i.e. *las normas de educación*.

60 Greetings

(a) Saying hello

When greeting a stranger or an adult you know only slightly:

Buenos días. Good morning. / Good day. / Good afternoon.

Buenas tardes. Good afternoon. / Good evening.

Buenas noches. Good evening. / Good night.

In a much more informal situation, you can greet people by just saying:

Hola. Hello. / Hi.

Hola, Marián. Hi, Marián.

An initial greeting is usually accompanied by a handshake (*darse la mano*), if you do not know the person well or between men. For family and closer friends (two women or a woman and a man), it is usual to *darse besos* – to kiss on both cheeks.

(b) Saying goodbye

These are the most common expressions:

¡Adiós!

¡Hasta luego!

However, there are a number of other ways of taking your leave, depending on what the other person is going on to do:

¡Hasta la vista! See you again!
¡Hasta mañana! See you tomorrow!
¡Buena suerte! / ¡Suerte! Good luck!
¡Buen viaje! Have a good journey!
¡Que lo pases bien! Have a good time!
¡Que aproveche! Bon appétit!

61 Formal and informal modes of address

Even for the Spanish, the use of *tú* or *usted* can be delicate. The point is that there are not always hard-and-fast rules: practice varies according to generation, social context, individual background, etc.

Tú is used between friends, members of family, to children and generally between strangers under the age of thirty; it is always used to speak to animals, in prayers and invocations and, in a heated argument, complete strangers can use *tú* in insults.

It is used more readily than the French *tu*, and almost always between persons who are on first-name terms. *Tú* should not be used to older strangers or persons in authority.

In formal situations adult strangers can be addressed as *Señor*, *Señora* or *Señorita*, but these titles should not be used constantly in a conversation once two people have met. When a young woman ceases to be *Señorita* to become *Señora* depends technically on her marital status, but, if you do not know this, on whether she looks under or over 25 years old; this term is rarely used in colloquial Spanish nowadays.

62 Introductions

As in English-speaking countries, if you have to introduce two people to each other, you should start by telling the woman the man's name, or the older person the younger person's name. In a formal context, introductions will run as follows:

Señora Castillo, permítame que le presente al señor Medina.
Encantado de conocerla, Señora Castillo.
Encantada.

Mrs Castillo, may I introduce you to Mr Medina?
How do you do?
How do you do?

In an informal situation, you can introduce two people more simply:

Isabel, tú no conoces a mi amigo Patricio, ¿verdad?
No, no lo conozco. Hola, Patricio.
Hola, Isabel, ¿qué tal estás?

63 Asking someone to repeat something

A familiar situation for the foreigner conversing with Spanish speakers is the need to slow down the other person and ask him or her to repeat things. In a formal situation, use:

Perdone, ¿podría repetirme la pregunta, por favor?
Excuse me. Would you mind repeating your question, please?

Perdón, no he entendido lo que ha dicho.
I'm sorry, I didn't hear / understand what you said.

Por favor, ¿le sería posible repetir eso un poco más despacio?
I'm sorry. Would you mind repeating that a little more slowly?

In informal situations, use:

¿Perdón, qué has dicho?
Sorry, what did you say?

No te he entendido.
I didn't quite get what you said.

¡Más despacio!
Slow down a bit!

The brief interjection, exactly equivalent to 'What?', is *¿Cómo?*

INFORMATION AND ADVICE

To ask for information and advice, an interrogative (question) form is often required (see section 58).

When you are talking about information or advice, note the use of both singular and plural forms of the following:

un consejo a piece of advice
consejos (several pieces of) advice

una información an item of information or news
informaciones (several items of) information or news

una noticia a piece of news
noticias (several pieces of) news

64 Asking for information

(i) To stop someone (in the street) to ask for information, use:

Perdone, Señor / Señora / Señorita . . .
Por favor, . . .
Excuse me . . .

(ii) To ask for information in a formal context (Tourist Office, reception desk, etc.), use one of the following:

¿Podría decirme dónde está la habitación 87?
Could you tell me where to find room 87?

¿Le sería posible explicarme cómo usar el bono-bus?
Could you explain to me how to use the bus travelcard?

Necesitamos cierta información sobre su empresa.
We need some information about your company.

¿Sabe qué hay que hacer para llamar a Argentina?
Do you know how to phone Argentina?

Este es el colegio mayor, ¿verdad?
This is the university hall of residence, isn't it?

(iii) Other questions may require one of the following interrogative forms:

> *¿Cómo podríamos ponernos en contacto con él?*
> How can we get in touch with him?

> *¿Dónde puedo comprar sellos?*
> Where can I buy stamps?

> *¿Por qué no te dio el médico una respuesta?*
> Why didn't the doctor give you an answer?

> *¿Cuándo hay que devolver el libro?*
> When should the book be returned?

> *¿Qué has pedido?*
> What did you ask for?

> *¿Qué tipo de perfume desea?*
> What sort of perfume are you looking for / would you like?

> *¿Cuál de los dos prefieres?*
> Which of the two do you prefer?

> *¿A qué hora abre la biblioteca?*
> What time does the library open?

> *¿Quién ha mandado el fax?*
> Who sent the fax?

65 Asking for advice

(i) More formal ways of requesting advice include:

> *Queremos pedirle consejo.*
> We'd like to / We want to ask your advice.

> *¿Podría aconsejarnos cómo actuar?*
> Could you advise us on how to proceed?

> *¿Podría proponernos otra fecha?*
> Could you suggest another date to us?

> *¿Podría recomendarnos un buen hotel en la misma zona?*
> Could you recommend us a good hotel in the same area?

> *¿Nos aconsejaría que le confiáramos la tarea a él?*
> Would you advise us to entrust the task to him?

> *¿En su opinión, qué deberíamos hacer?*
> In your opinion, what should we do?

(ii) In informal colloquial contexts, ways of asking advice include:

¿Me puedes aconsejar?
Can you give me some advice?

Necesito tu opinión.
I need your opinion.

¿Le llamo por teléfono, o sería mejor que le escribiera?
Shall I ring him, or would it be better to write?

¿Tú crees que es la persona adecuada para el empleo?
Do you think she is the right person for the job?

66 Giving information

To give information and advice, there exists a range of expressions from the tentative suggestion to the definite statement. For the use of the imperative to give orders, see section 47.

(i) To introduce the required information in a letter or in formal speech:

En respuesta a su pregunta, me permito remitirle a nuestro catálogo.
In reply to your question, I would refer you to our catalogue.

Para responder a lo que me pregunta, me gustaría señalarle que abriremos una nueva tienda en enero.
In reply to your question, I'd like to point out that we are opening a new shop in January.

(ii) In less formal contexts, information will often be introduced by one of the following phrases:

Bueno, . . .
Well, . . .

Bueno, mira, lo que yo digo . . .
Well, look, what I can say is that . . .

(iii) If your information takes the form of instructions, use one of the following:

Coja la segunda bocacalle a la derecha después del semáforo.
(imperative)
Take the second turning on the right after the traffic lights.

Sigue todo recto hasta llegar al cruce. (present tense)
You have to carry straight on until you get to the crossroads.

Si llamas al timbre, te abrirá mi hermana. (*si* + present tense)
If you ring the doorbell my sister will let you in.

67 Giving advice

(i) The following expressions range from the tentative to the emphatic:

Sería prudente esperar su respuesta.
It would be advisable to wait for his answer.

¿Me permite que le haga una sugerencia?
Might / May I make a suggestion?

Si no tiene inconveniente, esto es lo que podría hacer.
If you don't have any objection, this is what you could do.

Le aconsejaría que hablara con mi compañero.
I'd advise you to speak to my colleague.

¿Y si fueras a recogerla a la estación?
How about going and fetching her from the station?

¿Por qué no vamos andando?
Why don't we walk there?

¿Has pensado en pedirle ayuda?
Have you thought of asking him for help?

¿No se te ha ocurrido preguntar en la oficina de información?
Have you thought of asking at the information office?

Te sería de gran utilidad hacerlo así.
It would be very much in your interest to do it like this.

Sabes, lo que podrías hacer es escribirle.
You know, if you wanted, you could write to him.

(ii) To stress that the advice is your own point of view, you can preface your remarks by:

Yo, personalmente, no lo haría.
Personally, I wouldn't do it.

Hablando con franqueza, yo no confiaría en él.
To be honest, I wouldn't trust him / rely on him.

Yo en tu lugar, aceptaría su petición.
If I were you, I'd accept their request.

En mi opinión, te valdría más no decir nada.
In my view, you'd be better off saying nothing.

155

68 Dissuasion

The expressions in the previous section on giving information and advice can be used negatively to deter someone from a course of action. The following expressions are also useful:

Se ruega encarecidamente no enviar más de una solicitud.
< formal >
You are requested not to send more than one application.

Por favor, no tocar las flores. < formal >
Please do not touch the flowers.

No deberías guardarle rencor. < formal>
You shouldn't hold it against him.

¡Cuidado con los carteristas!
Watch out for pickpockets!

Me pregunto si no deberías esperar unos cuantos días.
I wonder whether you shouldn't wait for a few days.

Yo en tu lugar, tendría mucho cuidado de no perder el tiempo.
If I were you, I'd be careful not to waste my time.

Personalmente, me lo pensaría mucho antes de volver allí.
Personally, I'd think twice before going back there.

Mucho ojo, te arriesgas a tener que pagar una multa.
Careful, you risk having to pay a fine.

Vas a tener problemas si sigues así.
You'll be in trouble if you carry on like this.

AUTHORIZATION AND REQUESTS

Public notices frequently concern permission and prohibition –
what you can and cannot do. In conversation, different structures
will express the same concepts in more or less formal ways. See
section 47 for the use of imperative forms.

69 Seeking permission

(i) More formal ways of seeking permission include:

¿Me permite que me ausente (subj.) *esta tarde?*
Would you allow me to excuse myself from this afternoon's
session?

¿Sería posible que revisáramos (subj.) *ese punto?*
Might we go back over that point?

¿Está permitido fumar en el patio?
Is smoking allowed in the courtyard?

¿Te importaría mucho que no te acompañara?
Would you mind if I didn't come with you?

(ii) To seek permission in informal contexts:

¿Te importa que no vuelva (subj.) *mañana?*
Do you mind if I don't come back tomorrow?

¿Tenemos derecho a dos platos?
Are we entitled to two courses?

¿Puedo preguntarte algo?
May / Can I ask you something?

¿Me dejas que use (subj.) *tu coche?* Can I use your car?

70 Granting permission

(i) Public notices expressing authorization concisely:

Sólo se permite equipaje de mano
Only hand luggage is permitted.

Se aceptan tarjetas de crédito. Credit cards accepted.

(ii) In other formal contexts, permission may be conveyed as follows:

No tenemos ningún inconveniente en que lo retrase (subj.) *hasta mañana.*
We have no objection at all to your delaying it until tomorrow.

Aceptamos gustosos que nos envíe (subj.) *la respuesta por fax.*
We are quite agreeable to your sending your reply by fax.

No es necesario que hagas (subj.) *este ejercicio.*
There's no need for you to do this exercise.

Si es necesario, me lo podrá consultar mañana.
If necessary, you can consult me tomorrow.

Tienen ustedes derecho a un ejemplar gratuito.
You are entitled to a free copy.

(iii) To grant permission informally:

Por supuesto que te puedes quedar la llave.
Of course you can keep the key.

No hay ningún problema si quieres cogerte el día libre mañana.
That's fine if you want to take the day off tomorrow.

En caso de necesidad, te puedes ahorrar los trámites protocolarios.
If need be, you can skip the formalities.

71 Prohibitions

In many contexts, prohibition can be expressed by using, in the negative form, the structures for giving permission that are listed above. There also exist the following expressions specific to prohibition.

(i) Public notices expressing prohibition concisely:

No pisar la hierba.
Do not walk on the grass.

Prohibido aparcar.
No parking.

Prohibido fijar carteles.
No posters allowed.

(ii) In other formal contexts, prohibition is expressed by:

Te prohíbo que vuelvas (subj.) *a sacar el tema.*
I forbid you to bring up the subject again.

Me opongo firmemente a que aceptes (subj.) *el plan.*
I am most strongly opposed to your accepting the project.

Me es completamente imposible permitir tu ausencia.
I cannot give permission for you to be absent.

No puedes presentarte en la ventanilla sin el documento de identidad.
You cannot go up to the counter without your identity card (or some equivalent proof of identity).

(iii) Telling someone not to do something in informal contexts:

Esta noche no vas a salir.
You're not going out tonight.

No tienes que trabajar tanto.
You mustn't work so hard.

Ten ciudado de no molestarle.
Make sure you don't disturb him.

¡No se hable más, tú no pagas!
You're not paying, and that's that!

72 Offering to do something

Offers, requests and orders can vary from the peremptory to the most discreetly worded. In section 45b(iv) you will see that the use of a conditional as opposed to the present indicative often provides a more polite form, appropriate in cases where you do not know the other party well.

We can distinguish broadly between expressions appropriate to formal correspondence and transactions, and those occurring in everyday contexts.

(i) In formal correspondence or transactions the following forms may be used:

Nos complace ofrecer a todos nuestros clientes un descuento del diez por ciento.
We are pleased to offer all our customers a ten per cent discount.

Hoy ofrecemos descuentos especiales en el departamento de bricolage.
Today we are offering special discounts in the D.I.Y. department.

La empresa está dispuesta a ceder el alquiler.
The firm is willing to give up the lease.

(ii) In everyday contexts, offers may take the form of statements, questions or imperatives:

Si quieres, puedo ponerme en contaco con él.
I can get in touch with him if you like.

Podríamos invitarla el viernes próximo.
We could invite her for next Friday.

Estoy encantado de sustituirle.
I'm delighted to stand in for you.

Ya me encargaré del correo mientras estés (subj.) *de vacaciones.*
I'll take care of the mail while you're on holiday.

Ya me voy a ocupar yo de mandarles los nuevos precios.
I'll be responsible for sending them the new prices.

¿Desearía que viniera mañana? < formal >
Would you like me to come tomorrow?

¿Quiere que le reserve dos butacas? < less formal >
Do you want me to book two seats for you?

¿Quieres que te lleve a la estación?
Shall I drop you at the station?

Si te sirve, me podría quedar con Laura mañana.
If it helps, I could look after Laura tomorrow.

Hágame saber cualquier cosa que necesite. < formal >
Let me know if there's anything you need.

Dime si me necesitas.
Let me know if you need me.

Cuenta conmigo para le reunión del domingo.
You can rely on me for Sunday's meeting.

Al menos, déjame pagar los cafés.
Do let me at least pay for the coffees.

No, los helados son por mi cuenta. Te invito. < coll. >
No, I'll pay for the ice-creams. They're my treat.

73 Making requests

Again, it is helpful to distinguish between expressions used in public notices or formal correspondence, as opposed to everyday, informal ways of making requests. See also section 65.

(i) Requests made over public-address systems or in notices use certain formulae:

Se ruega a los señores pasajeros del vuelo de Iberia 606 se dirijan a la puerta 6.
Passengers for Iberia flight 606 should now proceed to gate 6.

Se ruega a los señores conductores regresen a sus vehículos.
Passengers with cars are asked to return to their vehicles.

★ Note that the *que* after *rogar* is often omitted.

Por favor, respeten la zona de no fumadores.
Please respect the no-smoking area.

La línea está ocupada. Por favor, llame más tarde.
The line is engaged. Please call back later.

(ii) In formal correspondence, other formulae occur (see also sections 108 and 113):

Sea tan amable de enviarnos su nueva dirección.
Please be kind enough to notify us of your new address.

161

Le agradeceríamos mucho que nos enviara (subj.) *una muestra.*
We should be most grateful if you would send us a sample.

Por favor, advierta el cambio de dirección.
Please / Kindly note the change of address.

(iii) In less formal circumstances, requests can be made more or less directly:

Nos gustaría visitar el Museo de Antropología.
We'd like to visit the Museum of Mankind.

¿Te puedo pedir un favor?
Could I ask you a favour?

¿Puedes prestarme tu libro?
Could you lend me your book?

¿Me puedes prestar 6.000 pesetas?
Could you lend me 6,000 pesetas?

74 Giving orders

Obviously, the imperative can be used to give orders (see section 47), but in many situations you may wish to avoid the instruction sounding too brusque, and alternative expressions may be more suitable.

Sírvete, por favor.
Please, help yourself.

Vamos a ver, ponte cómodo.
Please, do make yourself at home.

¿Me quieres volver a llamar mañana?
Could you call me back tomorrow?

AIMS, RESPONSIBILITIES AND ABILITIES

Expressions concerning your aims, responsibilities and abilities rely on a range of verbs or verbal phrases and adjectives. With some key verbs, such as *deber* or *poder*, different shades of meaning can be conveyed by the distinction between the present indicative and the conditional.

75 Aims and intentions

The future tense, or the use of *ir* + infinitive, can convey definite aims and intentions. Other verbs can convey more provisional future projects.

Asistiremos a la reunión de mañana.
We shall attend tomorrow's meeting.

Van a quedarse tres noches en Zaragoza.
They're going to spend three nights in Saragossa.

Espero dedicar dos semanas a este número de la revista.
I hope to spend two weeks on this issue of the magazine.

¿Va a pasar por la oficina mañana?
Will you be calling into the office tomorrow?

Tenemos la intención de lanzar este producto en marzo.
We're planning to launch the product in March.

¿Tienes idea de buscar otro trabajo?
Are you planning to look for a new job?

No tengo la más mínima intención de trasladarme este año.
I haven't the slightest intention of moving this year.

Queremos alquilar una casa en Altea.
We are thinking of renting a house in Altea.

Han dispuesto una reunión para las dos de la tarde. < formal >
They've organized a meeting for two o'clock.

Nos proponemos nombrar a dos altos directivos.
We are intending to appoint two senior managers.

76 Responsibilities and obligations

Remember that impersonal expressions of obligation when followed by que (*hace falta que, es necesario que*) require the subjunctive (see section 46b(vi).

(i) Formal expressions of responsibility or obligation include:

Lamento tener que informarle de que no nos es posible renovar su contrato.
I regret to inform you that we cannot renew your contract.

Me corresponde a mí poner punto final a la sesión.
It falls to me to bring this session to a close.

Es preciso que nos envíe (subj.) *una fianza antes de finales de mes.*
We require you to send us a deposit by the end of the month.

He insistido en que me manden (subj.) *una pieza de repuesto.*
I have insisted that they send me a spare part.

Es necesario reservar las butacas una semana antes de la representación.
Seats must be reserved a week before the performance.

Es indispensable que contacte (subj.) *con nosotros lo antes posible.*
It is essential that you contact us as soon as possible.

Será necesario que lo volvamos (subj.) *a discutir.*
We shall have to discuss the matter again.

Es mi deber justificar nuestra respuesta. < literary >
It is my duty to offer an explanation of our reply.

Ha recaído sobre mí nuestra representación en este congreso.
< formal >
It falls to me to be our representative at the conference.

(ii) Less formal expressions of obligation or responsibility include:

Tienes que llamar a mi hermana.
You must phone my sister.

Deberías prevenirla.
You should warn her.

Hay que tirar estos zapatos a la basura.
These shoes must be thrown away.

Tienes que ir al ayuntamiento.
You have to go to the Town Hall.

Tengo que trabajar el domingo.
I have to work on Sunday.

Me obligaron a quedarme hasta más tarde.
They forced me to stay until later.

Se supone que tengo que reemplazarla la semana que viene.
The implication is that I have to replace her next week.

Sí, hace falta que estés (subj.) *allí. Es indispensable.*
You must be there. It's essential.

(iii) Adverbs or adverbial phrases can be added to emphasize the degree of obligation:

Tienes que verla, sin falta.
You absolutely must see her.

Tenemos que invitarlo a la fuerza.
We have to invite him; there's no way out of it.

En cualquier caso, él es indispensable.
Whatever happens we can't manage without him.

Tendrás que venir aunque no te apetezca.
You must come whether you like it or not.

En el peor de los casos, tendremos que encontrar otro.
If worst comes to worst, we'll have to find someone else.

No debes tocarlo, pase lo que pase.
You mustn't touch it under any circumstances.

77 Abilities and competence

★ Note that Spanish distinguishes between *poder* – to be able to do something physically – and *saber* – to know how to do something, e.g.:

¿Sabes nadar?
Can you swim? (Do you know how to swim?)

¿Puedes nadar más rápido?
Can you swim faster? (Are you physically capable of swimming faster?)

(i) Formal expressions of ability or competence include:

Buscamos una secretaria que hable (subj.) *catalán.*
We are looking for a secretary who speaks Catalan.

Creo tener las cualidades necesarias para tener éxito.
I believe I have the qualities necessary to succeed.

¿Cree estar capacitado para dirigir este proyecto?
Do you think you are qualified to run this project?

Me es imposible confirmar estas noticias.
I cannot confirm the news.

Nos resulta imposible aceptar su proposición.
We are unable to accept your proposal.

(ii) Less formal expressions of ability or competence include:

¿Has conseguido dar con él?
Have you managed to track him down?

No puedo hacer nada.
There's nothing I can do.

No puedo creerlo.
I can't believe it.

PERSONAL TASTES

To express likes, dislikes and preferences, Spanish has a range of verbs and adverbial phrases. In most cases, adverbs can be added which express a more precise shade of feeling. Remember that structures on the lines of 'to like / dislike / prefer someone to do something' require the subjunctive (see section 46).

78 Likes

(i) The main way of expressing 'I like something' in Spanish is the verb *gustar*, used in the third person: *me gusta / gustan*, literally 'it / they please me'. The subject may be a singular or plural noun, or an infinitive.

Me gusta la música clásica.
I like classical music.

Me gustan los hoteles de Santander.
I like the hotels in Santander.

Me gusta pintar.
I like painting.

In the construction 'like / want someone to ...', the use of the subjunctive is required:

¿Te gusta que tus amigos vengan a verte?
Do you like your friends to come and see you?

Les gusta que vayamos a su casa los domingos.
They like us to drop in on them on Sundays.

The conditional of *gustar* is used in polite requests or suggestions:

¿Os gustaría venir al cine con nosotros?
Would you like to come to the cinema with us?

The verb *querer* can also be used in polite requests or suggestions:

Quisiéramos reservar una habitación.
We should like to book a room.

(ii) To qualify the extent to which one likes something, the following adverbs can be used:

Este artista me gusta enormemente / muchísimo / un montón
< coll. >.
I like this artist tremendously / particularly / a lot.

(iii) Other verbs / verbal phrases to express likes include:

Les encanta montar a caballo.
They love horse riding.

Lo que más nos gusta es ir a la playa.
What we like most is going to the beach.

Pilar es muy aficionada a este cantante.
Pilar is very keen on this singer.

La música popular ha complacido siempre a los turistas.
Traditional music has always been popular with tourists.

¿Te apetece salir a cenar?
Do you fancy going out for dinner?

A mi hija le pirra / chifla su último disco. < very coll. >
My daughter's crazy about their last album.

★ **(iv)** It is difficult to give a single translation of the English verb 'to enjoy'. Note the following possibilities:

¿Te gustó el concierto?
Did you enjoy the concert?

Lo pasamos muy bien en la fiesta.
We thoroughly enjoyed ourselves at the party.

Ha sido un placer conocerle.
I've very much enjoyed meeting you.

Los niños disfrutan mucho en casa de los abuelos.
The children enjoy themselves a lot at my parents'.

79 Dislikes

The phrases used to express likes (section 78) can be used in the negative to express dislikes. Other idioms to express dislike range from the formal to the markedly colloquial.

Detesta las reuniones que duran demasiado. < formal >
She hates meetings that last too long.

No soporta que la hagan (subj.) *esperar.*
She can't stand being kept waiting.

No aguanta que le llamen (subj.) *Toni.*
He can't stand being called Toni.

Aborrecía el tono de sus cartas. < formal >
He loathed the tone of their letters.

Las películas de ciencia ficción me aburren.
I get bored with science fiction films.

! *Me revientan los viajes largos en autobús.* < coll. >
I hate long coach journeys.

Me duele tener que hacerte esta crítica.
I deeply regret having to make this criticism of you.

! *Les joroba tener que levantarse tan pronto.* < very coll. >
They hate having to get up so early.

Me horroriza el peinado que lleva.
I think her hair style is frightful.

Les ha cogido manía a sus nuevos compañeros.
He has taken a dislike to his new colleagues.

80 Preferences

★ As well as with the verb *preferir*, preferences can be expressed in
Spanish by some other verbs or phrases:

¿Prefieres que vayamos (subj.) *ahora mismo o un poco más tarde?*
Would you prefer to go there straight away or later?

Prefieren que lleguemos (subj.) *por la tarde.*
They prefer us to arrive in the afternoon / evening.

Es preferible hacer una reserva anticipada.
It's better / preferable to make an advance booking.

Más valdrá que cojas 10.000Pts.
You'd better take 10,000Pts with you.

¡Más valdría que estudiaras (subj.) *con regularidad!*
It would be better if you studied regularly!

After three in the afternoon would suit us best.

El viernes por la tarde me viene bien.
Friday evening is fine with me / convenient for me.

El horario de tarde <u>es mejor</u> para ella.
The evening shift is more convenient for her.

La directora <u>a favorecido</u> a los alumnos de C.O.U.
The headmistress has given preference to pupils in the sixth form.

El Ayuntamiento <u>ha dado prioridad al</u> transporte público.
The Town Council has given priority to public transport.

<u>Será mejor que</u> le llamemos (subj.) *por teléfono.*
It'll be better to phone him.

81 Indifference

It is important to distinguish between polite expressions suggesting you are equally happy to do any of the things under discussion and statements of a total lack of interest.

(i) Polite expressions include:

La verdad es que no tengo <u>ninguna preferencia</u>. < formal >
To tell the truth, I have no particular preference.

Como quieras tú, a mí me da <u>lo mismo</u>.
It's up to you, I don't mind at all.

Sí, <u>cualquiera</u>, le da <u>igual</u>.
Yes. Any of them; he doesn't mind which.

(ii) To express a lack of interest:

No me importa, no me gusta la comida china.
I don't mind / care, I don't like Chinese food.

!! *¡A mí me importa un bledo!* < coll. >
<u>I</u> couldn't care less.

!! *¡No me da la gana de decírtelo!* < coll. >
I'm not telling you! / I don't damn well choose to tell you.

DIFFERENT VIEWPOINTS

Agreement, disagreement and opinions can be expressed briefly and categorically, often by one or two words, but in other contexts it may be important to phrase your point of view tactfully. The expressions suggested below include the most important brief responses as well as more formal expressions. Of course, paralinguistic gestures and facial expressions can play an important role in conveying your precise feelings!

82 Agreement

(i) To convey immediate agreement in a conversation:

Sí, de acuerdo. Yes, that's all right.
Vale. < coll. > O.K.
Desde luego. Of course.
Evidentemente. Obviously.
Efectivamente. Exactly, indeed.
Exactamente. Precisely.
Así es. That's it.

(ii) To elaborate on the fact that you agree when talking informally:

★ Remember the very basic distinction between *tener razón* (a person is in the right) and *ser cierto* (something is right / accurate).

Creo que tienes razón. I think you're right.

¡Ah, sí, es cierto, ya se ha ido! Yes, that's right, he's already left.

There are a number of expressions of agreement which include the phrase *de acuerdo*:

Bien, ¿estás de acuerdo en que sea (subj.) mañana?
Is it O.K. by you for tomorrow then?

Nosotros estamos de acuerdo en este punto.
We're in agreement on this point.

Cuando se entrevistaron, se pusieron de acuerdo.
They agreed / came to an agreement when they met.

Tendremos que ponernos de acuerdo en cuanto a la fecha.
We'll have to agree / come to an agreement on the date.

171

Mi padre está de acuerdo.
My father has agreed / is in agreement.

(iii) In more formal conversations or in writing, agreement can be expressed by:

¡Qué razón tiene al decir que no deberíamos hacer caso de las encuestas!
How right he is to say that we should not pay attention to opinion polls!

Estoy dispuesto a apoyarte.
I'm willing to give / lend you my support.

Nuestra empresa es favorable a esta proposición.
Our company is agreeable to this proposal.

Tras haber comprobado su ficha, creo que su petición es aceptable.
Having checked your file, I find your request quite acceptable.

¿Están dispuestos a aceptar las líneas generales del proyecto?
Are you prepared to accept the general outline of the project?

Nos adherimos a las conclusiones presentadas por nuestros representantes.
We stand by the conclusions put forward by our representatives.

83 Disagreement

The expressions listed in sections 82(ii) and (iii) can be used in the negative to express disagreement. For the use of the subjunctive after verbs of thinking / saying used negatively, see section 46.

(i) To convey immediate disagreement in a conversation:

No, nada. No, not at all.
No es cierto. That's not true / not right.
Por supuesto que no. Certainly not. / Of course not.
No entiendes nada. You just don't understand.
No tienes ni idea. You've got no idea.
No te lo crees ni tú. < coll. > Tell that to the marines.

(ii) To elaborate on the fact that you disagree in an informal conversation:

★ Remember the distinction between *estar equivocado* (a person is wrong / incorrect) and *no ser cierto* something is wrong / incorrect:

Estoy seguro de que estás equivocado. I'm sure you're wrong.

Lo que dijiste ayer no es cierto.
What you said yesterday isn't right / is wrong.

No están de acuerdo contigo.
They don't agree with you.

Para los niños, ése no es el caso.
It's not true as far as children as concerned.

Tu razonamiento se cae por su propio peso.
Your argument doesn't stand up.

En cuanto a eso, se equivocan.
They're wrong on that score.

(iii) In more formal conversations and writing, disagreement can be expressed by:

Me temo que no estoy de acuerdo con usted.
I am afraid I don't agree with you.

Siento tener que contradecirle, pero eso no es cierto.
I am sorry to have to contradict you, but that's not true.

Creo que ha cometido un error.
I think you've made a mistake.

Los hechos contradicen lo que usted sugiere.
The facts contradict what you're suggesting.

Tengo que oponerme firmemente a esta solución.
I must express my strong opposition to this solution.

Negamos categóricamente esa afirmación.
We categorically deny that statement.

84 Hedging your bets

There are times when you are asked to agree or disagree, but would rather hedge your bets! The following expressions may be useful.

(i) Short responses:

Es posible. Possibly. / It may be so.
Sí, más o menos. Yes, more or less.
En último extremo, sí. In the last resort, we could.
Sí, en principio. Yes, I suppose so.
Bueno, quizás. Well, perhaps.
A lo mejor, depende. Maybe, it depends.

(ii) To convey your unwillingness to commit yourself, in more formal contexts:

> *Si no me equivoco, es así.* If I'm not mistaken, that's how it is.
>
> *En realidad, no lo he pensado mucho.*
> I haven't really given it much thought.
>
> *Preferiría no tener que comprometerme.*
> I'd prefer not to have to commit myself.
>
> *Preferiría no pronunciarme sobre este tema.*
> I'd prefer not to comment on this question.

85 Opinions

(i) To suggest that what follows is a personal opinion, you can preface remarks by:

> *Para mí...* In my opinion...
> *Personalmente...* Personally...
> *Por mi parte...* As far as I'm concerned...
> *Según su portavoz...* According to their spokesperson...
> *Según dice el periodista...* According to the journalist...
> *En palabras de Eduardo...* In the words of Eduardo...
>
> *Si fuéramos a creer lo que dice este artículo...*
> If we / you can believe this article...

(ii) Verbal expressions to state a personal opinion include:

> *Soy de la opinión de que deberíamos consultárselo.*
> I believe that we should consult him.
>
> *Teníamos la impresión de que era lo que hacía falta.*
> We were under the impression that it was what was needed.
>
> *Piensa que no debería haber rechazado el trabajo.*
> She thinks I shouldn't have refused the job.
>
> *Consideran que sería muy complicado.*
> They consider that it would be too complicated.
>
> *Juzgué vuestra actuación demasiado peligrosa.* < formal >
> I considered your action to be too dangerous.

(iii) To ask someone else for their opinion:

> *¿Qué opinas? ¿Cuál es tu opinión?* What's your opinion?
>
> *¿Qué te parece el nuevo aeropuerto?*
> What do you think of the new airport?

Me gustaría saber lo que piensa usted del nuevo presidente.
I'd like to hear what you think of our new president.

Quisiera conocer su actitud ante este proyecto.
I should like to have your view on the project.

86 Expressing approval

(i) At the simplest level, approval may be expressed by a single adjective or short phrase of exclamation:

¡Perfecto! Perfect! Excellent!
¡Estupendo! Great! Fantastic!
¡Genial! Brilliant!
¡Vale! Good idea! Fine!

(ii) To elaborate on approval in an informal context:

Tienes toda la razón para quejarte.
You're quite right to complain.

Comprendo perfectamente que quieras (subj.) *participar.*
I quite understand your wanting to take part.

Me parece que es una idea estupenda.
I think it's an excellent idea.

Apoyo tu decisión. I support your decision.

(iii) To elaborate on approval more formally:

Mi esposa tiene su trabajo en gran estima.
My wife thinks very highly of your work.

Mi marido piensa que ha sido una conferencia admirable.
My husband thinks it was an excellent lecture.

Por fin han aprobado la construcción de una nueva estación.
They have finally approved the plans to build a new station.

¡Enhorabuena por haber encontrado una casa tan bonita!
Congratulations on finding such a lovely house!

El gran mérito de ese arquitecto es que escucha a sus clientes.
The architect's great strength is that he listens to his clients.

El comité ha acogido con entusiasmo su propuesta.
The committee has received your proposal warmly.

El ministro dio una opinión favorable sobre este informe.
The Minister gave a favourable opinion on this report.

87 Expressing disapproval

Disapproval can be expressed by using the expressions in sections 86(ii) and (iii) in the negative, as well as by the expressions given below. Adverbs provide a useful way to nuance the degree of your disapproval.

(i) To express disapproval by a short exclamation:

¡No, hombre, no es posible! Oh, no. You can't!
¡Es horrible! It's horrible!
!! *¡Da asco!* < coll. > It's disgusting!
! *¡Qué cara!* < coll. > What a bloody cheek!
¡Es escandaloso! It's outrageous!
¡Qué vergüenza! It's a disgrace!

(ii) To elaborate on disapproval in an informal context:

Está en contra del aborto. She is against abortion.

Me opongo totalmente a que te quedes (subj.) *allí solo.*
I won't hear of your staying there on your own.

Estoy harto de la gente que deja basura por todas partes. < coll. >
I'm fed up with people who drop litter everywhere.

No me perdona el que haya vendido (subj.) *el piso.*
He won't forgive me for selling the flat.

Es una lástima que no hayas hecho (subj.) *ningún progreso.*
It's a pity you haven't made any progress.

(iii) To elaborate on disapproval in a formal context:

No pudieron aceptar que yo me hubiera encargado (subj.) *de todo.*
They couldn't accept my taking responsibility for everything.

La dirección se opone con firmeza a las nuevas tarifas.
The management is strongly opposed to the new rates.

Tengo que protestar ante semejante injusticia.
I must protest at such an injustice.

El sindicato se ha pronunciado en contra de los cambios.
The union protested at the changes.

Desaprobamos que vuelvan (subj.) *a construir el mercado.*
We disapprove of any attempt to rebuild the market.

Es lamentable que no nos hayáis avisado (subj.) *antes.*
It is most unfortunate that you did not warn us earlier.

DEGREES OF CERTAINTY
AND POSSIBILITY

88 Certainty

Affirmative expressions of certainty and probability take the indicative. Compare this with the predominance of the subjunctive for expressions of possibility and doubt (sections 90 and 92).

(i) To convey certainty by a single word or short phrase:

¿Va a venir mañana? – Desde luego.
Will he come tomorrow? – Definitely. / Of course.

¿Los van a invitar? – Sí, por supuesto.
Will they be invited? – Yes, of course.

El candidato va a salir elegido, seguro.
The candidate is sure to be elected.

(ii) Fuller expressions of certainty rely mainly on adjectives or verbs. Among the useful expressions based on adjectives are, first, those with a personal subject:

Estoy seguro de que vas a triunfar.
I'm sure you'll succeed.

¿Estás seguro de que has echado la carta?
Are you sure you posted the letter?

Está convencida de que es la mejor solución.
She's convinced it's the best solution.

Están convencidos de que ha habido un error.
They're convinced there's been a mistake.

No van a cambiar de opinión, es una decisión tajante.
They won't change their minds. The decision's final.

Expressions with an impersonal subject to convey certainty include:

No va a haber temporada de verano. Es definitivo.
There won't be a summer season. That's final.

Es innegable que muchos niños necesitan ayuda.
It is certainly the case that many children need help.

Ya es seguro que el ministro va a dimitir.
It is now certain that the Minister is going to resign.

No hay discusión posible: estos pisos están muy deteriorados.
It is undeniable that these flats are badly run down.

(iii) Expressions of certainty based on verbs generally belong to a more formal register of speech, and include:

El gobierno ha confirmado este comunicado.
The government has confirmed this announcement.

La encargada del caso ha confirmado que ha habido diez heridos.
The woman in charge has confirmed that ten people have been injured.

¿Puede asegurar que se trata de un empleado de la casa?
Can you vouch for the fact that the person is employed here?

Puedo garantizar su seguridad.
I can guarantee your safety.

Hemos garantizado que la entrega se hará mañana.
We have guaranteed that the delivery will be made tomorrow.

Le aseguro que ingresé el dinero en mi cuenta ayer.
I assure you that I put the money into my account yesterday.

Testificaron que no se había llevado a cabo ningún experimento con animales.
They testified that no experiments on animals had taken place.

(iv) The word *duda* can be used in several expressions to make a categorical affirmation, but remember that *sin duda* means 'probably'.

No hay ninguna duda de que ganará la próxima vez.
Of course she'll win next time.

Sin lugar a dudas, se trata de un triunfo bien merecido.
There's no doubt that his success is well deserved.

Sin duda alguna, pagarían más en Suiza.
There's no doubt at all they'd pay more in Switzerland.

(v) Two expressions with *certeza* (*tener la certeza de que, saber con certeza que . . .*) convey a similar degree of affirmation:

Tengo la certeza de que ya me ha hecho esa pregunta.
I'm absolutely certain he's already asked me that question.

Sabe con certeza que le van a destinar a Japón.
He knows for certain that he's going to be posted to Japan.

89 Probability

For the use of the conditional tense to suggest that a statement is probably true, but not guaranteed, see section 45b(v).

(i) To convey that something is probable in a word or short phrase:

¿Vas a poner las baldosas tú mismo? – En principio, sí.
Are you going to lay the tiles yourself? – That's the idea.

¿Vas a ir a la boda? – Sin duda.
Are you going to the wedding? – Most probably.

¿Han ido de vacaciones a la costa? – Seguramente.
Have they gone on holiday to the seaside? – It's quite likely.

¿Fue tu madre la que llamó? – Probablemente.
Was it your mother who rang? – Probably.

¿De modo que ahora se va a dedicar al teatro? – Así parece.
He's going to take up acting now, is he? – So it seems.

(ii) The combination of the verb *poder* with the adverb *bien* provides the basis for a number of expressions of probability:

Bien pudiera ser que cogiese el tren.
I might well take the train.

Bien puede ser que llamen esta tarde.
They're quite likely to phone this evening.

Bien pudiera ser que necesitara tu coche el fin de semana.
I may well need your car over the weekend.

(iii) Other structures expressing probability include:

Es muy probable que Laura haga el papel de reina.
It's very likely that Laura will play the role of the queen.

Tengo muchas posibilidades de obtener una beca.
There's a very good chance that I'll get a grant.

Se supone que llegan en el tren de las seis.
So far as we know, they'll be arriving on the six o'clock train.

Tendrían que devolverte el dinero inmediatamente.
They should reimburse you immediately.

90 Possibility

Most constructions expressing 'the possibility that . . .' or 'doubt that . . .' are followed by the subjunctive. Compare this with the predominance of the indicative in expressions of certainty and probability (sections 88 and 89).

(i) Brief responses to indicate that something is possible include:

¿Está enfermo? – Es posible.
Is he ill? – Possibly. / Maybe.

¿Vas a necesitar el coche? – Quizás.
Are you going to need the car? – I might.

¿Vas a poder sustituirle? – Quizás más tarde.
Could you stand in for him? – Later, perhaps.

(ii) More elaborate expressions of possibility often use the verb *poder*:

Puede que se hayan perdido (subj.) *por el camino.*
They may have got lost on the way.

Puede que se les haya averiado (subj.) *el coche.*
It's possible their car's broken down.

¡Podrías pensar que lo ha hecho a propósito!
You might almost think that he did it deliberately.

(iii) Possibility can also be expressed by a range of idiomatic phrases:

Es fácil que no esté (subj.) *en condiciones de ayudarte.*
It's quite likely that he's not in a position to help you.

Nosotros os apoyaremos en la medida de lo posible.
We shall support you as far as we can.

Ha hecho todo lo posible para que salgas (subj.) *elegido.*
She's done everything she can to get you appointed.

Lo que propones es bastante factible.
What you're suggesting is quite feasible.

Sí, me parece que se trata de un proyecto realizable.
Yes, I think this plan could work.

A mí entender, sería un sucesor posible.
He'd make a possible successor, in my opinion.

91 Impossibility

The expressions to denote possibility listed in the previous section can be used in the negative to suggest impossibility.

(i) Other adjectival expressions for suggesting impossibility include:

Esa fecha nos resulta imposible.
We can't make that date.

Mi hijo está siempre intentando lo imposible.
My son's always trying to do the impossible.

Me gustaría viajar por todo el mundo, pero es un sueño irrealizable.
I'd like to travel all over the world, but it's an impossible dream.

El trato estaba condenado al fracaso.
The deal was bound to fail.

(ii) Other structures to express impossibility:

Es imposible excluirla del equipo.
She can't possibly be left out of the team.

Esa exigencia ha hecho imposible cualquier compromiso.
This demand has made any compromise impossible.

Es imposible / inadmisible que lo hagas (subj.) *tú en su lugar.*
It's out of the question for you to do it instead of him.

No podemos contemplar la posibilidad de vender el mobiliario.
There's no question of our selling off the furniture.

92 Doubt

(i) Spanish possesses the verb *dudar*, the cognate of the English verb 'to doubt'.

No hay por qué dudar de la autenticidad de esta firma.
There's no reason to doubt that the signature is genuine.

Dudo que haya tenido (subj.) *tiempo para hacerlo todo.*
I doubt if he has had time to do everything.

Siempre dudé que triunfara (subj.).
I always doubted that he would succeed.

(ii) Other verbal constructions to express doubt:

No sabía si tenía que despertarte.
I didn't know whether I should wake you up.

No me fiaba de lo que había dicho.
I didn't trust what he had said.

Nada indica que haya decidido (subj.) *regresar.*
There's nothing to suggest he's decided to come back.

Sospecho que no está capacitado.
I have a suspicion that he is not fully qualified (for the job).

(iii) Adverbial and adjectival constructions to express doubt:

El director no va a estar necesariamente de acuerdo.
The manager won't necessarily be in agreement.

Va a ser difícilmente convencida.
It will be difficult to persuade her.

Es poco probable que la tienda esté abierta el domingo.
It's unlikely that the shop's open on Sunday.

Es todavía dudoso que se presente a las próximas elecciones.
It is still doubtful whether she will stand at the next election.

El resultado es todavía incierto.
The outcome is still unsure.

El veredicto era discutible.
The verdict was open to question.

Es un procedimiento aleatorio.
The procedure leaves everything to chance.

COMPLAINTS AND EXPLANATIONS

93 Making complaints

(i) To make tentative or polite complaints:

Mire usted, he pedido el número 39 y el zapato que me ha sacado es el 38.
I'm sorry, but I asked for a size 39 and the shoe you've given me is size 38.

Creo que hay un error en la cuenta.
I think there is a mistake in the bill.

Me temo que ha habido un malentendido.
I'm afraid there's been a misunderstanding.

¿Podría pedirle que comprobara (subj.) *la cantidad?*
Could I ask you to check the amount?

¿Podría corregir la factura, por favor?
Would you correct the invoice?

(ii) To make more forceful or official complaints:

Quisiéramos hablar inmediatamente con el propietario.
We'd like to speak to the owner straightaway.

Tengo que presentar una queja sobre el estado de la habitación.
I must complain about the state of the bedroom.

Tengo que señalarle que esta escalera es muy peligrosa.
I must point out to you that this staircase is very dangerous.

Mi marido no puede soportar más ese ruido.
My husband can't stand that noise any longer.

La dirección no puede seguir ignorando sus faltas de asistencia.
The management can't continue to overlook your irregular timekeeping.

Si no se retracta de su acusación, me veré obligado a presentar una queja. < formal >
If you do not withdraw your allegations, I shall be forced to make an official complaint.

(iii) There are various adjectives to suggest that something is unacceptable, which can be used to strengthen complaints:

Encontramos inadmisible este procedimiento.
We find this course of action quite unacceptable.

La juzgo una actitud inadmisible.
I consider this attitude unacceptable.

Estos niños son francamente insoportables. < coll. >
These children are absolutely impossible / insufferable.

Es una falta de educación inexcusable.
It shows an unforgivable lack of manners.

Me parece un comentario imperdonable.
I consider that remark unforgivable.

Su pregunta está fuera de lugar.
Your question is inappropriate.

94 Making apologies

In Spanish, as in most languages, there are set formulae for making your apologies, and accepting those of someone else.

★ Constructions expressing 'I am sorry that / I regret that ...' are followed by a subjunctive (see section 46).

(i) Apologizing to friends:

At the simplest level, you may use one of these exclamations:

¡Perdón! Sorry!
¡Perdone! ¡Disculpe! My apologies!
Lo siento mucho. I'm really sorry.

Slightly more elaborate ways of apologizing and admitting responsibility include:

Ha sido culpa mía, perdóneme. It's my fault, I'm sorry.

Espero que no estés (subj.) *demasiado molesto conmigo.*
I hope you're not too upset with me.

Siento mucho haberle molestado.
I'm very sorry to have disturbed you / troubled you.

If you want to apologize but also suggest you are not entirely to blame, use *Lo siento mucho* and one of the following:

No lo he hecho a propósito. I didn't do it on purpose.

No pude hacer otra cosa.
There was nothing else I could do.
Sólo quería ayudarte.
I was only trying to help you.
No había otra posibilidad.
I didn't have any choice.

(ii) More formal apologies in conversation:

¡Perdóneme! (e.g. if you tread on someone's toes)
Oh, I'm sorry!
La culpa es mía.
It's my fault. / I'm to blame.
Sentimos mucho que la mercancía no haya llegado (subj.).
We're very sorry that the goods haven't arrived.
Me siento culpable por no haberos avisado.
I feel to blame for not letting you know.
Me temo que te he enfadado.
I'm afraid I've annoyed you.
El director lamenta muchísimo que nuestro fotógrafo no esté
(subj.) *aquí hoy.*
The manager is extremely sorry that our photographer isn't here today.
El alcalde os ruega que aceptéis (subj.) *sus disculpas. Tenía otro compromiso.*
The mayor sends his apologies. He had another engagement.
Tengo que reiterar nuestras excuses por este desafortunado incidente. < formal >
I can only repeat our apologies for this unfortunate incident.

(iii) To apologize in formal correspondence:

Por favor, disculpe nuestro retraso en contestarle.
Please forgive us for the delay in replying to you.
Le pido disculpas por nuestro error, que ya hemos rectificado.
I apologize for our error, which we have now corrected.
Lamentamos informarle de que nuestra tienda permanecerá cerrada durante todo el mes de agosto.
We regret to inform you that our store will be closed for the whole of August.

Lamentamos que la pieza no esté (subj.) *disponible en estos momentos.*
We regret that this (spare) part is not currently available.

La constructora pide disculpas por el ruido ocasionado por las obras.
The company apologizes for the noise caused by the building works.

95 Accepting apologies

(i) To accept apologies without reservation:

No pasa nada. It doesn't matter. / No harm done.
No se hable más. Don't mention it. / Say no more.
Olvídalo. Forget it.
No importa, déjalo. It doesn't matter, don't worry.

(ii) To accept an apology, but stress that the fault must not happen again:

Está bien, pero debes prestar más atención en el futuro.
I forgive you, but you should take more care in future.

Esperemos que esto no vuelva a ocurrir.
Let us hope it doesn't happen again.

96 Asking for and offering explanations

(i) Asking someone for an explanation:

This may be a neutral request for information (as in the first two examples below), or a demand that the person addressed should justify himself / herself (as in the subsequent examples).

¿Podrías explicarme las instrucciones de uso?
Could you explain the instructions to me?

¿Me puedes explicar lo que pasa?
Can you explain to me what's happening?

Tengo que pedirte que me expliques (subj.) *tu decisión.*
May I ask you to explain your decision?

Espero que puedas (subj.) *explicar tu ausencia.*
I hope / trust you can account for your absence.

¿Cómo piensa justificar este retraso?
How do you intend to justify this delay?

(ii) Offering an explanation:

¿Quiere usted que le explique (subj.) *la estructura de nuestra sociedad?*
Would you like me to explain to you our company's structure?

Si quiere, le enseño cómo funciona la máquina.
If you like, I'll show you how the machine works.

Permítame que le explique nuestro razonamiento.
Allow me to explain our reasoning to you.

Si me lo permite, intentaré aclarar la razón de este malentendido.
If you will allow me, I'll try to explain the reason for this misunderstanding.

Me quería hacer ver los obstáculos.
He wanted to point out the obstacles to me.

Mi colega podrá darle cuenta de nuestros progresos.
My colleague will be able to tell you all about our progress.

Tengo que disculparme por mi comportamiento de ayer.
I must apologize for my conduct yesterday.

No quiero ir. Voy a dar el pretexto de que tengo una reunión.
I don't want to go. I'll make the excuse that I've got a meeting.

97 Giving explanations

Constructions for giving explanations rely heavily on prepositions / prepositional phrases, conjunctions, or verbs.

(i) Prepositions / prepositional phrases:

A causa de la niebla, decidió no coger el coche.
He decided not to take the car because of the fog.

Debido a vacaciones del personal, la biblioteca permanecerá cerrada los lunes.
The library will be closed on Mondays because of staff holidays.

Por una demanda excepcional, la mercancía se ha agotado.
Supplies have been exhausted as a result of exceptional demand.

Debido a la saturación de las líneas, no podemos contestar a su llamada.
Since all the lines are engaged, we cannot answer your call.

En vista del mal tiempo, la fiesta será suspendida.
In view of the bad weather, the fête will be cancelled.

Vistos los sacrificios que ha tenido que hacer, intentaremos recompensarle.
In view of the sacrifices you've had to make, we shall try to recompense you.

Gracias a su generosidad, podremos arreglar la iglesia.
Thanks to his generosity, we shall be able to repair the church.

Las excavaciones se llevaron a cabo con la ayuda de una subvención municipal.
The excavations were completed with the help of a grant from the local council.

Gracias a una inversión considerable, van a aumentar su volumen de negocios.
They'll increase their turnover thanks to large-scale investment.

A pesar de la lluvia, salimos.
We went out despite the rain.

Por falta de personal, nos vemos obligados a cerrar al mediodía.
Because of staff shortages, we are forced to shut at lunchtime.

(ii) Conjunctions which indicate an explanation:

No puedo ir porque tengo una cena esta noche.
I can't come because I've got a dinner tonight.

Ya que existe el riesgo de un atentado, tendrán que aumentarse los controles de seguridad.
Because there is the risk of an assassination attempt, security checks will have to be increased.

Realizó sus estudios en México, por lo que habla muy bien el español.
She did her training in Mexico, so she speaks good Spanish.

Nos hemos quedado sin dos empleados, así que vamos retrasados con el correo.
We've lost two members of staff, so we're behind with the mail.

Necesitan un estudiante de biología. Fue por eso por lo que pensé en ti.
They need somebody studying biology. That's why I thought of you.

Debido a que trata un tema de actualidad, este autor es muy apreciado.
This author is highly thought of because he writes about a topical subject.

Yo me encargaré de las invitaciones, a condición de que tú me mandes (subj.) la lista de direcciones.
I'll take care of the invitations, provided you send me the address list.

Volvimos ayer, aunque querían que nos quedáramos (subj.) un día más.
We came back yesterday, although they wanted us to stay a day longer.

No quise llamar al timbre por si acaso estábais ya en la cama.
I decided not to ring the bell in case you were already in bed.

(iii) Verbal constructions used to give an explanation:

La erosión la causan principalmente los elementos.
The erosion is caused mainly by adverse weather.

La riña se produjo por un choque de temperamentos.
The quarrel stemmed from a clash of temperaments.

Este tipo de mal se remonta a las condiciones de vida de aquella época.
This kind of misfortune could be traced back to living conditions at the time.

Su éxito se podría atribuir a su entusiasmo.
His / Her success could be attributed to his / her enthusiasm.

La crisis se puede explicar por la falta de inversiones.
The crisis can be explained by the lack of investment.

INVITATIONS

98 Giving an invitation

(i) When talking informally, to friends or close colleagues:

¿Te gustaría venir a tomar algo?
Would you like to come for a drink?

¿Quieres venir a la fiesta de presentación de mi libro?
Will you come to the party for the launch of my book?

Mañana vamos a tener una fiesta de inauguración del piso. Espero que podáis venir los dos.
We're having a housewarming party tomorrow. I hope you can both come.

¡Te invito a celebrar la noticia en un restaurante!
Let me take you out to lunch / dinner to celebrate the news.

Vamos al teatro, yo invito.
Let's go / We'll go to the theatre. It's my treat. / It's on me.

¿Estás libre para tomar una copa con nosotros?
Are you free to come and have a drink with us?

(ii) When issuing an invitation more formally:

Espero que se puedan unir a nosotros para la cena del domingo.
We hope you'll be free to join us for dinner on Sunday.

Estaríamos encantados si pudieran venir con nosotros.
We'd be delighted if you could join us.

Tenemos el gusto de invitarles a la inauguración de la exposición.
We'd like to invite you to the opening of the exhibition.

99 Accepting an invitation

(i) Brief or informal acceptance:

Sí, yo me apunto. Yes, with pleasure. / Count me in.
Muy amable, gracias. That's very kind of you, thank you.
Sí, de todas todas. Yes, sure / definitely.
Ah, nos apetece mucho. We'll be very happy to come.

(ii) More formal verbal acceptance:

Es muy amable de tu parte.
That's most kind of you.

Acepto encantado.
I'm delighted to accept.

Será un gran placer ir con ustedes.
We'll be very happy to go with you.

Estaremos encantados de asistir a la ceremonia.
We'll be delighted to attend the ceremony.

100 Declining an invitation

(i) Brief or informal refusal:

Es una lástima, pero no puedo.
What a pity. I can't.

Desgraciadamente, nos es imposible la semana que viene.
Unfortunately, we can't make next week.

Me hubiera encantado, pero ya tenía otros planes.
I'd have loved to, but I've already got something on.

Lo siento mucho, pero tenemos otro compromiso esa noche.
I'm really sorry, but we've got another engagement that evening.

(ii) More formal refusal:

Lo siento mucho, pero estamos comprometidos hasta finales de julio.
I'm so sorry, but we aren't free until the end of July.

Lamento mucho no poderme unir a ustedes.
I'm most sorry that I shan't be able to join you.

Es muy amable de su parte, pero tengo un compromiso anterior.
It's very kind of you, but I have a prior engagement.

Desgraciadamente, me es imposible aceptar su invitación.
Unfortunately, I am unable to accept your invitation.

USING THE TELEPHONE

Speaking a foreign language on the phone is often daunting, but the task becomes easier if you know some of the standard responses you are likely to hear, and if you have worked out in advance what you want to say.

If you have to give a telephone number, it is usual to split it up into groups of two digits, given together, e.g. 0865-515479 would be given as 08.65.51.54.79, i.e. *cero ocho, sesenta y cinco, cincuenta y uno, cincuenta y cuatro, setenta y nueve.*

101 Answering the phone

(i) There are several standard ways of answering a call, but it never consists of simply giving the number (as many people do in Britain).

> *Dígame.* Hello.

> *Hotel Granada, buenos días.*
> Granada Hotel, good morning / good afternoon.

(ii) To check if you have the right number:

> *¿Es la señora Ormaechea?*
> Is that Mrs Ormaechea?

> *¿Es el (número) 23 87 93?*
> Is that 23 87 93?

(iii) If you have the wrong number, you will hear:

> *No, se ha equivocado (de número).*
> No, you've got the wrong number.

> *¿A qué número llama?*
> What number did you want?

> *No, le han cambiado de número.*
> No, he's no longer on this number.

102 Getting put through

(i) To ask for the person you want:

¿Puedo hablar con Lola, por favor?
Could I speak to Lola, please?

Quisiera hablar con el director.
I'd like to speak to the manager.

Extensión 4234, por favor.
Extension 4234, please.

¿Podría ponerme con la señora Viñaspre, por favor?
Could you put me through to Mrs Viñaspre, please?

(ii) The person who answers or is putting you through may say:

¿De parte de quién?
Who is it calling?

Ahora mismo le pongo.
I'm putting you through.

La extensión está comunicando. ¿Quiere esperar?
The extension's engaged. Would you like to hold?

El señor de Gregorio no contesta.
Mr de Gregorio isn't answering.

(iii) An operator or secretary wishing to put a call through to a given person will say:

Hay una llamada personal para la señorita Tricio.
There's a personal call for Miss Tricio.

Le llama la señora Sáez de Salamanca. ¿Quiere contestar a la llamada?
Mrs Sáez is calling from Salamanca. Will you take the call?

Tengo al señor Ridruejo en la línea.
Mr Ridruejo is on the line for you.

103 Leaving a message

(i) To ask someone to phone you:

¿Podrías darme un telefonazo esta tarde?
Could you give me a ring this afternoon / evening?

¿Podría decirle a la señora Foronda que me llame más tarde?
Could you ask Mrs Foronda to ring me back later?

Su colega puede contactar conmigo esta tarde. Le voy a dar mi número.
Your colleague can get in touch with me this afternoon / evening.
I'll give you my number.

(ii) Taking a message for someone:

¿Quién tengo que decir que ha llamado?
Who shall I say rang?

¿Quiere dejar algún recado?
Would you like to leave a message?

¿Puedo dejarle un recado?
Can I leave a message for him / her?

¿Quiere que le diga que le llame?
Shall I get her / him to ring you back?

Deje su mensaje después de la señal. (answering machine)
Please speak after the tone.

104 Ending a conversation

Bueno, tengo que colgar. Hasta luego.
Well, I must ring off. Bye. / Cheerio.

Bueno, tengo que dejarte. Hasta luego, entonces.
I must ring off. Well, goodbye then.

Adiós. Un abrazo. Cheerio. All my love. / All the best.

Bueno, hasta el domingo entonces. OK, till Sunday then.

105 The operator and reporting problems

(i) Reporting faults:

Esta línea es muy defectuosa / tiene un defecto.
The line is very bad.

Te entiendo muy mal. ¿Puedes hablar un poco más alto?
It's a bad line. Can you speak up?

Se ha cortado la comunicación.
We were cut off.

(ii) Directory enquiries:

¿Puede darme <u>el número de</u> la Caja Rural de Haro?
Can you give me the number of the Caja Rural in Haro.

¿Cuál es <u>el prefijo de</u> Portugal, por favor?
What's the code for Portugal, please?

Lo siento, pero este abonado <u>no está en la guía.</u>
I'm sorry, but the customer is ex-directory.

No aparece <u>nadie bajo ese nombre.</u>
We have no person listed under that name.

(iii) Official recorded messages:

El número que solicita está fuera de servicio.
The number you want is not available.

Todas las líneas están ocupadas. Por favor, llame más tarde.
All the lines are engaged. Please try later.

WRITING LETTERS

Correspondence is subject to convention in most languages, and so it is in Spanish, where the formulae for opening and closing a letter are plentiful. The choice is rarely arbitrary: how you address your correspondent, and how you sign off, are indicative of how you see your relationship with the other person. Below you will find detailed guidance on the appropriate form for the context. You may well come across subtle variations in letters you receive from Spanish correspondents.

In common types of correspondence – requests, complaints, making a reservation and so forth – there are set phrases which most writers will use. To demonstrate how these work in an authentic context, examples are given in the form of short letters on key subjects. With some adaptations, these should serve as basic models. You may observe that conventional phrases tend to be longer in Spanish – especially the equivalents of 'Yours sincerely' and 'Yours faithfully'.

106 Beginning and ending letters

(a) Heading official letters

For formal correspondence it is normal either to use headed paper or to put your name and address (including the postcode) at the top of the letter.

Below this, on the left-hand side, put the title, name and address of the person to whom the letter is addressed. The titles *Sr / Sra / Srta* are given here, or you can use *D.* (*Don / Doña*):

> *Sra Pilar Ovejas*
> *D. Jesús Ayúcar*

Usually both are given:

> *Sra Dª*
> *Sr D.*

The date should be put on the right-hand side, a little higher than the name of the addressee. Remember that months are written with a small letter. It is usual to write the day of the month and the year in figures, but the month as a word, with or without the preposition *de*, as with the year. It is also possible to write the date only in figures:

27 de febrero de 1992
27 febrero 1992
27 / 2 / 1992

Below the name of the addressee, on the left (or if you prefer, immediately below the letter heading), you can include:

s / ref. . . . Your ref. . . .
n / ref. . . . Our ref. . . .
Asunto: . . . Re: . . .

> *Sra Angeles Castillo*
> *9 Oxford Road*
> *Oxford OX3 0TS*
>
> *16 / 9 / 1992*
>
> *Sr D. Juan José Ramos*
> *Departamento de Contabilidad*
> *Bodegas del Norte*
> *Avenida de La Paz, 98*
> *26005 Logroño*
>
> *s / ref. AD / 7 / 92*
> *Asunto: Precios 1993*

(b) Addressing your correspondent

For any official letter (e.g. business, to hotels) addressed to a person who is not known to you personally, or only in a formal capacity, use:

Muy señor mío / Estimado señor Dear Sir
Muy señora mía / Estimada señora Dear Madam

If you are writing to a person in an important position, whom you do not know personally, or only formally, it is preferable to use *Señor / Señora* + title:

Señor Jefe de Estudios Dear Director of Studies
Señora Directora Dear Headmistress

For professional correspondence, when writing to a colleague or counterpart whom you know, one can use:

Querido Señor Del Barco Dear Mr Del Barco

Querida Señora Rupérez Dear Mrs / Ms Rupérez

For informal letters to personal friends with whom you are on first name terms, use:

Queridos Fernando y Pilar

Querida Montse

A variant of this, particularly appropriate when writing to friends with whom you have a slightly more formal relationship (e.g. friends of an older generation) is:

Querido amigo / Querida amiga / Queridos amigos

(c) Ending letters

The enormous number of formulae used to end Spanish correspondence can seem bewildering, so this section offers examples of the most important ones for different contexts.

For a formal (business) letter which began *Señor / Señora*, the equivalent to 'Yours faithfully' is:

Le saluda atentamente.

For a formal letter to someone in an important official position (M.P., Director, etc.), a more respectful equivalent of 'Yours faithfully' is:

Le saluda respetuosamente.

For a formal letter to a person with whom you have had some professional contact, the equivalent of 'Yours sincerely' is:

Le saluda cordialmente.

For a personal letter to acquaintances or friends you do not know closely – in other words, those you would address as *usted* in Spanish – equivalents of 'Yours ever' / 'All good wishes' include (in descending order of formality):

Un atento saludo

Un cordial saludo

Afectuosos saludos

Con todo mi afecto

For personal letters to close friends or family – those you would address as *tú* in Spanish – equivalents of 'love' / 'love and best wishes' include:

> *Un fuerte abrazo*
> *Besos*
> *Besos y abrazos*
> *Con todo mi cariño*

107 Informal letters

When you are writing a general 'newsy' letter to friends, the style can be informal, and the content will obviously depend on the situation. The example below gives ideas for some standard phrases for thanks, good wishes and so forth.

Oxford, 25 / 8 / 92

Querido Eduardo:

Muchas gracias por tu carta desde Santander. Me encantó recibir noticias tuyas y saber que te lo estás pasando muy bien en los Picos de Europa. Siento haber tardado tanto en contestarte, pero he tenido un montón de trabajo todo el mes. Además, me tengo que cambiar de casa a finales del verano, y me he pasado un montón de tiempo buscando piso. Un amigo me había ofrecido que compartiera con él la casa, pero es un poco cara. De todas maneras, ya te mandaré mi nueva dirección cuando la sepa, y quizás puedas venir a verme en septiembre. ¡A ver si es posible!

Pepe y yo lo pasamos fenomenal cuando estuvimos de vacaciones contigo. A propósito, Pepe te manda sus recuerdos; los dos tenemos muchas ganas de volver a verte muy pronto. Hasta entonces recibe un abrazo muy fuerte de

Claudia

Oxford, 25 / 8 / 92

Dear Eduardo,

Many thanks for your letter from Santander. It was great to get your news
and to hear that you are having a good time in the Picos de Europa. I'm
sorry it's taken me a while to reply, but I've had a lot of work to do in the
last month. Also, I've got to move house by the end of the summer, so I've
spent a hell of a lot of time looking for a new flat. A friend suggested that I
share his place, but it's a bit expensive. Anyway, I'll send you my new
address when I know it and perhaps you'll come to see me in September?
I'd be delighted if you could.

Pepe and I had a wonderful time when we were on holiday with you.
Incidentally, I mustn't forget that Pepe said to send you his love. We're both
looking forward to seeing you very soon.

With love from
Claudia

108 Making reservations and bookings

(a) To the Tourist Office for a list of hotels and campsites

Oficina de Información y Turismo
Calle de La Rioja, 66
66007 Logroño   Orense, 12 / 8 / 92

Estimados señores:

Estamos planeando visitar su región en el mes de septiembre y le
agradecería mucho que me mandara una lista de hoteles y campings
en las cercanías de Ezcaray. También, me gustaría recibir
alguna información sobre excursiones en autobús desde Ezcaray o
Santo Domingo.

Muchas gracias y un cordial saludo.

Oficina de Información y Turismo
Calle de La Rioja, 66
66007 Logroño   Orense, 12 / 8 / 92

Dear Sir / Madam,

We are planning to visit your region in September, and I should be grateful
if you could send me a list of hotels and campsites near Ezcaray. I would also
like some information about trips by coach from Ezcaray or Santo Domingo.

Thanking you for your advice,

Yours faithfully,

(b) To a hotel to ask about the availability of rooms

> *Hotel Casa Vasca*
> *Calle Mayor, 33*
> *22009 Haro, La Rioja*   *12 / 4 / 92*
>
> *Estimados señores:*
>
> *Quiero pasar una semana con mi familia en Haro, del 2 al 9 de junio,
> y necesitaríamos dos habitaciones dobles con baño. ¿Podrían
> enviarnos los precios correspondientes, con desayuno o a media
> pensión?*
>
> *Se despide con un cordial saludo*

Dear Sir or Madam,

I wish to spend a week with my family in Haro, from 2 to 9 June, and we
should need two double bedrooms with bathroom. Could you send us your
prices for bed and breakfast and half-board?

Yours faithfully,

201

(c) To confirm a hotel booking

Señor D. A. Ridruejo
Hotel Viñaspre
Avenida del Cantábrico, 102
65332 Santander

Estimado señor Ridruejo:

He recibido el folleto informativo y los precios de su hotel y le escribo
para confirmar mi reserva de una habitación individual para las 4
noches del 12 al 15 de junio. Deseo una habitación con baño y
desayuno, al precio de 6.500 pesetas por noche. ¿Sería tan amable de
confirmarme la reserva lo antes posible?

Se despide atentamente

Dear Sir,

I have received the brochure and prices for your hotel and am writing to
confirm my reservation for a single room for four nights from 12 to 15 June.
I would like a single room with bathroom and breakfast, at the daily rate of
6500 pesetas. Could you send me a confirmation of the reservation as soon
as possible?

Yours faithfully,

(d) To reserve a place in a campsite

Camping Los Chopos
Santillana del Mar
Cantabria   *22 / 3 / 93*

Estimados señores:

Vamos a visitar su región del 15 al 25 de abril. ¿Podrían reservarnos
una plaza en su camping para estos días y enviarnos una lista de
precios? Se trata de un grupo de 2 adultos y 2 niños, con una tienda
de campaña y un coche.

A la espera de sus noticias, se despide atentamente

Dear Sir or Madam,

We are visiting your region from 15 to 25 April. Could you reserve us a pitch at your campsite for this period and send us your current prices? We shall be a party of two adults and two children, with a tent and car.

Looking forward to hearing from you,

Yours faithfully,

(e) To book furnished holiday accommodation

Sra Dª Dora Sáez
Calle de la Peña, 12
Islallana, La Rioja   *9/2/93*

Estimada Señora Sáez:

La Oficina de Turismo de Calahorra me ha proporcionado su nombre y dirección y le escribo para preguntarle si su casa estará disponible para alquilar la primera quincena de abril. Si lo está, ¿podría decirme el precio de la misma? Se trata de un grupo de 4 adultos.

¿Me podría dar también alguna información sobre las habitaciones y si disponen de ropa de cama?

Se despide atentamente

Dear Señora Sáez,

I have received your address from the Tourist Office in Calahorra, and am writing to ask whether your house will be available for the first two weeks in April. If so, could you let me know the price? We will be a group of four adults.

Could I also ask you for some further information about the rooms and the provision of bed-linen?

Yours sincerely,

109 Letters of complaint

(a) To a shop in respect of an unsatisfactory purchase

Textiles El Hogar
Plaza del Mercado, 34
98456 Zaragoza   *12 / 11 / 92*

Estimados señores:

Lamento tener que informarles que no estoy satisfecho con la calidad del mantel de algodón que compré en su establecimiento la semana pasada.

Después de haberlo usado sólo una vez, lo lavé en la lavadora, teniendo buen cuidado de seguir las instrucciones de lavado. Con todo, los colores han desteñido y el mantel ha quedado inservible.

Por lo tanto, me gustaría solicitar la devolución de la totalidad del importe del artículo en cuestión, 2.900 pesetas.

Se despide atentamente

Dear Sir or Madam,

I regret to inform you that I am dissatisfied with the cotton tablecloth which I bought from your shop last week.

After using it only once, I put it through the washing-machine, taking great care to follow the washing instructions. Despite this, the colours ran, with the result that I am unable to use the tablecloth again.

I would therefore ask you for a refund of the full price of the article, i.e. 2900 pesetas.

Yours faithfully,

(b) To an estate agent in respect of unsatisfactory accommodation

Inmobiliaria Turia
Calle de Manuel de Falla, 122
88000 Valencia   *20 / 10 / 92*

Estimados señores:

Lamentamos tener que dirigirles una carta de queja, pero estamos muy poco contentos con respecto al apartamento que ustedes nos facilitaron en la urbanización Los Naranjos. Habíamos solicitado un apartamento de dos habitaciones en una zona tranquila. Sin embargo, sin previo aviso, nos proporcionaron uno muy pequeño, de un solo dormitorio y en una zona muy ruidosa, sobre todo por las noches.

A mi llegada intenté contactar con ustedes para comunicarles mi descontento, pero su oficina permaneció cerrada durante toda la semana que pasamos en Valencia.

Consideramos que su agencia no nos ha proporcionado el servicio que esperábamos. Por lo tanto me veo obligado a pedirles la devolución de al menos el 50 por ciento del alquiler que pagamos.

Se despide atentamente

Dear Sir or Madam,

We regret that we must register our disappointment in respect of the flat you provided for us in Los Naranjos. We had requested a two-bedroom flat in a quiet area. However, without prior notification, you gave us a very small one-bedroom flat, in an area which was distinctly noisy, especially in the evenings.

Upon my arrival, I attempted to contact you to express my dissatisfaction, but your office was closed for the whole of the week we stayed in Valencia.

We consider that your agency has failed to treat our booking with the care we would expect. I must therefore ask you to refund at least 50 per cent of the rent we paid you.

Yours faithfully,

(c) To an individual in respect of unacceptable / unneighbourly behaviour

Sr D. Francisco Gordo
Calle Tormento, 17
34500 Madrid   8/9/1992

Estimado señor Gordo:

He dudado mucho antes de decidirme a escribir esta carta.

He alquilado la casa de al lado de la suya para el mes de septiembre, con la esperanza de pasar unas vacaciones tranquilas. Sin embargo, sus hijos han tomado la costumbre de pasar horas delante de nuestra casa arreglando sus motos y escuchando música a todo volumen. En varias ocasiones les he señalado que esto nos causaba una gran molestia, pero mis quejas no han servido de nada.

Quisiera rogarle que les repitiera mi queja, ya que creo que deberíamos llegar a una solución aceptable para todos.

Se despide atentamente

Dear Mr Gordo,

It is with some hesitation that I write to you.

I rented the house next to yours for September, hoping to enjoy a quiet holiday. However, your sons have taken to spending hours outside our house repairing their motorbikes and listening to very loud music. On several occasions I have pointed out to them that this was causing us considerable annoyance, but my complaints have had no effect.

Could I ask you to back me up? In this situation, I feel that we need to find a neighbourly solution.

Yours sincerely,

(d) To a public body in respect of unsatisfactory service

Oficina de Turismo
98723 San Pablo   1 / 04 / 1993

Estimados señores:

*Lamento tener que informarles que los datos del folleto sobre San
Pablo que me enviaron en marzo propenden, cuando menos, a
confundir al usuario.*

*Su folleto afirma que en San Pablo hay tres campings, cuando, en
realidad, no queda más de uno. Por otro lado, la exposición 'El
Románico del Camino de Santiago', que su folleto tanto elogia, se
clausuró en febrero.*

*Tengo que decirles que nuestra estancia en San Pablo fue muy
decepcionante.*

Le saluda atentamente

Dear Sir or Madam,

I regret to inform you that the information in the brochure on San Pablo
which you sent me in March is, to say the least, misleading.

Your brochure says that San Pablo has three public campsites, whereas in
fact there is now only one. Furthermore, the exhibition on 'El Románico del
Camino de Santiago', which your brochure warmly recommends, closed in
February.

I am forced to say that we were disappointed by our stay in San Pablo.

Yours sincerely,

110 Letters concerning employment

(a) Seeking vacation / short-term employment

Editorial Universal
Departamento de Personal
Paseo de Pamplona, 68
77867 Zaragoza   *7 / 6 / 93*

Asunto: empleo durante el verano

Estimados señores:

Me gustaría trabajar en España durante mis vacaciones de verano y le agradecería mucho que tuviera la bondad de decirme si su empresa dispone de puestos de carácter temporal. Estoy libre del 1 de julio al 15 de septiembre, y podría trabajar de secretaria, recepcionista o auxiliar administrativa.

Con la esperanza de una respuesta afirmativa, le mando adjunto mi curriculum vitae.

Se despide atentamente

Dear Sir or Madam,

Re: application for a vacation post

I should like to work in Spain during the summer vacation, and should be grateful if you could inform me whether your firm offers temporary posts. I am available from 1 July until 15 September, and am willing to work as a secretary, receptionist or in a clerical post.

In the hope that you may be interested in my application, I enclose my C.V.

Yours faithfully,

(b) Applying for a job as an au pair

Sra Dª P. Foronda
Calle Lagasca, 66
23098 Zaragoza   *14 / 6 / 93*

Estimada señora Foronda:

He visto en Heraldo de Aragón su anuncio pidiendo una au pair para el mes de julio. El empleo sería ideal para mí, ya que me gustan mucho los niños pequeños, y estoy interesada en pasar una temporada en España para practicar y mejorar el español; es por ello por lo que le adjunto mi curriculum vitae.

Si acoge favorablemente mi solicitud, ¿podría indicarme cuál sería la paga y el horario de trabajo?

Se despide atentamente

Dear Mrs Foronda,

I saw your advertisement in the *Heraldo de Aragón* for an au pair for July. The post would be ideal for me, since I am very fond of small children, and would like to spend some time in Spain to improve my Spanish. I enclose my C.V. for your attention.

If you are interested in my application, might I ask you about the allowance you would pay and the hours I would be expected to work?

Yours sincerely,

(c) Applying for a post advertised in the press

> *Caja Norte*
> *Departamento de Personal*
> *Calle Jorge Vigón, 66*
> *00923 Logroño*   *26 / 11 / 1993*
>
> *Asunto: oferta de empleo de traductor / a*
>
> *Estimados señores:*
>
> *En respuesta a su anuncio publicado en El País, estoy interesado en solicitar el puesto arriba mencionado. Adjunto mi curriculum vitae.*
>
> *Si ustedes lo desean, estaré dispuesto a acudir, para una entrevista, a su oficina.*
>
> *Les saluda atentamente*

Dear Sir or Madam,

Re: application for the post of translator

In response to your advertisement in *El País*, I would like to apply for the above vacancy. Please find enclosed my C.V.

If you wish, I shall be available for interview at your offices.

Yours faithfully,

(d) Accepting a written offer of a post

> *Galerías AS*
> *Departamento de Personal*
> *Vía de la Hispanidad, 99*
> *23009 Zaragoza*   *1 / 9 / 1993*
>
> *A la atención de D. Enrique Ansó*
>
> *Estimado señor Ansó:*
>
> *Muchas gracias por su carta del 28 de agosto en la que me ofrece el puesto de secretaria bilingüe, en su empresa, a partir del 15 de septiembre. Las condiciones que propone en su carta me son totalmente aceptables, y me alegra mucho poder aceptar este empleo.*
>
> *Un cordial saludo*

Dear Mr Ansó,

Thank you very much for your letter of 28 August, offering me the post of bilingual secretary in your firm, with effect from 15 September. All the conditions outlined in your letter are perfectly satisfactory and I am extremely pleased to accept the post.

Yours sincerely,

(e) Letter of resignation

Hotel Marqués de la Ensenada
Calle Iruña, 6
09088 Pamplona   *7 / 9 / 1993*

A la atención de la Directora de Personal

Estimada señora Tricio:

Le escribo para comunicarle que he decidido continuar mis estudios universitarios y, por lo tanto, tengo que dejar mi empleo de recepcionista en su hotel. Estaría dispuesto a trabajar hasta finales de mes, a menos que puedan reemplazarme antes.

Se despide cordialmente

Dear Ms Tricio,

I am writing to inform you of my decision to go back to university, and so I must ask you to accept my resignation from the post of receptionist at your hotel. I shall be happy to work until the end of the month, unless you can find a replacement earlier.

Yours sincerely,

111 Curriculum vitae

Applications for jobs in Spain will usually require a C.V. to be submitted. The example below gives the standard headings, and some indications of appropriate information.

CURRICULUM VITAE

APELLIDO: *Berrozpe*

NOMBRE: *Pilar*

DIRECCIÓN: *Calle Pablo Iglesias, 90, 09088 Madrid*

TELÉFONO: *91-315 08 72*

FECHA Y LUGAR DE NACIMIENTO: *3 / 10 / 1962, Logroño*

ESTADO CIVIL: *Divorciada*

ESTUDIOS UNIVERSITARIOS: *Licenciada en Ciencias Económicas,
Explotaciones Agropecuarias, Universidad
Autónoma de Madrid, 1985*

EXPERIENCIA DE TRABAJO: *Industrias Cárnicas del Ebro S.A. (1986–88)
Bodegas Marqués de Vallejo (1988–)*

AFICIONES: *Cine, historia del arte, judo*

CURRICULUM VITAE

SURNAME: Berrozpe

FIRST NAMES: Pilar

ADDRESS: Calle Pablo Iglesias, 90, 09088 Madrid

TELEPHONE NUMBER: 91-315 08 72

DATE AND PLACE OF BIRTH: 3 October 1962, Logroño

MARITAL STATUS: Divorced

UNIVERSITY EDUCATION: Degree in Economics and Farming
Universidad Autónoma de Madrid, 1980–85

WORK EXPERIENCE: Industrias Cárnicas del Ebro S.A. (1986–88)
Bodegas Marqués de Vallejo (1988–)

OUTSIDE INTERESTS: Cinema, history of art, judo

Testimonials, references and authorizations

(a) Brief testimonials

> *Por la presente, yo, Javier Palacios, Director del Museo Municipal de Mérida, confirmo que Laura Gregorio ha ocupado en este Museo el puesto de Conservadora Ayudante entre el 1 de enero de 1989 y el 30 de junio de 1993, y que ha realizado su trabajo con toda eficiencia y profesionalidad.*
>
> *Mérida, 1 de julio de 1993*

To whom it may concern

I, Javier Palacios, Director of the Museo Municipal de Mérida, hereby confirm that Laura Gregorio has been employed under me as an Assistant Curator from 1 January 1989 to 30 June 1993, and that she has fulfilled her duties satisfactorily.

Mérida, 1 July 1993

> *Yo, Isabel Alvarez, catedrática de la Universidad de Zaragoza, certifico que Pilar Ovejas ha asistido con regularidad a las clases de Derecho Internacional I.*
>
> *Zaragoza, 7 de julio de 1993*

To whom it may concern

I, Isabel Alvarez, Professor at the University of Zaragoza, declare that Pilar Ovejas has regularly attended the classes on International Law I.

Zaragoza, 7 July 1993

(b) Personal references

> *Viajes La Rosa de los Vientos*
> *Avenida de la Paz, 1*
> *25000 Salamanca*
>
> *Estimados señores:*
>
> *Me complace mucho recomendarles encarecidamente a Nela Rioja, con la que he trabajado 5 años. Su personalidad es extraordinaria y merece toda confianza.*
>
> *En cuanto a su capacidad profesional, me gustaría destacar su larga experiencia en el mundo del turismo y sus grandes conocimientos de francés e italiano.*
>
> *Les saluda atentamente*

Dear Sir or Madam,

I am pleased to recommend Nela Rioja to you most warmly. I have worked with her for five years. Her character is exemplary, and you may have every confidence in her.

In respect of her professional qualities, I should like to highlight her long experience in tourism and her perfect command of French and Italian.

Yours faithfully,

(c) Giving authorization to a proxy

> *Yo, el abajo firmante Fernando Garnica, autorizo a la señora Ramona Sáez a que me represente en la compra de Viajes Extremo Oriente.*
>
> *Dado en Valencia, a 6 de marzo de 1993.*

I, Fernando Garnica, hearby authorize Mrs Ramona Sáez to act on my behalf in the purchase of Viajes Extremo Oriente.

Valencia, 6 March 1993

113 Commercial correspondence

(a) Enclosing brochures and information for a client

Artespaña
Avenida del Cid, 99
09090 Burgos   *9 / 7 / 93*

Estimados señores:

Agradecemos su carta del 2 de julio. <u>Les remitimos un folleto informativo sobre</u> nuestras tiendas en el Reino Unido. Si desean recibir <u>más información sobre</u> nuestros establecimientos del resto de Europa, con muchísimo gusto se la proporcionaremos.

Estaríamos encantados de trabajar con Artespaña, y esperamos tener noticias suyas en un futuro próximo.

Les saluda atentamente

Dear Sirs,

Thank you for your letter of 2 July. Please find enclosed a brochure about our shops in the United Kingdom. If you would like to receive further information concerning our shops in the rest of Europe, we shall be happy to furnish it.

We would be delighted to work with Artespaña, and hope that we may hear from you in the near future.

Yours faithfully,

(b) Asking for a quotation

Instalaciones Eléctricas
Paseo de Pereda, 66
67866 Santander

Estimados señores:

En relación a nuestra conversación sobre la instalación de dos nuevas cocinas en nuestro restaurante, <u>les agradeceríamos mucho que nos remitiesen lo antes posible el presupuesto.</u>

Reciban nuestro atento saludo

Dear Sir,

Following our discussion concerning the installation of two new kitchens in our restaurant, I should be grateful if you could send me your quotation as soon as possible.

Yours sincerely,

(c) Placing an order

Directora de Ventas, Riauto
Calle del Norte, 7
67896 León

Estimada amiga:

Muchas gracias por el envío de su catálogo. Estamos muy interesados en comprarles a ustedes piezas de repuesto. A continuación, paso a detallarle los artículos que necesitamos nos entreguen a la máxima urgencia:

xxxxxx
xxxxxx
xxxxxx

En los próximos días, en cuanto hayamos finalizado de realizar el stock de nuestro almacén, prepararemos el siguiente pedido.

Le saluda atentamente

Dear Madam,

Thank you for sending us your catalogue. We are anxious to purchase spare parts from your firm. We should like to request that the following articles be delivered a.s.a.p.:

xxxxxx
xxxxxx
xxxxxx

Within the next few days we will have our next order ready, on completion of stock-taking in our store.

Yours sincerely,

(d) Apologizing for a delayed order

Director Gerente
Cooperativa de Viticultores
Carretera de Logroño, s / n
88786 Cenicero

Apreciado señor:

Lamentamos mucho que su pedido todavía no se haya despachado, y le ofrecemos nuestras más sinceras disculpas. El artículo que solicita está agotado en estos momentos, pero volverá a estar disponible la semana próxima, cuando se lo enviaremos sin tardanza.

Rogando disculpen las molestias que les hemos ocasionado, se despide atentamente

Dear Sir,

We regret the fact that your order has not yet been expedited and we wish to express our apologies. The article you request is currently out of stock. However, it will be available as from next week and we shall forward it to you without delay.

We would ask you to accept our apologies for the inconvenience caused.

Yours faithfully,

(e) Asking for an urgent reply to an earlier letter

Diario El Norte
Calle Vieja, 12
20220 Bilbao

Estimados señores:

A menos que se deba a un retraso en los servicios postales, me temo que no han contestado a mi carta de 4 del corriente relativa a los derechos de reproducción de unas fotografías que aparecieron en su periódico.

Por tratarse de un asunto de cierta urgencia, le agradecería mucho que enviara su contestación al recibo de la presente.

Se despide atentamente

Dear Sir or Madam,

Unless there has been some delay in the postal service, you would appear not to have replied to my letter of 4 March, concerning the right to reproduce certain photos which appeared in your newspaper.

As this is a matter of some urgency, I should be most grateful if you could reply by return of post.

Yours faithfully,

 Press announcements

(a) Births

Nacimientos	Births
Ernesto Fernández, de Calahorra, y Pilar San Juan, de Tarazona, tienen el placer de comunicar el nacimiento de su hijo, Eduardo. Zaragoza, 7 de julio de 1993.	Ernesto Fernández, of Calahorra, and Pilar San Juan, of Tarazona, take pleasure in announcing the birth of their son, Eduardo. Saragossa, 7 July 1993.

(b) Engagements

Compromisos	Engagements
Nos complace anunciar el compromiso de la señorita María José Sánchez con el señor Antonio Melón. Córdoba, 6 de julio de 1993.	We are pleased to announce the engagement of Miss Maria José Sánchez to Mr Antonio Melón. Córdoba, 6 July 1993.

(c) Marriages

Enlaces matrimoniales	Marriages
Rubén Palacios y Silvia Pérez tienen el placer de comunicar su enlace matrimonial, que se celebró, en la intimidad, el pasado día 9 de octubre. Avila, 12 de octubre de 1993.	Rubén Palacios and Silvia Pérez are pleased to announce their marriage, which was celebrated quietly on 9 October. Avila, 12 October 1993.

(d) Deaths

Defunciones	Deaths
El señor Pedro Fragua falleció en el día de ayer a los 79 años de edad. La conducción del cadáver y el funeral tendrán lugar en la intimidad familiar. Sevilla, 6 de abril de 1993.	*Mr Pedro Fragua passed away yesterday at the age of 79. The funeral service will be a private family occasion. Seville, 6 April 1993.*

(e) Seasonal greetings

La Casa del Chocolate les desea un próspero Año Nuevo.
The Casa del Chocolate wishes you a Happy New Year.

Deseamos a todos nuestros clientes una Feliz Navidad y un Próspero Año Nuevo.
We wish all our customers a Merry Christmas and a Prosperous New Year.

(f) Opening of a new firm

La Galería EcoCentro tiene el placer de invitarle a la inauguración de su nueva tienda (Calle Sierpes, 66), el próximo viernes, 9 de octubre.
The Galería EcoCentro is pleased to invite you to the opening of its new shop (66, Calle Sierpes) next Friday, 9 October.

(g) Change of address

El Círculo Mercantil se complace en anunciar la dirección de su nueva sede, que, a partir del 1 de enero, será: Calle de Castilla, 42.
As from 1 January, the Círculo Mercantil will be relocated at the following address: 42, Calle de Castilla.

115 Official invitations and replies

The examples in this section are all based on formal written usage. For inviting friends, family or informal acquaintances, see sections 98 to 100.

(a) Issuing an invitation to a reception or function

Julián García Romera y María José Sánchez Alonso agradecerán a los Señores de Colmenares su asistencia a la recepción que ofrecerán el viernes 7 a las 20 horas.
Julián García Romera and María José Sánchez Alonso are pleased to invite Mr and Mrs Colmenares to a reception on Friday 7, at 8 p.m.

Con ocasión de la apertura de la nueva oficina de Crédito Agrícola, tenemos el gusto de invitarles a un cóctel, el martes 22 de abril, a las 11.30 h.

To mark the opening of our new branch of Crédito Agrícola, we are pleased to invite you to a cocktail party on Tuesday 22 April, at 11.30 a.m.

(b) Accepting an invitation

Dolores del Río agradece mucho su invitación y le confirma gustosa su asistencia el próximo día 30 de marzo.

Dolores del Río thanks you for your kind invitation for 30 March, which she accepts with great pleasure.

El Director de Revista Europa asistirá con gran placer al cóctel que ha de celebrarse con ocasión de la apertura de la nueva oficina de Crédito Agrícola.

The Manager of Revista Europa will be very pleased to attend the cocktail party to mark the opening of the new branch of Crédito Agrícola.

(c) Declining an invitation

Dolores del Río agradece mucho su invitación, pero lamenta no poder asistir por tener otro compromiso anterior ineludible.

Dolores del Río thanks you for your kind invitation, but regrets that she is unable to accept owing to a prior engagement.

El Director de Revista Europa agradece a Crédito Agrícola su invitación al cóctel del 22 de abril y lamenta no poder aceptarla debido a un compromiso anterior.

The Manager of Revista Europa thanks Crédito Agrícola for their kind invitation to the cocktail party on 22 April, but regrets he will be unable to attend owing to a prior engagement.

(d) Wedding invitations and replies

Manuel Ayúcar García	*Pedro Martinez Pascual*
Amaya Irazola Oraá	*Carmen López Posadas*

Se complacen en participarle el enlace de sus hijos

Alfonso y Ana

y tienen el gusto de invitarle a la ceremonia que tendrá lugar el día 12 de octubre, a las 18.30 h., en la Iglesia Parroquial de San Miguel, y a la cena que se servirá a continuación en el Hotel El Saler.

Calle Albufera, 57	*Avda. de la Paz, 66*
Tfno. 445 67 78	*Tfno. 315 08 74*

Valencia, 1993
S.R.C.

Manuel Ayúcar García	Pedro Martinez Pascual
Amaya Irazola Oraá	Carmen López Posadas

request the pleasure of your company at the marriage of

Alfonso and Ana

at the Church of San Miguel on Saturday, 12th October, at 6.30 p.m. and afterwards at the Hotel El Saler.

Valencia, 1993
R.S.V.P.

Idoya Garrido Aguirre agradece la invitación al enlace matrimonial de Alfonso Ayúcar Irazola y les confirma gustosa su asistencia, a la vez que aprovecha esta ocasión para expresarles a los contrayentes y a sus familias su más sincera enhorabuena.

Idoya Garrido Aguirre offers Mr and Mrs Ayúcar her warmest congratulations on the forthcoming marriage of their son, Alfonso, and is pleased to accept their kind invitation.

Idoya Garrido Aguirre agradece muchísimo la invitación al enlace matrimonial de Alfonso Ayúcar Irazola, y desea expresarles a los contrayentes su más sincera enhorabuena, lamentando no poder asistir, debido a compromisos ineludibles.

Idoya Garrido Aguirre offers Mr and Mrs Ayúcar her warmest congratulations on the forthcoming marriage of their son, Alfonso, but regrets that she is unable to accept their kind invitation owing to previous engagements.

WRITING ESSAYS

Students of Spanish may be required to write an essay on a topical or literary subject. This section offers some 'skeleton' structures for constructing a cogent and well-expressed argument.

It is worth remembering that the quality of an essay will be judged on three criteria: relevant and well-informed content; incisive and well-organized argument; and correct and idiomatic use of Spanish. On the first two points, the most essential key to success is to read the question closely, so that you answer it precisely, and then construct a balanced and thorough plan. Obviously, different types of essays require different approaches, but in almost all cases a plan (and essay) will work through the following stages:

(1) Brief general introduction to the subject
(2) Interpretation of the precise implications of the question
(3) Indication of how the essay will proceed
(4) The main body of the argument, subdivided as appropriate
(5) General conclusions, related back to the question

In general, the style of an essay in Spanish needs to be formal. This means avoiding over-colloquial expressions, and becoming familiar with the idiom of formal written Spanish, as demonstrated throughout this section. You may initially find this register rather impersonal, even pompous, but remember that in Spanish the distinction between the informal spoken language and formal written style tends to be more pronounced than in English. With practice, you should be able to select some of the phrases you find particularly useful, and make them part of your own active vocabulary.

116 General introduction

(i) For a direct approach to the terms of the question:

La afirmación del título plantea una cuestión fundamental.
The observation in the title raises a basic question.

La afirmación de Ortega plantea claramente el problema de la injusticia.
The statement by Ortega raises very clearly the problem of injustice.

Esta cita del documento de 'Amigos de la Tierra' nos enfrenta con el difícil problema de la relación entre el hombre y el mundo en el que vive.
This quotation from the document by 'Friends of the Earth' confronts us with the difficult problem of the relationship between man and the world in which he lives.

En el origen de <u>la reflexión de este autor</u> subyace una idea profundamente pesimista de la condición humana.
The author's observation is based on a deeply pessimistic view of man's condition.

<u>El título con el que nos encontramos</u> está expresado de manera que destaca la idea del deber ciudadano.
This title is phrased in a way which emphasizes the idea of civic duty.

(ii) For a more general introduction to the subject, before coming on to the terms of the question:

<u>Cualquier análisis</u> de la calidad de una novela <u>implica la cuestión del</u> papel del lector.
Any analysis of the strengths of a novel begs the question of the role of the reader.

El desarrollo del transporte público es un problema de vital importancia, ya que <u>afecta a nuestra vida cotidiana.</u>
The development of public transport is a crucially important problem, since it affects our everyday lives.

<u>Vivimos en un mundo / en una época en que</u> todos los valores tradicionales se ponen en cuestión.
We are living in a world in which / at a time when all the traditional values are being called into question.

Las fuentes de energía son el objeto de <u>muchas investigaciones actuales.</u>
Sources of energy are the object of a great deal of current research.

El 'asunto Vicario' <u>estuvo presente en la prensa</u> meses y meses.
The 'Vicario' affair was in the headlines for several months.

Hace veinte años un artista <u>provocó un escándalo</u> al declarar que los museos eran algo inútil.
Twenty years ago an artist caused an outcry when he declared that museums were useless places.

117 Interpreting the question

(i) Defining the essence of the question:

La pregunta se puede reinterpretar de la siguiente manera: ¿Cuál es al papel del trabajo en el mundo actual?
The question can be reinterpreted / reformulated as follows: what is the role of work in the world today?

El problema se reduce a lo siguiente: ¿existirá la C.E.E. de aquí a un siglo?
In short, what we need to ask is whether the EEC will still exist a hundred years from now.

El meollo de la cuestión es si los títulos están sobrevalorados.
Are academic qualifications overvalued? This is the heart of the problem.

Así, la cuestión es en qué medida se puede justificar la censura.
The question is therefore one of how far censorship can be justified.

Este comentario nos conduce a preguntarnos cuál es al futuro de la industria informática.
This remark invites us to wonder what is the future of the computer industry.

(ii) Stating what aspects are / are not relevant:

Para tratar del tema de la inquietud religiosa, es importante considerar las obras de Santa Teresa.
If we wish to examine the subject of religious anxiety, it is important to look at the work of Santa Teresa.

Esta opinión merece examinarse más de cerca.
This point of view deserves closer consideration.

Es importante profundizar en el concepto del progreso.
We need to examine more closely the notion of progress.

Hay que precisar la naturaleza de estas reservas.
We need to specify the precise nature of these reservations.

Dejaremos de lado la situación de Estados Unidos, que es un caso especial.
We shall leave aside the situation of the USA, which is a special case.

225

En este artículo, <u>nos abstendremos de hablar de</u> la historia del período de entreguerras.
In this article, we shall not discuss the history of the period between the two wars.

<u>Nos vamos a atener al</u> caso de las grandes ciudades.
We shall confine ourselves to the case of cities.

Al tratar este tema <u>debemos evitar</u> caer en la trampa de lo tópico.
In discussing this subject, we must avoid falling into the trap of clichés.

118 Outlining the plan and transitions

(i) To introduce a first section:

Hay que tener en cuenta varios factores: <u>en primer lugar,</u> el actual estado de cosas; <u>después,</u> la probable evolución de nuestras necesidades; y, <u>finalmente,</u> los riesgos políticos.
Several factors must be taken into consideration: first, the present state of affairs; secondly, the likely development of our needs; and finally, the political stakes.

<u>Primeramente,</u> sería conveniente sopesar las ventajas para los trabajadores.
First we should weigh up the advantages for the workers.

<u>Ante todo,</u> hay que constatar la destrucción de selva tropical.
We should first of all note the loss of tropical rain forests.

<u>Vamos a empezar por</u> investigar la situación de la mujer.
We shall start by examining the position of women.

<u>La primera cuestión que se presenta</u> es la de la seguridad.
The first issue to arise is that of safety.

Sería imposible tratar este tema sin plantear <u>una cuestión previa.</u>
It would be impossible to deal with this subject without raising a preliminary question.

<u>Esta continúa siendo la objeción principal,</u> como demostraremos <u>más tarde</u> en todo detalle.
This is still the main objection, as will be shown later in full detail.

(ii) To draw a logical consequence from an argument:

De donde se concluye que la televisión por satélite ofrece muchas ventajas.
It follows that satellite television offers many advantages.

Así pues, la mayoría de los cinéfilos prefieren las películas en versión original.
Thus most cinema-goers prefer films in the original language.

Entonces, tenemos que reconocer la importancia de los grupos ecologistas.
We must therefore recognize the importance of the ecological lobby.

Luego este sistema es demasiado caro.
This system is therefore too expensive.

Ahora bien, este proyecto conlleva cierto número de riesgos.
However, this plan involves a number of risks.

(iii) To move on to another complementary argument:

Pero nuestra discusión quedaría incompleta si dejáramos de considerar otro de sus aspectos fundamentales.
But our treatment of the subject would be incomplete if we failed to look at another fundamental aspect.

En este momento, hay que examinar un segundo criterio.
At this point a second criterion must be examined.

A este respecto, se impone un segundo argumento.
At this stage there is a second argument we must take into consideration.

En lo concerniente a los jóvenes, so observa una tendencia paralela.
As far as young people are concerned, there is a parallel tendency.

Del mismo modo, los holandeses experimentaron un contratiempo.
Similarly, the Dutch experienced a setback.

Lo que es más, estas máquinas son de un mantenimiento complicado.
Furthermore, these machines are complicated to service.

Lo mismo se puede aplicar a las personas de la tercera edad.
The same is true for retired people.

Además, podríamos citar igualmente el caso de Oviedo.
Besides, we could also cite the case of Oviedo.

(iv) To move on to an opposing argument:

Sin embargo, este punto de vista no se puede aceptar totalmente.
However, this point of view cannot be entirely accepted.

Por lo tanto, en la interpretación de esta situación, existen dos criterios opuestas.
However, there are two opposing schools of thought on the interpretation of this situation.

Por una parte, las importaciones han aumentado, pero, por la otra, las exportaciones no han disminuido.
On the one hand, imports have gone up, but on the other hand exports have not fallen.

Por un lado, se necesitan más profesores, pero al mismo tiempo no hay licenciados suficientes.
On the one hand, we need more teachers, but on the other hand there are not enough qualified candidates.

Alternativamente, se podría contemplar la reducción del número de vehículos privados.
Alternatively, we might envisage a reduction in the number of private vehicles.

Pero, podríamos refutar tal interpretación de las estadísticas.
However, we could reject this interpretation of the statistics.

Tras la consideración de estos dos puntos de vista, vamos a demostrar que no son irreconciliables.
After considering these two points of view, we shall show that they are not irreconcilable.

119 Defining key terms

(i) Explaining the need for definition:

Debemos concentrar nuestra atención en los términos 'ciudadano' y 'estado'.
We should focus our attention on the terms 'citizen' and 'state'.

Tenemos que explicar la expresión empleada por Valle-Inclán.
We need to define the expression used by Valle-Inclán.

228

'Libertad' es una palabra clave que tendremos que comentar.
'Freedom' is a key word and one which requires analysis.

Es necesario que nos detengamos en la frase 'cada uno según su experiencia'.
The phrase 'each according to his experience' needs further comment.

Tendríamos que hacer constar que la definición de 'amistad' que se ofrece en la cita es incompleta.
Thus we should note that the definition of 'friendship' given / suggested in the quotation is incomplete.

(ii) Establishing various meanings of a term or expression:

En la formulación del título, el término 'europeo' tiene que entenderse en su sentido originario.
In the wording of the title, the term 'European' has to be understood in its primary sense.

Hay que entender este término en su sentido más amplio.
This term should be understood in its wider meaning.

Esta expresión se usa tanto en un sentido literal como figurado.
This expression is used in both a literal and a figurative sense.

En este contexto, la palabra 'loco' debería entenderse en su significado literal.
In this context, the word 'mad' should be understood in its literal sense.

El segundo de estos dos sentidos es el que el título implica.
It is the second of these two meanings which is implied in the title.

(iii) Giving synonyms and antonyms:

La frase 'unión libre' expresa el estado civil de las personas que viven juntas sin estar casadas.
The expression 'unión libre' refers to the status of two people who are living together, but are not married.

Es una cuestión de los colegios privados, es decir, de los centros religiosos.
It is a question concerning private schools, that is, religious establishments.

La palabra 'verde' es, prácticamente, sinónima de 'ecologista'.
The word 'green' is effectively synonymous with 'ecologist'.

Esta frase se aproxima a la definición propuesta por Unamuno.
This phrase comes close to the definition suggested by Unamuno.

Es importante no confundir estos dos términos.
It is important not to confuse these two terms.

Los adjetivos 'generoso' y 'tacaño' se pueden considerar antónimos.
The adjectives 'generous' and 'mean' can be considered as direct opposites.

Esta definición es distinta de la ofrecida por el primer autor en cuestión.
This definition is different from the one given by the first author under consideration.

Esta interpretación difiere del significado más común de la palabra.
This interpretation is different from the usual meaning of the word.

120 Giving examples

Por ejemplo, todos los españoles conocen a Montserrat Caballé.
For example, all Spanish people have heard of / know Montserrat Caballé.

Esto afecta a varias regiones, por ejemplo, Asturias y Galicia.
This concerns several regions, for example, Asturias and Galicia.

Citemos, a título de ejemplo, las novelas de Miguel Delibes.
Take, for example, the novels of Miguel Delibes.

La literatura contemporánea nos proporciona muchos ejemplos.
Contemporary literature offers numerous examples.

Podemos defender este argumento citando como ejemplo las películas de Buñuel.
We can support this argument by reference to the films of Buñuel.

Utilizaremos la hipótesis de un estudiante que ha terminado el bachillerato y quiere ingresar en la facultad de derecho.
Let us take the hypothetical case of a student who has passed the 'bachillerato' and wants to study law at university.

Sería suficiente citar el ejemplo de los Juegos Olímpicos.
We can simply give the example of the Olympic Games.

Esta poesía ilustra la desesperación de Machado.
This poem illustrates Machado's despair.

El crecimiento de la economía alemana demuestra la importancia de una política centralizada.
The growth of the German economy shows the importance of centralized policy.

Como prueba de esta afirmación de puede citar el caso de Goya.
The case of Goya confirms this claim.

121 Supporting an argument

Estaría justificado afirmar que esta época no se repetirá.
We could justifiably assert that this period will not recur.

Es de justicia decir que la calidad de vida de los ancianos deja mucho que desear.
It is fair to say that the quality of life experienced by old people leaves a good deal to be desired.

Podemos afirmar rotundamente que el gobierno nunca adoptará este proyecto.
We can state unreservedly that this plan will never be adopted by the government.

Los hechos confirman el optimismo de los empresarios.
The optimism of the businessmen is supported by the facts.

La evidencia nos permite sostener esta opinión.
The facts enable us to maintain this point of view.

Que un niño necesita a sus padres es un hecho innegable.
It is undeniable that a child needs its parents.

Me gustaría destacar el hecho de que han sido los jóvenes los que han iniciado esta reforma.
I would like to highlight the fact that it was young people who introduced this reform.

122 Opposing an argument

Por supuesto, existe también el reverso de la moneda.
There is also, of course, the other side of the coin.

Sería injusto aceptar inmediatamente todos estos razonamientos.
It would be unfair to accept all these arguments immediately.

Ya no se puede sostener la opinión de que sólo la mujer se tiene que ocupar de los niños.
It is no longer possible to hold the view that only women should take care of children.

El mayor reproche que podemos hacer a algunos urbanistas es su falta de imaginación.
The most serious charge we can level against certain town-planners is their lack of imagination.

Tenemos que expresar ciertas reservas en cuanto a esta solución.
We must confess to some reservations regarding this solution.

Cierto número de factores hacen imposible una respuesta sencilla.
A number of factors make it impossible to give a simple answer.

Esta afirmación se ha rechazado por completo.
This claim has been totally rejected.

Ciertos eruditos han rechazado este argumento.
Certain scholars have rejected this argument.

Los resultados de la investigación echan por tierra esta observación.
The results of the inquiry disprove this observation.

Tal razonamiento merece una condena sin paliativos.
This argument deserves to be dismissed out of hand.

123 Conclusions

En última instancia, tenemos que admitir la cita de Unamuno.
In the last analysis, we have to concur with the words of Unamuno.

Al término de nuestro análisis, es conveniente hacer balance.
In conclusion, it is fitting to weigh up the arguments.

Ante estos comentarios, <u>se puede deducir que</u> no compartimos el punto de vista del autor.
From these remarks it may be inferred that we do not share the author's point of view.

<u>Con dicha reserva</u>, ciertamente considerable, aceptaría la opinión de Clarín.
With this reservation, which it must be said is an important one, I would accept Clarín's opinion.

<u>Este esbozo</u> nos permite destacar la importancia del arte moderno.
This summary underlines the importance of modern art.

FORMAL REPORTS AND ADDRESSES

This section covers writing reports on projects, research, business achievements and so forth. The register of language is also suitable for formal verbal reports, such as a report to a board meeting, or a lecture at a conference.

124 Reporting observations

(a) Key verbs and verbal phrases

Hemos observado un descenso en el desempleo.
We have noticed a drop in unemployment.

El presidente hizo notar que dicha situación no podía continuar.
The chairman made it clear that the situation could not continue.

Hemos asistido a una ralentización del crecimiento económico.
We have witnessed a slowdown in economic growth.

Varios equipos han constatado el mismo fenómeno.
Several teams have noted the same phenomenon.

Mi colega ha indicado ya que esperamos continuar con esta investigación.
My colleague has already indicated that we hope to continue with this research.

El biólogo ha asegurado que dicha investigación no puede hacer ningún daño a las plantas.
The biologist has given his assurance that the research can in no way be harmful to plants.

El jefe del proyecto dejó claro que estaba dispuesto a tomar nuevas medidas.
The head of the project made it clear that he was ready to adopt new measures.

El doctor dejó patente en su informe previo esta evolución.
The doctor clearly noted this development in his earlier report.

El físico ha expuesto su tesis sobre la causa de este efecto.
The physicist has explained his theory about the cause of this effect.

Mi libro trata de <u>explicar por qué</u> este sector de la sociedad está marginado.
My book seeks to explain why this sector of the population is underprivileged.

Deberíamos <u>analizar</u> los resultados.
We should analyse the results.

Queremos <u>analizar</u> en detalle este caso ya que es una excepción de la regla.
We want to examine this case in detail, since it is an exception to the rule.

Sería difícil <u>resumir</u> en unas pocas palabras lo que hemos logrado este año.
It would be difficult to summarize what we have achieved this year in just a few words.

(b) Key nouns

La dirección ha redactado <u>un informe</u> del año 1992–93.
The management has written a report on the year 1992–93.

El Ministro del Medio Ambiente va a pronunciar su <u>discurso</u> esta noche.
The Minister for the Environment will be making his speech tonight.

Con ocasión de la asamblea general, presentó <u>una comunicación</u> sobre las excavaciones.
At the Annual General Meeting, she gave a paper on the excavations.

Seguramente se habrán fijado en la primera observación hecha por el director en su <u>comunicado</u>.
You will probably have noticed the first observation that the Director makes in his report.

Cada estudiante tendrá que preparar <u>una exposición</u>, que habrá de presentar ante la clase.
Each student will be required to prepare a paper which he will deliver to the class.

Mi colega nos ha ofrecido <u>un perfil</u> del problema.
My colleague has given us an outline of the problem.

Esta <u>constatación</u> va a sorprender a algunos profesionales.
The observation will be a surprise to some in the profession.

La <u>declaración</u> del presidente fue muy aplaudida.
The President's statement was greeted with loud applause.

Tengo que hacer algunas precisiones sobre este punto.
I must give some clarification on this point.

Los accionistas esperan un análisis detallado de estos datos.
The shareholders expect a detailed analysis of the data.

El estudio en profundidad del equipo chileno presentaba unos interesantes hallazgos.
The thorough study by the Chilean group offered some interesting findings.

Reporting conclusions

Quisiera hacer balance de la situación financiera.
I should like to give a summary of the financial situation.

En la presente coyuntura, cualquier análisis tiene que ser considerado provisional.
At the present moment, any analysis must be considered provisional.

¿Qué conclusiones se pueden extraer de estos datos?
What conclusions can be drawn from these facts?

La policía ha concluido que se trata de un atentado cometido por terroristas.
The police have concluded that it was an outrage perpetrated by terrorists.

Como resultado, el Occidente tendrá que reducir el consumo de petróleo.
As a consequence, the West will have to reduce its oil consumption.

Se concluye que cada demanda tiene que ser considerada en función de nuestros recursos.
It follows that each request must be considered in relation to our resources.

Ahora está muy claro que, en ciertos casos, la medicina alternativa puede ayudar.
It is now clearly established that alternative medicine can help in certain cases.

Este diagrama muestra dos tendencias opuestas.
This chart shows two opposing trends.

Estos resultados han mostrado una nueva tendencia inquietante.
The results have shown a disturbing new trend.

Este experimento <u>va a resultar</u> inútil.
This experiment will prove to be worthless.

Este proyecto <u>tendrá el efecto de</u> mejorar la calidad de vida de los habitantes de las ciudades.
The project will have the effect of improving the quality of life of city-dwellers.

126 Methods of research

(i) People involved in carrying out research

un(a) investigador(a)	a researcher, research worker
un(a) cobayo / -a	a guinea pig
una persona interrogada	a person interviewed
un(a) erudito / -a	a scholar
un(a) científico / -a	a scientist / a man / woman of learning

(ii) Forms of research

un análisis	an analysis
una investigación	an inquiry / (piece of) research
una prueba	a test
un experimento / una experiencia	an experiment
investigaciones	research
un sondeo	an opinion poll

(iii) Methods of research

un aparato	a piece of equipment / apparatus
una consigna (de seguridad)	a (safety) instruction
un paso a seguir	a step to follow
un dispositivo	a device
una muestra	a sample
el material	material / apparatus
un procedimiento	a procedure, method
un proceso	a process
una técnica	a technique

Making predictions

Los expertos han hecho una predicción alarmante en cuanto al número de accidentes de carretera.
Specialists have made a disturbing prediction about the number of road accidents.

Según las predicciones del Instituto de la Salud, para el año 2000 vamos a comer menos carne.
According to the predictions of the Institute of Health, we shall eat less meat by the year 2000.

No nos atrevemos a hacer ninguna predicción.
We dare not risk any predictions.

No hay que perderse en conjeturas.
We must not get lost in hypotheses.

Por lo que respecta a la evolución del mercado, sólo podemos aventurar hipótesis.
As far as the development of the market is concerned, we can only venture hypotheses.

A corto / largo plazo, podemos esperar un aumento de nuestro volumen de negocios.
In the short / long term, we can hope to see an improvement in our turnover.

La médico estima que el problema desaparecerá en unos seis meses.
The doctor reckons that the problem will disappear within about six months.

PART 3

Word power

Angeles Pérez

SELECTIVE GLOSSARIES OF IDIOMS AND SYNONYMS

128 Building on verbs

Verbs are the backbone of a language – and one of the greatest sources of worry to foreign speakers. Part 1 reviewed the use of the different tenses and moods in Spanish (sections 39–47). This section lists idiomatic structures and expressions based on common verbs, together with key compound forms. Irregular verbs are marked *, referring you to the table of conjugation of common irregular verbs in Appendix 4 (pp. 345–61).

abrir to open

★ Note past participle: *abierto*

abrir algo con un cuchillo to cut something open
abrir un caso to start proceedings
abrir una cuenta (bancaria) to open a bank account
abrir un grifo to turn on a tap
abrir los ojos a la realidad to open one's eyes to reality
en un abrir y cerrar de ojos in a flash
abrirse (1) to open
      (2) < slang > to leave

    ¿Nos abrimos? < slang > Shall we go?

entreabrir (1) to half-open
          (2) to leave (a door) ajar
dejar la ventana entreabierta to leave the window ajar

reabrir to reopen

acabar (1) to finish
      (2) to finish off, to kill off
acabar un trabajo to finish a job
acabar con algo to put an end to something

    Tenemos que acabar con eso. We must put an end to that.

acabar con alguien to be the end of someone

    Este niño acabará con nosotros. This boy will be the end of us.

acabar de hacer algo (1) to have just done something
                       (2) to finish doing something
     Acabo de llegar. I've just arrived.
     Madrid, acabado en d. Madrid, ending in a 'd'.

acabarse (1) to finish
            (2) to run out

     Se nos ha acabado el café. We've run out of coffee.
     ¡Se acabó! < fam. > That's it! / That's enough! / It's all over!
     Cuando se acabe, se acabó. < fam. > That's all there is.
     Es el cuento de nunca acabar. It's a never-ending story.

actuar (1) to act, to perform
          (2) to behave
          (3) to do something, to take action

Note the accents in *actúo, actúas, actúa, actuáis, actúan, actúe, actúes,*
actúe, actuéis, actúen.

actuar con prudencia to act with care
actuar de forma extraña to act strangely

     Hay que actuar cuanto antes. Something must be done as soon as
       possible.
     No saben actuar. They can't act.

acusar (1) to accuse (law)
          (2) to show, to register
          (3) to acknowledge (e.g. receipt of something)

acusar (a alguien) de algo / de haber hecho algo to accuse (someone) of
  something / of having done something

     ¿De qué se le acusa? What is he / she charged with?
     Su cara acusaba cansancio. His / her face betrayed weariness.
     Por la presente, acuso recibo de la mercancía. I hereby
       acknowledge receipt of the goods.

acusarse (1) to confess
            (2) to be noticed, noted

     Se ha acusado una subida de precios. An increase in prices has
       been noted.
     No tienes que acusarte de nada. You shouldn't blame yourself for
       anything.

excusar to excuse

excusar a alguien to excuse someone, to present someone's apologies
excusar a alguien (de algo / de hacer algo) to exempt someone (from
   something / doing something)
   Excusamos decirles que . . . We do not need to tell you that . . .
excusarse to excuse oneself, to apologize
   Se excusó por llegar tarde. He apologized for being late.

alojar to accommodate, to put up

alojarse to stay, to lodge
   ¿Dónde te alojas? Where are you staying?
   El tumor se aloja cerca de la matriz. The tumour is lodged near the
      womb.

desalojar to evacuate, to clear the people out of a place
   La policía desalojó el edificio. The police cleared the building.
   El juez ordenó desalojar la sala. The judge ordered the court
      (room) to be cleared.

andar* (1) to walk
         (2) to go (e.g. clock)
         (3) < fam. > to be

andar de pique (con alguien) to get on badly (with someone)
andar en algo (1) to be engaged in something
              (2) to mess about with something
andar haciendo algo to be doing something
andar mal de algo (e.g. el corazón) to have problems (with your heart)
andar por los (treinta) to be about (thirty)
andar tras algo / alguien to be after someone / something
ir andando to walk
   Anda mal de la cabeza < fam. > He's lost his marbles.
   ¡No andes en mi armario! Don't rummage in my wardrobe!
   Creo que andan en negocios de construcción. I think they're
      involved in the construction business.
   Siempre andas comprando cosas raras. You're always buying
      strange things.
   Seguro que la niña anda haciendo algo. I'm sure that child is up to
      something.
   No quiero ir andando. I don't want to walk there.
   ¿Cómo andamos hoy, Pedro? How are we today, Pedro?

243

No ando muy bien de dinero. I'm a bit hard up.
Mi madre anda un poco pachucha. My mother's rather ill.
Debe de andar por las 12.000 ptas la habitación. The room must
    be about 12,000 pesetas.
Este reloj no anda. This watch doesn't work.
¡Anda, pero si eres tú! What a surprise, it's you!
¡Anda, anda! no digas bobadas. < fam. > Come on, don't talk
    nonsense!
¡Andando! Let's go! / Off you go!
Dime con quién andas y te diré quién eres. < proverb > You can
    tell a man by the company he keeps.

andarse

andar(se) con cuidado to take care
andarse con rodeos / por las ramas to beat about the bush
andarse con tonterías to mess about

> *Todo se andará.* All in good time.

desandar to go back over, to undo

> *No se puede desandar lo andado.* You can't undo what's already
> been done.

animar (1) to liven up, to add interest to, to brighten up
         (2) to encourage
         (3) to animate, to give life to

animar una fiesta to liven up a party
animar a alguien (a hacer algo) to encourage someone (to do something)

animarse

> *¡Anímate a venir hombre!* Come on, why don't you come along?
> *¡Anímate!* Cheer up!
> *Nunca se animan a salir a cenar.* They never feel like coming out to
> dinner.

desanimar to discourage, to depress

> *Esa noticia desanimaría a cualquiera.* News like that would
> dampen anyone's spirits.

desanimarse to get discouraged, to lose heart

reanimar to revive

apreciar (1) to appreciate
          (2) to value
          (3) to see (and appreciate)

Sabes que te aprecian. You know they appreciate you.
Desde aquí no se aprecia. You can't see it properly from here.

despreciar(se) (1) to despise
              (2) to reject
              (3) to underestimate

despreciar a alguien to despise someone

Despreciaron la oferta. They rejected the offer.
No desprecies a tus amigos. Don't look down on your friends.
Se desprecian. They despise each other.

armar (1) to arm (weapons)
       (2) to build, to assemble
       (3) to load (machine)

armarla to kick up a fuss

Ese niño siempre la está armando. That child's always kicking up a
   rumpus.

armar un lío to create trouble / a problem
armarse to arm oneself
armarse de valor / paciencia to stiffen one's resolve / patience
armarse un lío to get confused

No consigo armar estas piezas. I can't manage to assemble these
   pieces.
¡Ahora sí que la hemos armado! Now we've done it!

atar to tie, to fasten

atar cabos (sueltos) to tie up loose ends, to put two and two together
atar corto a alguien < fam. > to keep someone on a tight rein

atar(se) los cordones to do up / tie one's shoelaces

estar atado to be very busy
estar con las manos atadas < lit. & fig. > to have one's hands tied
estar atado de pies y manos to be bound hand and foot

desatar to untie, to undo, to unfasten

desatarse (1) to break out
          (2) < fam. > to go wild

Se desató una tormenta. A storm broke out / burst.
Bebió dos vasos de más y se desató. He / she had too much to
   drink and went wild.
De pronto, se desató en improperios contra mí. He / she suddenly
   broke out into a stream of insults against me.

atender* (1) to help, to assist
(2) to pay attention, to listen

atender por el nombre de to answer to the name of
no atender a razones not to (be willing to) see reason

> *En seguida le atiendo.* I'll be with you in a minute.
> *¿Ya le atienden?* Are you being attended to?
> *¿Qué médico le atiende?* Who is your doctor?
> *Bien, ahora atiende.* Well now, listen carefully.

desatender to neglect, to ignore, to pay no heed to

desatender una llamada to ignore a phone call
desatender un negocio to neglect a business

entender to understand

> *Ya me entiendes.* You know what I mean.

entenderse:

entendérselas con alguien to have it out with someone

bajar (1) to lower, to reduce
(2) to descend

bajarle los humos a alguien to take the wind out of someone's sails, to
   take someone down a peg or two
bajar la guardia to drop one's guard

> *Baja tu ropa de arriba.* Bring your clothes down from upstairs.
> *¡Bájate de ahí!* Get down from there!
> *¡Bájate del burro!* Don't be so stubborn!

bajarse to bend down, to get down

rebajar to reduce, to lower, to lessen

rebajarse ante alguien to bow before someone

buscar to look for, to seek

Note the 'qu' in *busqué*, and in the present subjunctive, i.e. *busque,
busques, busque, busquemos, busquéis, busquen.*

buscar una aguja en un pajar to look for a needle in a haystack
buscar camorra < slang > to be looking for trouble
buscar una palabra en el diccionario to look up a word in the
   dictionary
buscar una salida < lit. & fig. > to look for a way out
buscarle tres pies al gato < fam. > to split hairs, to look for trouble
   (where there's none)

estar buscado por la policía to be wanted by the police
mandar a buscar (algo / a alguien) to send for (something / someone)
venir a buscar a alguien to come / call for someone

> *Esos buscan tu dinero.* They're after your money.
> *El que busca, encuentra.* Seek and you shall find.

buscarse to get

buscarse la vida to make a living

Note the construction

> *Se busca chica para niños.* Au pair needed.
> or *Se busca(n)* (e.g. criminals) Wanted

rebuscar to search carefully for

caber* to fit, to go into

> *No cabe en sí.* He is very full of himself. / He's over the moon.
> *Cabe la posibilidad de que . . .* There is the possibility of . . .

caer* to fall, to hang down (e.g. hair)

al caer la noche at nightfall
caer enfermo to fall ill
caer en la cuenta (de algo) to realize (something)
caer como moscas to drop like flies
dejar caer algo to drop a hint (e.g. in a conversation)
estar al caer to be about to arrive / happen
no caer del burro to be stubborn, to refuse to change one's mind

> *¿Por dónde cae la biblioteca?* < fam. > Whereabouts is the
>   library?
> *¡Ya caigo!* < fam. > I see now! / Now I get it!
> *No caigo.* < fam. > I don't get it. (e.g. a joke) / I can't remember.
> *Me caen bien / mal.* I like / don't like them.
> *Este año la Semana Santa cae en abril.* Easter is in April this year.

caerse to fall down

caerse redondo to faint / to fall in a heap

> *Ese libro está que se cae a trozos.* That book is falling apart / is
>   falling to pieces.
> *Esos se caen de tontos.* < coll. > They couldn't be more silly / stupid.

recaer to relapse, to fall on

recaer (las sospechas) en / sobre alguien to fall on someone (suspicion)

> *Había dejado de fumar, y he vuelto a recaer.* I'd stopped smoking,
>   but now I've fallen into the habit again.

cambiar to change, to alter

cambiar de chaqueta < fig. > to change sides, to turn one's coat
cambiar de idea to change one's mind
cambiar de mano to change hands
cambiar para bien / mal to change for the better / worse
cambiar de tema to change the subject

> *Le vendrá bien cambiar de aires.* A change of air will do him / her good.

cambiarse to get changed, to get dressed

descambiar to exchange

> *Tengo que descambiar estos pantalones.* I have to exchange these trousers.

cantar (1) to sing, to call
(2) < coll. > to smell bad

> *¡Cómo canta ese queso!* < fam.> That cheese smells really bad!

cantar las cuarenta < fam. > to call trumps / to give a ticking off

> *Eso ya es otro cantar.* < fam. > That's another story / That's better.

cobrar to charge, to get paid

por cobrar unpaid

> *¿Me cobra por favor?* Can I pay, please?
> *Si lo haces mal, ¡cobras!* < fam. > If you make a mess of it, you're in for it! / You're going to cop it!
> *Espero cobrar mañana.* I hope I'll get paid tomorrow.

cobrarse to take

> *El terremoto se ha cobrado 10 vidas.* The earthquake has taken / claimed 10 lives.

coger to catch, to take

Note: 'g' becomes 'j' before 'a' and 'o' as in *cojo, coja, cojamos, cojáis, cojan.*

coger un autobús to catch a bus
coger cariño a alguien to take a liking to someone, to get fond of someone
coger un catarro to catch a cold
coger a alguien desprevenido / de nuevas to take someone by surprise
cogerla con alguien to have it in for someone
coger el sentido (de algo) to gather the meaning (of something)

coger la puerta < coll. > to leave, to clear out
coger al toro por los cuernos < fig. > to take the bull by the horns
coger las cosas al vuelo < fig. > to be quick on the uptake

  Prefiero coger un taxi. I'd rather take a taxi.

coger una mona < slang > to get drunk

cogerse to get, to catch

cogérsela < slang > to get drunk

acoger to welcome, to receive

acoger con los brazos abiertos to welcome with open arms

encoger to shrink

recoger to gather, to pick up

recoger datos to collect data
recoger las velas to furl the sails

  Te recojo a las 5. I'll pick you up at 5.
  El que siembra recoge. As you sow so you shall reap.

recogerse to assemble, to go home, to go to bed, to retire

colgar* to hang, to hang up (phone)

colgar el / los hábito(s) < fig. > to give something up, to throw in the
  towel
estar colgado < slang > to be hooked (on drugs) / to be at a loose end

  No cuelgue por favor. Hold the line, please.
  ¡Me ha colgado! He's hung up on me!

descolgar to pick up (the phone)

  Alguien ha dejado el teléfono descolgado. Somebody's left the
    phone off the hook.

descolgarse con una tontería < coll. > to come out with a silly remark

correr to run, to rush, to speed, to flow

correr a ayudar a alguien to run to help someone
correr con los gastos to pay / bear the expenses, to foot the bill
correr como un loco to run like mad
correr peligro to be in danger
hacer correr la voz to spread rumours / the word
el mes que corre the current month
en los tiempos que corren as things are at present, in these times

  ¡Corre! Hurry up!

Es preferible dejarlo correr. It's better to let things be.
Corre la silla un poco para la derecha. < fam. > Move your chair
   to the right a bit.

correrse (1) to move (up)

!!   (2) < slang > to have an orgasm

descorrer to draw back (e.g. curtains)

recorrer to go over, to travel, to 'do'

recurrir to resort to, to turn to (person), to appeal

costar* to cost

cueste lo que cueste whatever it costs
a precio de costo at cost price

   Eso te costará caro. That will cost you dear.
   ¿Qué / cuánto cuesta aquel bolso? How much is that handbag,
      please?
   Le cuesta mucho hacer amigos. He / she finds it difficult to make
      friends.

acostar to put (someone) to bed, to lay down

acostarse to go to bed, to lie down

recostar to lean something (on)

recostarse to lie down, to lie back

dar* to give

dar(le) algo a alguien to give someone something
dar(le) la bienvenida a alguien to welcome someone
dar a entender que to make someone believe that, to imply / hint that
dar esquinazo a alguien < slang > to dodge someone, to give
   someone the slip
dar una fiesta to give / have a party
dar permiso para to give permission (to do something)
dar un premio to give a prize
dar que hablar to cause people to gossip
dar(le) la razón a alguien to say someone is right, to agree with
   someone
dar el visto bueno to give the go-ahead / OK
estar dale que te dale / dale que te pego (a algo) < coll. > to insist on
   something, to bash away at / harp on something
darle a alguien < fam. > to hit someone

Daría cualquier cosa por... I'd give anything for...
por si vienen mal dadas < fam. > for a rainy day
Me da lo mismo. It's all the same to me.
No consigo dar con la solución. I can't find the answer.
¡Qué más da! Never mind! / What does it matter!
Me da (en la nariz) que... I have the feeling that...
Acaban de dar las 4. The clock has just struck four.
Tu habitación da a la calle. Your room overlooks the street.
Me parece que no va a dar para todos. I don't think there's going
    to be enough for everybody.
Esta cuerda no da. This rope is too short.
¡Dale! < fam. > Come on! Again!

darse to devote oneself (to)

darse aires to put on airs
darse a la bebida to take to drink
dárselas de algo to claim to be something
darse el lote con alguien < slang > to have it off with someone
dársela con queso a alguien < fam. > to fool someone
darse / pegarse un baño to take a bath, to go for a swim
darse por vencido / a to give in

decir* to say, to tell

decir que sí / no to say yes / no
decir mentiras to tell lies
decirle cuatro verdades a alguien to tell someone a few home truths
decir la verdad to tell the truth
decir tonterías to talk nonsense

es decir that is to say
por así decirlo as it were
quiero decir... I mean...
sin decir palabra without a word
sobra decir que needless to say that
¡Dígame! Hello! (answering the phone)
Se dice fácil, pero... It's easy to say, but...
Dicho y hecho. No sooner said than done.
¿Cómo dice? Pardon?
¿Lo dices en serio? Are you serious?
Yo no diría tanto. I wouldn't say that much.
¡Quién lo hubiera dicho! Who'd have thought that!
Eso dice mucho de tu actitud. That says a lot about your attitude.

decirse to be said, to be called

> *Se dice que lo asesinaron.* They say he / she was murdered.
> *¿Cómo se dice eso en español?* How do you say that in Spanish?

bendecir to bless

contradecir to contradict, to be contrary to

contradecirse to contradict oneself, to contradict each other

desdecir(se) to withdraw (a statement), to contradict (oneself)

maldecir to speak ill of, to slander

predecir to predict, to foretell

predecir el futuro to tell the future

dormir* to sleep, to be asleep, to anaesthetize, to deaden

dormir como un niño / a pierna suelta to sleep soundly
dormir como un tronco to sleep like a log
dormir la mona < slang > to sleep it off, to sleep off a hangover
dormir tranquilo to rest easy, to sleep with an easy mind
dormirse to fall asleep / to oversleep
dormirse en los laureles to rest on one's laurels

echar to throw / to give out / to put in, to add

echar las cartas to tell fortunes (in cards)
echar (le) la culpa a alguien to blame someone, to put the blame on
  someone
echar de menos to miss
echar algo en falta to miss something
echar en falta (+ infinitive) to miss (doing something)
echar un vistazo a algo to take a look at something

> *¿Cuántos años le echas?* How old do you think he / she is?

echarse to lie down, to have a rest

echarse a (+ infinitive) to start (doing / to do something)
echarse calle abajo to set off down the street

estar* to be, to stay

estar a (diez pesetas el kilo) to be (10 pesetas a kilo)
estar al (+ infinitive) to be about to do something:

> *Están al llegar.* They're about to arrive.

estar por (+ infinitive) to feel like / be in favour of doing something

> *Eso está por ver.* That remains to be seen.

estar como en casa to feel at home
estar enfermo / a to be ill
no estar para (bromas) not to be in the mood for (jokes)
estar sin gorda / perra < fam. > to be broke
estar con gripe / sarampión to have flu / measles

> *Estoy que me muero por verlo.* < fam.> I can't wait to see it.
> *Pedro está que muerde / trina / rabia* < fam. > Pedro is hopping mad.
> *Estamos en el hotel de la esquina.* We're staying in the hotel on the corner.
> *Esto ya está.* This is ready / finished / done.
> *Ya está.* That's it.
> *¡Está regalado!* < fam. > It's a bargain! / It's a gift!
> *Así están las cosas.* That's how things are.

haber* to have (used to form the perfect / compound tenses)

hay there is / are
hay que (+ infinitive) we have to, it is necessary to
no hay más que (+ infinitive) one only has to:

> *No hay más que verlo, está agotado.* You only have to look at him to see he's exhausted.
> *Hay que terminarlo para el lunes.* It's got to be finished by Monday.
> *¿Qué hay?* < fam. > Hi! / What's up?
> *No hay de qué.* You're welcome. / Don't mention it.

hablar to speak, to talk

hablar (inglés) to speak (English)
hablar en favor de to put in a good word for, speak in favour of
hablar con alguien por teléfono to talk to someone on the phone

> *Hablo en serio.* Seriously. / I'm serious.
> *No sé para qué hablo, no me haces ni caso.* I don't know why I bother talking, you take no notice of what I say.
> *¡Mira quién fue a hablar!* Look who's talking!
> *¡(De eso) ni hablar!* No way! / That's out of the question!

hablarse:

> *Se habla francés.* French spoken here.
> *Se habla de unos 300 heridos.* There is talk of 300 people injured.

hacer* to do, to make

hacer algo adrede to do something on purpose
hacer el amor to make love
hacer dedo < fam. > to hitch-hike
hacer las camas to make the beds
hacer la casa to clean the house
hacer cola to queue
hacer la comida to cook, to make lunch
hacer como que to pretend, to act as if
hacer un examen to take an exam
hacer el ridículo to make a fool / spectacle of oneself
hacer lo que uno puede to do one's best
hacer todo lo posible por (+ infinitive) to do one's very best to
estar (algo) demasiado hecho to be overcooked

   ¡*Trato hecho!* That's a deal!

Note that *hace* occurs in many common expressions about the weather:

   Hace frío / calor. It's cold / hot.
   Hace muy bueno. The weather is fine.
   Hace de tormenta. It's stormy.
   Hace viento. It's windy.
   Hace un tiempo (+ adjective). It's (adjective) weather.

hacerse (+ adjective) to become, to grow, to turn (+ adjective)

hacerse cura to become a priest
hacerse alto to grow taller
hacerse daño to hurt oneself
hacerse a la idea to get used to the idea
hacerse ilusiones to delude oneself, to be under a delusion

   El niño se ha hecho muy mayor. The boy has grown up a lot.

deshacer to undo, to unmake, to unpack

deshacer la maleta to unpack the suitcase

deshacerse to melt

deshacerse (de algo / alguien) to get rid (of something / someone)

rehacer to redo, to remake

ir* to go

ir a (+ infinitive) to be going to do something
ir al grano to go / get straight to the point
ir a pie to walk
ir en coche to drive, to go by car

ir en serio to be serious

no vaya a ser que (+ subjunctive) you / we don't want

    Este reloj no va bien. This watch is not working properly.

    ¿No irás a comprarlo, verdad? You are not going to buy it, are you?

    ¿Cómo va todo? How are things going?

    A mí, ni me va ni me viene. < coll. > It's nothing to do with me.

    ¿Cuánto te va (que no viene)? How much do you bet (he's not
      coming)?

    ¡Vaya cochazo! What a terrific car!

    Vaya, vaya . . . Well, well, well . . .

    Bueno, a lo que iba, . . . Well, as I was saying . . .

    ¡Vamos! Come on! / Come off it! / Go on!

    ¡Ya voy! I'm coming!

    ¿Por dónde se va a Madrid? Which way is Madrid?

    Esa chaqueta no te va con esos pantalones. That jacket doesn't go
      with those trousers.

irse to go away, to leave

    ¡Vete! Go away! / Clear off!

morder* to bite

morder el anzuelo to take the bait

estar que muerde < fam. > to be hopping mad

morderse la lengua to bite one's tongue, to hold one's tongue

perder* to lose

perder (el) contacto (con alguien) to lose contact (with someone)

perder la costumbre de (+ infinitive) to lose the habit of (doing
    something)

perder el hilo to lose the thread (e.g. a story)

perder peso to lose weight

perder el tiempo to waste one's time

saber perder to be a good loser

salir perdiendo to lose out (on a deal)

    ¡Tú te lo pierdes! It's your loss!

    Ese carácter tuyo te perderá. That bad temper of yours will be
      your downfall.

    Esta botella pierde. This bottle leaks.

perderse to lose oneself, to get lost, to lose one's way

    Me temo que nos hemos perdido. I'm afraid we're lost.

    ¡Piérdete! < coll. > Get lost!

portar to carry
portarse to behave
portarse bien / mal to behave well / badly

aportar to bring, to contribute

comportarse to behave, to act
comportarse de forma extraña to behave in a strange way

deportar to deport

exportar to export

importar (1) to matter
(2) to import
>
> *Me importa un rábano / bledo / pito.* < coll. > I don't care two
> hoots.
> *No importa.* It doesn't matter.
> *No me importa.* I don't care.
> *¿Te importa?* Do you mind?
> *Y a ti ¿qué te importa?* < coll. > What's it to you anyway?

soportar to stand, to bear

transportar to transport, to carry

prender to catch / to fasten, to pin
prender fuego a algo to set light to something, to set on fire

prenderse to catch fire

aprender to learn

comprender to understand / to include / comprise
comprenderse to understand each other

emprender to start, to undertake
emprenderla con alguien to have it out with someone
emprender el regreso to start back
emprender la retirada to begin to retreat
emprender un viaje to set off / start on a journey

reír* to laugh
hacer reír to be funny
>
> *Todo el mundo le ríe las gracias.* Everybody laughs at his funny
> remarks.

¡No me hagas reír! Don't make me laugh! / That's absurd!

reírse to laugh

reírse a / en la cara de alguien to laugh in someone's face
reírse de algo to laugh at something
reírse de alguien to make fun of someone
reírse con alguien to laugh with someone, to have a good time with
  someone

> *Me río de tus amenazas.* I treat your threats with derision.
> *Quien ríe el último ríe mejor.* He who laughs last laughs longest.

sonreír to smile

> *La fortuna te sonríe.* Fortune is smiling on you.

salir* to go out, to leave

salir a cenar to go out for dinner, to dine out
salir a alguien to take after someone

salirse to leave, to get out

> *¡Se me salen por los ojos!* < fam. > I'm fed up with them!

sentir* to feel, to be sorry

sentir un ruido to hear something / a sound

> *Siento molestarle pero . . .* I am sorry to bother you but . . .
> *Lo siento.* I'm sorry.
> *Siento mucho lo de ayer.* I am very sorry about yesterday.

sentirse to feel

> *No me siento bien.* I'm not feeling well.

asentir to nod, to assent

consentir to consent, to allow, to spoil (e.g. a child)

> *Eso no lo consiento.* I won't allow that.
> *Les consientes demasiado.* You're spoiling them.

resentirse to resent, to be offended / to suffer, to feel the effects (of)

tener* to have

Note the structure *tener que* (+infinitive) to have (to do something):

> *Tengo que estudiar.* I have to study

tener que (+ infinitive) *algo / tener algo que* (+ infinitive) to have to do something / to have something (to do):

> *Tengo cuatro libros que leer.* I have four books to read.

tener (20) años to be (20) years old

tener buen saque < slang > to have a good appetite

tener (a alguien) al corriente to keep (someone) up to date

tener (algo) en cuenta to take (something) into account

tener frío / calor to be cold / warm / hot

tener miedo to be afraid

tener muchas tablas < fam. > to have a lot of experience / a strong stage sense

tener la negra < fam. > to have a run of bad luck

tener la palabra to be the speaker / have the floor (e.g. at a meeting)

tener prisa por (+ infinitive) to be in a hurry to (do something)

tener (a alguien) a raya to keep (someone) at bay

tener razón to be right

tener la sartén por el mango < fam. > to be in control, to have the whip hand

tener sed to be thirsty

tener sentido to make sense

tener un sueño to have a dream

tener suerte to be lucky

tener (a alguien) en vilo to keep (someone) in suspense

> *¿Cuántos años tienes?* How old are you?
> *Aquí tiene(s).* Here you are.
> *Sólo tenías que pedirlo.* You only had to ask.

tenerse:

> *No me tengo de risa.* I can't stop myself laughing. / I'm helpless with laughter.

abstenerse de (+ infinitive) to abstain / refrain from (doing something)

atenerse to follow, to stick (to)

contener to include, to comprise, to contain

contenerse to control / restrain oneself

detener to arrest, to hold, to stop

detenerse to stop

mantener to keep, to maintain

mantener una conversación (con alguien) to have a conversation (with someone)

mantener las distancias (con alguien) to keep (someone) at a distance /
  at arm's length

retener to retain, to keep, to hold back

sostener to support, to defend, to maintain

sostenerse to hold oneself up, to stand, to continue, to remain

tirar to throw, to pull

tirar de la cadena to flush the toilet / pull the chain
tirar a la derecha / izquierda to turn right / left
tirar el dinero to waste money / throw money away
tirar (a alguien) de la lengua to draw someone out / make someone
  talk
tirar piedras contra su propio tejado to do oneself down
tirar la toalla < fam. > to give in, to give up, to throw in the towel

> *Ese abrigo tiene que tirar hasta la primavera.* That coat has to last
>   till spring.
> *Este pantalón me tira un poco de aquí.* These trousers are a bit
>   tight here.
> *Vamos tirando.* < fam. > We're getting by / managing.

tirarse to throw oneself

estirar to stretch, lengthen

estirarse to stretch (one's limbs)

retirar to withdraw, to retract, to pull back

retirarse to retreat, to withdraw, to go home, to go to bed

valer* to cost, to be worth

valer la pena (algo) to be worth it / worth the trouble
valer la pena (+ infinitive) to be worth (doing something)

> *¿Cuánto vale aquella blusa?* How much is that blouse?
> *Tu chaqueta no me vale.* Your jacket doesn't fit.
> *Ya vale* < fam. > That's fine. / That's enough. / That'll do.
> *No hay pretexto que valga.* There's no excuse for it.

valerse:

valerse de algo / alguien to make use of something / someone
no poder valerse not to be able to manage, to be helpless

> *Todavía me valgo por mí mismo.* I can still manage by myself.

venir * to come

venir al mundo to come into the world
venir al pelo to suit down to a 't'

> *¡Venga!* Come on / Come off it!
> *¡Venga ya!* < coll. > That's a bit too much!
> *Nos vino con una historia increíble.* He came out with an
>   incredible story.

venirse to come

contravenir to contravene, to infringe

convenir to be suitable, to suit

convenir en (+ infinitive) to agree (to do something)

> *Conviene recordar que . . .* It is advisable to remember that . . .
> *Sueldo a convenir.* Salary to be agreed.

prevenir to prevent, to warn (someone)

ver * to see, to watch

ver las estrellas to be in terrible pain / to see stars
ver una película to watch a film (on T.V.) / to see a film (cinema)

> *por lo visto* apparently
> *Se veía venir.* It was bound to happen.

prever to foresee, to anticipate

proveer to provide, to supply

proveerse to provide oneself (with something)

129 Building on nouns

You will probably be familiar with the literal meaning of most of the
nouns given below. This section lists some of the common
idiomatic expressions in which they are also used, and which are a
key to word power in Spanish.

amor (m.) love

amor propio self-respect
amoríos (mild) love affairs, infatuations
hacer algo por amor al arte to do something for the sake of doing it
¡Por (el) amor de Dios! < fam. > For God's sake!

Son cosas del amor. All's fair in love and war.

El amor es ciego. < fam. > Love is blind.

asunto (m.) business (deal), matter, subject

asuntos familiares family matters

asuntos legales legal matters

tener un asunto con alguien < coll. > to have an affair with someone

No es asunto mío. It's nothing to do with me.

Métete en tus asuntos. < coll. > Mind your own business.

¡No es para tanto el asunto! What a lot of fuss about nothing!

¿Qué asunto tienes entre manos? What are you up to?

Mal asunto. That looks bad. / Bad news.

bandeja (f.) tray

pasar la bandeja to pass the collection box / tray

servir algo en bandeja < fig. > to give (someone) something on a plate

Me lo pusieron en bandeja.
They gave it to me on a plate.

bandera (f.) flag, banner

a banderas desplegadas openly, freely, with colours flying

los colores de la bandera the colours of the flag

con la bandera a media asta with the flag at half mast

bajar / levantar la bandera to lower / to raise the flag

jurar bandera to swear allegiance (to)

¡Esta tortilla está bandera! < coll. >
This omelette is great!

boca (f.) mouth

abrir boca to get one's appetite going

la boca de incendios water hydrant

decir algo de boquilla / con la boca pequeña / chica to say something
    without really meaning it

no decir esta boca es mía to keep very quiet

estar bocas < slang > to be broke

estar oscuro como la boca de un lobo to be as black as night / pitch-
    black (of a place)

partirle la boca a alguien < coll. > to smash someone's face in

ser un bocazas < coll. > to be a big mouth

taparle la boca a alguien < slang > to buy someone's silence / keep someone quiet

Me lo has quitado de la boca.
You took the words right out of my mouth.

¡Cierra la boca! < coll. > Shut up!

La historia está en boca de todos.
The story is the talk of the town.

Me quedé con la boca abierta. < fam. >
I was speechless.

La noticia irá de boca en boca.
The news will spread.

Se me hace la boca agua.
My mouth is watering.

bota (f.) boot

colgar las botas to hang one's boots up
morir con las botas puestas to die with one's boots on
ponerse las botas to stuff oneself, over-eat

brazo (m.) arm

el brazo derecho (de alguien) (someone's) right-hand man
un brazo de gitano Swiss roll
con los brazos abiertos with open arms
coger a alguien en brazos to take someone in one's arms
echarse en brazos de alguien to throw oneself into someone's arms
estar(se) con los brazos cruzados to be doing nothing / stand idle

Cuando los vi iban del brazo.
They were walking arm in arm when I saw them.

No daré mi brazo a torcer.
I won't change my mind.

No te quedes ahí de brazos cruzados.
Don't just stand there doing nothing.

Este niño está demasiado acostumbrado a los brazos.
This child is too used to being picked up.

breva (f.) (early) fig

de higos a brevas once in a blue moon
¡No caerá esa breva! < coll. >
We won't be that lucky! / That'll be the day!

262

cabeza (f.) head

asentir con la cabeza to nod in agreement
cabeza de serie leader of the group / seeded player
cabeza de turco scapegoat
de pies a cabeza from top to toe, completely
andar de cabeza to be in a terrible rush / in a tizzy
ir de cabeza to go to the dogs
ir en cabeza to be the leader
levantar cabeza to get better, to improve
perder la cabeza por alguien to lose one's head over someone
romperse la cabeza to wrack one's brains
sentar la cabeza to settle down
tener la cabeza cuadrada to be inflexible
ser un / una cabeza de chorlito < fam. > to be scatterbrained
subírsele a alguien algo a la cabeza to go to someone's head (e.g. wine, power)
tener la cabeza hueca < fam. > to be empty-headed
tener la cabeza más dura que una piedra < fam. > to be as stubborn as a mule
tener la cabeza a pájaros / tener pájaros en la cabeza to be a bird-brain, to be in a tizzy
tener mala cabeza to be scatter-brained

Van a rodar cabezas.
Heads will fall.

¿Pero, dónde tienes la cabeza?
What are you thinking of?

Eso no tiene ni pies ni cabeza.
That makes no sense at all.

Perdón, tenía la cabeza en otra parte.
Sorry, I was miles away.

cara (f.) face

cara a cara face to face
echar algo a cara o cruz to toss a coin over something
echarle cara < fam. > to be shameless, to tough it out
lavarle la cara (a algo) to spruce (something) up
plantar(le) cara a alguien to stand your ground against someone
sacar la cara por alguien to stand up for someone
tener / ser una cara dura < fam. > to be barefaced / brazen
tener cara de pocos amigos / de perro < fam. > to have a long face

¡Qué cara tienes! < fam. >
You've got a nerve! / What a cheek!

Siempre digo las cosas a la cara.
I always tell people things to their face.

Siempre me lo estás echando en cara.
You're always throwing that back in my face.

No lo niegues, lo llevas escrito en la cara.
Don't deny it, it's written all over your face.

¡Debería caérsete la cara de vergüenza!
You should be thoroughly ashamed of yourself!

Si le veo, le rompo la cara. < fam. >
If I see him, I'll smash his face in.

cola (f.) (1) tail, queue
          (2) glue

!! *la cola / colita* < slang > penis, cock
un piano de cola a grand piano
ponerse en la cola to join the queue
saltarse la cola to jump the queue

Tuvimos que hacer cola media hora.
We had to queue for half an hour.

Ese jersey no pega ni con cola con ese pantalón. < fam. >
That sweater doesn't match those trousers.

corazón (m.) heart

el as de corazones the ace of hearts
una operación a corazón abierto open-heart surgery
las revistas del corazón women's magazines, romance magazines
no tener corazón to be heartless
tener un gran corazón to be very kind-hearted

Te lo digo de corazón / con el corazón en la mano.
I say this with my hand on my heart / in all sincerity.

Tiene un corazón que no le cabe en el pecho.
He's kind-hearted.

Siempre te llevo en el corazón.
You're always in my thoughts.

Me parte el corazón verte así.
It breaks my heart to see you like that.

cosa (f.) thing

una cosa lleva a otra one thing leads to another
Entre unas cosas y otras . . . What with one thing and another . . .

¡Qué cosas! < fam. >
Dear me! / Good grief!

Esas cosas me ponen nervioso.
Things like that make me nervous / jittery.

¡Qué cosas tienes!
What on earth's up with you?

Será cosa de cinco minutos.
It'll only take five minutes.

Se quedaron como si tal cosa.
They acted as if nothing had happened / as if nothing had been said.

No te preocupes, es cosa mía.
Don't worry, it's my problem.

cuerpo (m.) body

el cuerpo de policía police force
dedicarse a algo en cuerpo y alma to throw oneself into something
    body and soul
una foto de cuerpo entero / de medio cuerpo full / half figure photo
ir a cuerpo to go out without (a coat / jacket) on
luchar cuerpo a cuerpo to fight hand-to-hand

A este vino le falta cuerpo.
This wine is insipid / hasn't much body.

No me lo pide el cuerpo. < fam. > I don't fancy it.

El proyecto va tomando cuerpo. The project is taking shape.

dedo (m.) finger

(4) dedos de ancho (4) fingers wide
chuparse los dedos to lick one's fingers
el (dedo) anular ring finger
el (dedo) corazón middle finger
el (dedo) gordo < fam. > thumb
el (dedo) índice index finger
el (dedo) meñique little finger
el (dedo) pulgar thumb
nombrar a alguien a dedo to appoint someone by the old-boy system /
    on a whim

265

poner el dedo en la llaga to touch on a sore spot
no tener dos dedos de frente < fam. > to be dim

Cuidado, no te pilles los dedos con ese asunto.
Careful you don't get your fingers burnt with this.

¿Te crees que me chupo el dedo? < coll. >
Do you think I'm stupid?

Ni siquiera movió un dedo para ayudarnos.
He didn't lift a finger to help us.

Podría contarlos con los dedos de la mano.
I could count them on the fingers of one hand.

diente (m.) tooth

dar diente con diente to shiver / to have one's teeth chatter
decir algo / hablar entre dientes to mumble something / to speak under
   one's breath
enseñar los dientes to show one's claws
un diente de leche a milk-tooth
estar con los dientes to be teething
hincarle el diente a algo < fam. > to get one's teeth into something
ir armado hasta los dientes to be armed to the teeth
tender buen diente < fam. > to have a healthy appetite

No me lo enseñes, que se me pondrán los dientes largos. < fam. >
Don't show it to me – I'll go green with envy.

lengua (f.) tongue, language

irse de la lengua < fam. > to talk too much
morderse la lengua to bite one's tongue
tener la lengua muy larga < fam. > to talk too much

¿Te ha comido la lengua el gato? < fam. >
Cat got your tongue?

Me encanta darle a la lengua con mis amigas.
I love gossiping with my friends.

El inglés es mi segunda lengua.
English is my second language.

Espera, lo tengo en la punta de la lengua. < fam. >
Just a moment, it's on the tip of my tongue.

mano (f.) hand

abrir la mano to ease up, to show a more liberal spirit

dar(le) la mano a alguien to shake hands with someone
dejado de la mano de Dios < fam. > God-forsaken
entregar algo en mano to deliver something by hand
estar en buenas manos to be in good hands
hecho a mano handmade
lavarse las manos de algo to wash one's hands of something
mano a mano together, on equal terms
mano de obra labour
meterle mano a alguien < coll. > to grope someone
poner manos a la obra to set to work, get down to work
de primera / segunda mano first- / second-hand
tener mano izquierda to be tactful, to have a light touch

¿Me echas una mano con la cena?
Can you give me a hand with dinner?

La manzanilla fue mano de santo. < fam. >
The camomile tea was heaven-sent / did the trick.

Les pillamos con las manos en la masa. < fam. >
We caught them with their hands in the till / red-handed.

El asunto está en manos de la comisión investigadora.
The affair is in the hands of the investigative commission.

Menos mal que no llegaron a las manos.
Thank God they didn't start fighting.

Habrá que meter mano a ese asunto. < fam. >
We'll have to get down to work on that.

Ese Juan tiene la mano muy larga. < slang >
That boy Juan is a bully.

Esos dos se traen algo entre manos.
Those two are planning something.

La clase se le ha ido de las manos.
The class has got out of control.

Se me ha ido un poco la mano con la sal.
I've overdone it a bit with the salt.

No se te ocurra ponerme la mano encima.
Don't even think of laying a finger on me.

nariz (f.) nose

hinchar las narices a alguien < slang > to get up someone's nose
Me cerraron la puerta en las narices. < fam. >
They shut the door in my face.

Se lo llevaron delante de sus (propias) narices.
They took it right under his nose.

Esa gente me tiene hasta las narices. < coll. >
I'm sick of those people.

¡Deja de meter las narices donde nadie te llama! < slang >
Stop sticking your nose into other people's business!

Son unos idiotas de (tres pares de) narices. < coll. >
They are complete idiots.

Lo hice porque me salió de las narices. < coll. >
I did it because I jolly well felt like it.

¿A que no tienes narices para decírselo a la cara? < coll. >
I bet you haven't got the guts to say it to his face.

ojo (m.) eye

a los ojos de in the eyes of
comer con los ojos to have eyes bigger than your stomach / belly
comerse a alguien con los ojos to leer at someone
mirar a alguien con buenos / malos ojos to look favourably /
    unfavourably on someone
no pegar ojo < fam. > not to get a wink of sleep
ser un cuatro ojos < slang > to be a four-eyes

¿Puedes echarle un ojo al niño?
Could you keep an eye on the baby?

Aquel señor no nos quita ojo. ¿Le conoces?
That man hasn't taken his eyes off us. Do you know him?

No vemos la situación con los mismos ojos.
We don't see eye to eye over the situation.

Nos costó un ojo de la cara. < fam. >
It cost us an arm and a leg.

No tiene ojos más que para sus hijos.
He only has eyes for his children.

Se les iban los ojos tras el pastel.
They couldn't keep their eyes off the cake.

Creo que Pedro te ha echado el ojo. < fam. >
I think Pedro has got his eyes on you.

¡Ojo! < fam. > Watch out!

Quiero echarle una ojeada al motor.
I want to have a quick look over the engine.

oro (m.) gold

de oro gold
el Siglo de Oro the Golden Age
nadar en oro to be rolling in money
prometer el oro y el moro < fam. > to promise heaven and earth

No lo haría (ni) por todo el oro del mundo.
I wouldn't do it for all the money in the world.

Ana vale su peso en oro.
Ana is worth her weight in gold.

Se acordaban de una niña de cabellos de oro.
They remembered a little girl with golden hair.

pie (m.) foot

al pie de la letra literally
estar de pie to stand, to be standing
estar al pie de cañón < fam. > to be on the job / hard at it
estar con un pie en el hoyo < coll. > to be at death's door
hacer algo con los pies < coll. > to make a botch / bungle of
ir a pie to walk, go on foot
ir con pies de plomo to be very careful / tread gingerly
nacer de pie(s) to be lucky / to fall on one's feet
una nota a pie de página a footnote
poner los pies en polvorosa < fam. > to take to one's heels

A sus pies, señora. < formal >
Your servant, ma'am.

No intentes buscarle tres pies al gato.
Don't try to split hairs. / Don't look for trouble (where there is none).

Empecé con buen / mal pie.
I got off on the right / wrong foot.

Les das el pie y te toman la mano. < fam. >
Give them an inch and they'll take a yard.

Es un caballero de los pies a la cabeza.
He's a gentleman from top to toe.

Llevo en pie desde esta mañana.
I've been on my feet since morning.

Lo que dices no tiene ni pies ni cabeza. < fam. >
What you're saying makes no sense. / There's no sense in what you say.

punto (m.) point, dot

desde mi punto de vista from my point of view
punto y coma semi-colon
dos puntos colon
punto y aparte new paragraph
punto (y seguido) full stop
puntos suspensivos ellipses
punto de encuentro meeting-point
punto medio mid-point
punto negro black spot
punto por punto one after the other
poner los puntos sobre las íes < fam. > to dot one's 'i's and cross
    one's 't's

Siempre lo cuenta con puntos y comas. < fam. >
He always tells things in great detail.

La carne estaba en su punto.
The meat was done just right.

He dicho que no, ¡y punto!
I've said no, and that's final!

Estábamos a punto de salir.
We were just about to go out.

El fútbol es su punto fuerte.
Football is his strong point.

vida (f.) life

buscarse la vida to make a living / to look for a job
nivel de vida standard of living
de por vida for life
hacerle la vida imposible a alguien to make life impossible for someone
tener siete vidas to have nine lives

Seguro que te cuenta su vida y milagros. < fam. >
He's bound to tell you his life story.

Es una amiga de toda la vida.
She's a lifelong friend.

En la / mi vida he visto nada igual.
I've never seen anything like it in my life.

¡Menudo tren de vida llevas! < fam. >
What a lifestyle you have!

¿Cómo se gana la vida? How does he earn his living?

Han tenido una vida muy dura.
They've had a very hard life.

vista (f.) sight

conocer a alguien de vista to know someone by sight
echar un vistazo a algo to have a (quick) look at something
hacer la vista gorda < fam. > to turn a blind eye
ser corto de vista to be short-sighted

A primera / simple vista me parece que . . .
At first sight I think . . .

En vista del dinero que tenemos, no vamos de vacaciones.
In view of our finances, we're not going on holiday.

¡Tierra a la vista!
Land ahoy!

¡Hasta la vista! < fam. >
See you! / I'll be seeing you!

No pierdas de vista el bolso.
Don't let that bag out of your sight.

⓲ Colourful adjectives

You will be familiar with the main colour adjectives in Spanish used in their literal sense. Many of them also give rise to some idiomatic figurative expressions. Even with the word *color*, you have:

cambiar de color / chaqueta to change sides
darle color a una cosa to dress something up
de colores coloured
una foto en color colour photo
ir de (blanco) to be dressed in (white)
perder el color to go white (of a person)
ponerse de todos los colores < fam. > to blush, to go red
subírsele a uno los colores to blush, to go red
tirando a verde greenish
ver la vida / las cosas de un solo color to be blinkered / narrow-minded

Un color se le iba y otro se le venía. < fam. >
His colour came and went.

¿De qué color es? What colour is it?

Es (rojo) / de color (rojo). It's (red).

Note: The word *color* can be omitted in Spanish, e.g. *Es (rojo)*.

271

amarillo / -a yellow

estar amarillo to be pale / to look ill
las páginas amarillas the yellow pages

azul blue

azul celeste light blue
azul marino navy blue
azul turquesa turquoise
de sangre azul blue-blooded
ser el príncipe azul to be Prince Charming

blanco / -a white

un blanco < fam. > a glass of white wine
el blanco del ojo the white of an eye
un cheque en blanco a blank cheque
dar carta blanca a alguien to give someone free hand / 'carte blanche'
dar en el blanco to hit the nail on the head / strike home
decir primero blanco y después negro < fam. > to say first one thing, then another
dejar algo en blanco to leave a gap / to leave (a piece of paper) blank
estar en blanco < fam. > not to have a clue
estar más blanco que una pared / sábana < fam. > to be as white as a sheet
una hoja en blanco a blank piece of paper
estar sin blanca < slang > to be skint
ir de punta en blanco to be in one's Sunday best / all dolled up
pasar la noche en blanco < fam. > not to sleep a wink
(el) pescado blanco white fish
una película / foto en blanco y negro a black and white film / photograph
ser el blanco de todas las miradas to be the centre of attention
verso blanco blank verse

¿Qué prefieres: blanco o tinto?
Do you prefer white or red (wine)?

gris grey

las células grises / la materia gris grey cells / grey matter
un día gris a grey / dull day
gris perla light grey
gris marengo dark grey

ser una persona gris to be a grey / dull person
tener el pelo gris to have grey hair

El futuro se presenta gris. The future looks bleak.

negro / -a black

el cine negro black cinema
dinero negro illegal hot money
estar negro / -a < fam. > to be furious / hopping mad
la magia negra black magic
el mercado negro black market
(tan) negro como el carbón / azabache jet black / pitch black
pasarlas negras < fam. > to have a tough time of it
tabaco negro dark tobacco
tener la negra < fam. > to have lousy luck
verlo todo negro to take a gloomy view about things

Me las vi negras para arreglar el coche.
I had a hell of a problem getting the car repaired.

Siempre fue la oveja negra de la familia.
He was always the black sheep of the family.

morado / -a purple

un moratón a bruise
pasarlas moradas < fam. > to have a rough time (of it)
ponerse morado (a / de algo) < fam. > to stuff oneself
ponerse morado de frío to go blue with cold
poner(le) el ojo morado a alguien to give someone a black eye

rojo / -a red

rojo de labios lipstick
al rojo vivo red hot
estar en números rojos to be in the red
ponerse rojo / -a to get sunburnt
ponerse rojo / -a como un pimiento / tomate < fam. > to blush, to go
  as red as a beetroot

rosa pink

estar como una rosa < fam. > to be in the pink
ver(lo) todo de (color de) rosa to view things through rose-tinted
  spectacles

verde green

el verde grass / lawn / green
los verdes the Greens
verde botella bottle-green
un chiste / una película verde a dirty joke / blue film
estar verde to be unripe
estar más verde que una lechuga (de algo / alguien) < fam. > to be
   green
poner verde a alguien < fam. > to be nasty about someone
un viejo verde < coll. > a dirty old man
zonas verdes green zones

131 Key synonyms

Both in speech and in writing, a wide vocabulary is a mark of good
style. For that reason alone, it is useful to find synonyms for
overused words. For English learners of Spanish there is the further
point that in formal style, e.g. reports and essays, *tener, estar, decir*
and other common verbs simply do not occur as frequently as 'to
have', 'to be', 'to say' in English. Cultivating some of the synonyms
below will help you to move towards 'real' Spanish.

bueno / -a good

Este no es el momento más oportuno.
This is not the best time.

Agradezco sus preciados consejos.
I appreciate your valuable advice.

El cambio ha resultado muy positivo.
The change has proved very beneficial.

El ejercicio es beneficioso para la salud.
Exercise is good for your health.

como as / like

Vendrá a la reunión en calidad de árbitro.
He will come to the meeting as (in the capacity of) an arbitrator.

Se me consultó, al igual que a otros.
I was consulted, as were others.

Está buscando una casa similar a la mía.
She's looking for a house like / similar to mine.

decir to say

Anunció que las tropas se retirarían.
He said / announced that the troops would withdraw.

La compañía afirmó que es una buena inversión.
The company said / stated that it is a good investment.

El acusado asegura no conocer a la víctima.
The accused says / claims the victim was unknown to him.

El portavoz declaró que el gobierno no cambiará de política.
The spokesperson said / declared that the government will not change
    its policy.

importante important

Es esencial demostrar que tenemos buena fe.
It's essential to show our good will.

La nueva ley presenta dos problemas fundamentales.
The new law creates two basic problems.

La libertad de prensa es de capital importancia.
The freedom of the press is of prime importance.

Aún más significativo es el caso de . . .
Even more important is the case of . . .

Su influencia es considerable.
He is a very important influence.

malo / -a bad

El producto puede tener efectos nocivos.
This product is likely to have bad / harmful effects.

Las consecuencias podrían ser nefastas.
The consequences could be terrible / devastating.

Ha ocurrido en un momento funesto.
It has happened at a terrible time.

muchos lots / a lot of

Un gran número de estudiantes prefiere este sistema.
A good many students prefer this system.

Han invertido una cantidad considerable de dinero.
They have invested a considerable sum of money.

Un nutrido número de ciudadanos viajará este fin de semana.
A large number of people will travel this weekend.

un problema a problem

Está además la cuestión de la inmigración.
There is also the problem / question of immigration.

La importación y exportación ocuparán el centro del debate.
Imports and exports will be the main problems / subjects under
   discussion.

ser to be

El libro representa una nueva interpretación de la época.
The book is / offers a new interpretation of the period.

Resulta evidente, pues, que no quieren llegar a un acuerdo.
It is clear, therefore, that they don't want to reach an agreement.

La solución consiste en adoptar otra actitud.
The solution is to adopt a different attitude.

serio / -a serious

La situación es muy grave.
The situation is extremely serious.

Han demostrado una falta de interés inquietante.
Their lack of interest is serious / worrying.

El tema tiene una importancia transcendental para el país.
It is a matter of extreme seriousness for the nation.

tener to have

El informe consta de / comprende tres partes.
The report has three parts.

Todavía abrigan esperanzas.
They still have hope.

La policía dispone de tres días para encontrar al asesino.
The police have three days to find the murderer.

Poseen dos casas en el campo.
They have two houses in the country.

Esta solución presenta muchas ventajas.
The solution has / offers lots of advantages.

132 Popular expressions and slang

Popular expressions and slang (*argot*) are a tricky area for foreign speakers. They may not be familiar with this register of language from their more formal studies – and in any case, slang changes quite fast. Some of the popular idioms of the late 1960s may produce laughter or incomprehension among today's teenagers. The use of popular expressions, and more particularly slang, is often indicative of a sense of group identity (peer groups at school, close colleagues at work, friends), and foreign speakers therefore need to be sure they are choosing an appropriate context in which to display their varied vocabulary. In other words, it is helpful to recognize all the expressions listed below, but if in doubt stick to the more formal equivalent in your own speech!

I have indicated by **!** or **!!** expressions which range from the somewhat vulgar to those distinctly liable to shock in some company. An attempt has been made to use the same register in the English as in the Spanish. It is interesting to note that while some areas of human activity – food, money, sex – are rich in slang in both languages, in other cases Spanish has a common popular term for which there is no real equivalent in English, e.g. *un bólido, un coche*. Those who believe languages betray the mentalities of those who speak them may care to think further . . .

	SLANG / POPULAR TERM		MORE FORMAL EQUIVALENT
!	*abrirse*	to make a move	*irse*
!!	*acojonarse*	to chicken out	*acobardarse*
	aguantar el tipo	to keep cool	*mantener la compostura*
!	*ahuecar el ala*	to make a move	*marcharse*
!!	*amariconado*	queer / effeminate	*afeminado*
	anormal	idiotic	*estúpido*
!	*de buen año*	fat	*gordo / -a*
!!	*estar hecho una(s) braga(s)*	to be knackered	*estar muy cansado / -a*
	buscarle las cosquillas a alguien	to wind someone up	*provocar*
	el caballo < slang >	heroin	*heroína*
!	*un cachas*	a handsome man	*un hombre atractivo*
	cada dos por tres	constantly	*todo el tiempo*

277

SLANG / POPULAR TERM		MORE FORMAL EQUIVALENT
la caja tonta	the box	*el televisor*
cambiar de agua al	to take a leak	*ir al servicio*
canario < slang >		
cantarle las cuarenta	to give someone	*reñirle a alguien*
a alguien	a bollocking	
cañón < slang >	great	*fenomenal*
la coca < slang >	cocaine	*cocaína*
coger (algo) < coll >	to get something	*entender*
! *coger(se) una mierda*	to get pissed	*emborracharse*
cogerse una mona	to get pissed	*emborracharse*
colega < slang >	mate	*amigo / compadre*
como una chiva	like crazy	*loco*
! *un coñazo*	a pain in the arse / neck	*un aburrimiento*
!! *¡coño!*	Christ!	*¡porras!*
correrse una juerga	to go out on the town	*irse de juerga*
corriente y moliente	run of the mill	*ordinario / normal*
un corte < slang >	a slash	*un navajazo*
currar < coll. >	to work / to graft	*trabajar*
el currelo < coll. >	work / grind	*el trabajo*
un china < slang >	a piece of dope	*cantidad de hachís (para un cigarro)*
¡Chínchate! < fam. >	tough luck!	*¡Te fastidias!*
!! *chingar*	to piss someone off	*fastidiar*
de chiripa	by chance	*de casualidad*
chocolate < slang >	dope	*hachís*
la chola < fam. >	bonce	*la cabeza*
un chollo	a bargain	*una ganga*
chorizar < slang >	to nick	*robar*
un chorizo < slang >	tea leaf / thief	*un ladrón*
! *chorra*	luck	*suerte*
! *una chorrada*	something stupid /easy	*una tontería*
de chunga < coll. >	jokingly	*en broma*
chungo < slang >	naff	*estropeado / enfermo*
una chupa	jacket	*cazadora*
chuparle la sangre a alguien	to bleed someone dry	*sacarle hasta el último céntimo a alguien*
! *chuparse el dedo*	to be stupid	*ser un ingenuo*
un chupóptero < slang >	ponce	*un parásito*
un churro	something naff	*una birria*

SLANG / POPULAR TERM		MORE FORMAL EQUIVALENT
! ¡Y un churro!	You're dreaming!	¡Qué te lo has creído!
chutarse < slang >	to mainline / to shoot up	inyectarse droga
dar un plantón	to stand up	no ir a una cita
! gilipollas	idiot	idiota
guay	great	bueno
! hacer el chorras	to act stupidly	hacer el tonto
!! la hostia	really good	muy bueno
!! joder	to screw	hacer el amor
!! una leche	blow	golpe
mundial	terrific	fabuloso
la pasma < slang >	the old bill / cops	la policía
la pasta < slang >	money	el dinero
un pelas < slang >	taxi driver	taxista
un pelele	idiot	idiota
! pillar a alguien en bragas	to catch someone with his trousers down	pillarle desprevenido
pirarse	to clear out	largarse
un pitillo	cigarette / fag	cigarrillo
un planchazo	disappointment	desilusión
salido < coll. >	horny	excitado
el talego < slang >	the nick	la cárcel
el tiesto	head	cabeza
! un(-a) tío / -a	bloke / girl	chico / -a
tocarle las narices a alguien	to wind someone up	irritar

279

FALSE FRIENDS

False friends are words which look almost or completely identical in Spanish and English but have different meanings in each. The following two sections give you a selection of these 'false friends' which can cause misunderstandings. Section 133 deals with true false friends (i.e. words which do not share the same meaning in both languages). Section 134 deals with partial false friends (i.e. when there is some degree of overlap, but also some distinction).

⓫ True false friends

True false friends are words which have a different meaning in Spanish and English.

actual current, present
> *la situación actual* the present situation
> (the actual situation *la situación misma*; in actual fact *en realidad*)

la actualidad the (T.V.) news

actualmente at present, currently
> (actually *de hecho, realmente, en realidad*)

advertir to warn
> (to advertise *anunciar(se), poner un anuncio*)

una balanza scales, Libra (zodiac)
> (balance *equilibrio* (m.); to lose one's balance *perder el equilibrio*; to balance *equilibrar*; the balance (bank account) *el saldo*)

bravura fierceness, bravery
> (bravura (mus.) *brío*)

cándido / -a naive; snow-white
> (candid *franco / -a*; a candid opinion *una opinión franca*)

la comodidad convenience, comfort
> (a commodity *un producto, artículo, una mercancía*; commodities *géneros*)

complaciente affable, kind, helpful
(complacent *satisfecho / -a*)

una conferencia a lecture, speech, long-distance phone call
(a conference *un congreso*)

consecuente consistent
(consequent *consiguiente*)

un curso a course (e.g. Education)
(course (food) *plato*; the main course *el plato principal*; in due
course *a su debido tiempo / en el momento oportuno*)

un (a) diputado / -a an M.P.
(deputy *sustituto, suplente; subdirector*)

las divisas foreign currency
(a device *un mecanismo, aparato; emblema*)

efectivo cash
(effective *eficaz; logrado*)

los efectivos members of staff, number of people involved, forces

energético / -a related to energy; *los recursos energéticos* energy
resources
(energetic *enérgico / -a* (of people))

el equipamiento facilities
(equipment *material, equipo*)

un estor a blind, shutter
(store *almacén*; a department store *unos grandes almacenes*)

eventual possible; temporary
(the eventual date *la fecha definitiva*)

eventualmente possibly
(eventually *finalmente, al final*)

una fábrica a factory
(*fabric tela* (f.); *estructura* (f.))

un(a) físico / -a a physicist
(a physician *un (a) médico*)

genial < coll. > brilliant, clever, great
(genial *amable, simpático / -a*)

un grado degree
  (grade *clase; nota* (f.), *resultado* (m.) (exams))

un inconveniente a disadvantage
  (inconvenient *que no viene bien, incómodo*; an
    inconvenience *una molestia*)

una instancia an application (form); request
  (an instance *un caso, ejemplo*; for instance *por ejemplo*)

largo / -a long
  (large *gran, grande*; at large *en general*; to be at large *estar en
    libertad / suelto*; largely *en gran parte*)

una lectura reading
  (a lecture *una conferencia; un sermón*)

una librería a bookshop
  (a library *una biblioteca*)

noticia a piece of news; *las noticias* the news
  (notice (1) *aviso* (m.); until further notice *hasta nuevo aviso*
       (2) *letrero* (m.); to put up a notice *poner un anuncio / letrero*
       (3) *atención* (f.))

pena sadness
  ¡Qué pena! How sad! / What a pity!
  (pain *dolor* (m.); to be in pain *tener dolores*; I have a pain in my
    back. *Me duele la espalda.*; to be a pain *ser una pesadez*)

el petróleo crude oil
  (petrol *gasolina* (f.))

una pila a battery
  (a pile *un montón*)

un preservativo a condom
  (preserves *conservas* (f.), *confitura* (f.); a preservative *un
    conservante*)

prevenir to warn
  (to prevent *evitar, impedir*)

una prima a bonus
  (prime *principal, primordial*; *de primera, selecto*)

la propiedad property; ownership
  (propriety *corrección* (f.), *conveniencia* (f.), *decoro* (m.))

282

una receta a recipe
    (receipt *recibo* (m.), *factura* (f.); *ingresos* (m.) (e.g. net / gross
    receipts *ingresos netos / brutos*); to acknowledge receipt of
    something *acusar recibo de algo*)

resumir to summarize
    (to resume *reanudar*; to resume one's seat *volver a sentarse*; a
    resumé *un resumen*)

sensible sensitive (person); *notable; un aumento sensible* a marked
increase
    (sensible *razonable, sensato / -a*)

sensiblemente markedly, notably
    (sensibly *de forma razonable / sensata*)

simpático / -a nice, friendly
    (sympathetic *comprensivo / -a, compasivo / -a*)

ulterior later, subsequent
    (ulterior motive *doble intención*)

134 Partial false friends

Partial false friends are those which only sometimes have the same
meaning in Spanish and English.

anunciar to announce
    (announcer *locutor, presentador / -a* (T.V., radio, etc.))

asegurar (1) to insure (person / object)
         (2) to assure

asistir to attend, to be (at)
    (to assist, help *ayudar*)

asumir to assume, to take on (responsibility, task)
    (to assume / suppose *suponer*)

atender to attend, to pay attention, to deal with; to look after (e.g.
hospital)
    (to attend (e.g. a meeting) *asistir*; to attend school *asistir al
    colegio*)

un canapé a settee, sofa; *canapé*
    (canopy *dosel* (m.); canopy over bed *baldaquino* (m.))

un caso (1) instance, case
        (2) case, lawsuit
        (3) attention, heed, notice
    (case *maleta* (f.) (suitcase), *joyero* (m.), *caja* (f.), *vitrina* (f.))

la circulación (1) traffic
        (2) circulation (of blood)

un compromiso (1) compromise, settlement
        (2) engagement
            un anillo de compromiso an engagement ring
        (3) obligation, commitment
        (4) an embarrassing situation

un control (1) an inspection, check-point
        (2) control, restriction

una discusión (1) an argument, quarrel
        (2) a discussion
    discutir por algo to argue over something
    discutir (sobre / de) algo to discuss something

disponer de to have available / to have at one's disposal
    (to dispose of / to get rid of *desembarazarse de, deshacerse de*)

excitar (1) to arouse (sexually)
        (2) to excite (but beware of unintentional *'malentendidos'* in
        view of (1))
    (to excite emotions *provocar / levantar pasiones*)

la facilidad ease, facility for doing something
    (facilities *instalaciones* (f.), *infraestructura* (f.), *equipamiento* (m.))

un familiar a relative
    (familiar *familiar*)

una figura figure
    (figure (numbers) *número* (m.), *cifra* (f.), *suma* (f.); *diagrama* (m.))

importante (1) important
        (2) large, big (especially numbers)
    un número importante de a large number of

una intervención (1) operation (medical)
        (2) a speech (at meeting, conference, etc.)
        (3) an intervention

justo (1) correct, right, fair, just
        (2) a tight fit / squeeze
        (3) just (for emphasis): *Es justo lo que quería.* It's just what I
        wanted.

local (1) local
        anestesia local local anaesthetic
        las noticias locales the local news
        (2) *el local* the premises
        (locals *vecinos* (m.); the local *bar* (m.))

nombrar a alguien (1) to appoint someone
                (2) to name someone

una nota (1) a mark, grade
        (2) a note
        (3) a note, message
        to take notes *tomar apuntes / notas*
        (a bank note *un billete*)

un permiso (1) leave (of absence)
        estar de permiso to be on leave (e.g. from army)
                (2) permission

las relaciones relations, relationship
        (relations / relative *parientes familiares* (m.) / *familia* (f.))

el resto the remainder, the rest
        el resto de los asistentes the rest of the people present
        los restos leftovers (of food)
        (a rest, break *un descanso*)

rudo rough, coarse, harsh, rude
        (rude / impolite *grosero, de mala educación*)

el sexo (1) male or female sexual organs
        (2) sex

una sociedad (1) a firm, company
                (2) a society
        una sociedad pública a state-run company
        (a public (limited) company *una sociedad / empresa que cotiza en
        bolsa*)

soportar to put up with, to bear, to support
        (to support (financially / morally) *ayudar; apoyar*)

susceptible (1) likely to
                    (2) susceptible, touchy

la tensión (1) blood pressure
                    (2) tension, stress

una unión a union (act of joining)
                    (a trade union *un sindicato*)

único / -a (1) only, single
        Es el único ejemplar que nos queda. It's the only copy we have left.
                    (2) unique

un verso (1) line (of poetry)
                    (2) verse (as opposed to prose)
        en verso in verse
        (a verse of poetry *una estrofa*)

ENGLISH BORROWINGS

With the passage of time it is common for one language to be influenced by another, and particularly for items of vocabulary to be borrowed. In the late twentieth century, Spanish has been constantly bombarded by the influence of English – or more often, American English. This phenomenon has given rise to polemical debate, and some official Spanish quarters seek to prevent new terms becoming accepted. This section gives examples of well-established borrowings, as well as recent acquisitions; it also shows how some of them have changed their meanings after becoming part of the Spanish language and how they have been adapted to Spanish grammar and structure. When the Spanish word occurs as frequently as the foreign borrowing, it has been indicated here next to the English.

It is important to remember that English words are generally pronounced according to Spanish pronunciation rules.

un babi children's overall
un best-seller bestseller (book)
un bistec (filete) a steak
un boom boom
un box horse-box, (racing car) pit
unos bóxer (calzoncillos largos) boxer shorts
un boy scout
un brunch brunch
una cámara cine-camera
un camping camping, camp-site
un casete (magnetofón) cassette player
una casete (cinta) cassette
el claxon horn
un cóctel / coctel cocktail, cocktail party
un compact compact disc
un compact disc C.D. player
un cowboy cowboy
un crac crack (noise), crash (finance)
el crack crack (drug)
un crismas (tarjeta de Navidad) Christmas card
el críquet cricket

un champú shampoo
un (vuelo) chárter charter flight

dopar (se) to dope (oneself)
el doping drug-taking (especially in connection with sports)

un elepé (L.P.) an LP
un eslogan slogan
un esmoquin (or smoking) a dinner jacket
el estrés stress
un estudio bedsit, studio-flat
expres: un tren expres a fast train, *una cafetera expres*
   an espresso coffee machine, *una olla expres* a pressure cooker

un (a) fan fan
un fax fax
un flash flash, newsflash
un flirt flirt
flirtear to flirt
un ferry ferry
el footing jogging (*el jogging* is more recent)
el fútbol football
un futbolín table football, bar football
un gángster gangster
un gay gay person (pronounced 'gei')
el golf golf
groggy dazed (boxing)
al grill grill

hacer autostop to hitch-hike
el hall hall
un handicap handicap
un(a) hippy / hippie hippy
un hobby (una afición) hobby
un hooligan hooligan (only used with reference to football
   matches)

el jazz jazz music
unos jeans (vaqueros) pair of jeans

un líder political leader
un lifting facelift

un(a) manager manager (in sport), director
el márketing marketing
el motocross motocross
la música country country music
la música pop pop music

unos pantis (medias) pair of tights
un parking car park, parking place
un pícnic picnic
el pimpón (or *ping-pong*) table tennis
un playboy playboy
un pub pub
un puzzle jigsaw puzzle

el relax relaxation, relaxing
el rock and roll rock and roll
un(a) roquero / -a a rocker

un sandwich toasted sandwich
un sandwich frío sandwich
un self-service self-service restaurant
un set set (tennis)
unos shorts (bermudas) pair of shorts
un slip / eslip pair of underpants, swimming costume for men
un spot / espot T.V. advertisement
el squash squash
un stop stop sign, junction at which you must stop

un tícket (billete) bus, underground or shop ticket

un vídeo video cassette recorder, video cassette
un videoclip video-clip
el voleibol (balonbolea) volley ball

un walkie-talkie walky-talky
un walkman (unos cascos) walkman
un wáter toilet
el waterpolo waterpolo
un weekend (fin de semana) weekend
un whisky glass of whisky

un(a) yuppie yuppie

el zápping zapping

PROVERBS

Proverbs encapsulate popular wisdom, which frequently transcends linguistic and cultural barriers. Hence, some proverbs are almost identical in Spanish and English. Others only exist in one language, perhaps reflecting something about the mentality or preoccupations of its speakers.

The list below provides a selection of common proverbs in Spanish, with their English equivalent (sometimes with a literal translation in parentheses).

135 Relationships and people

No es con quien naces sino con quien paces.
It's not with whom you're bred but with whom you're fed (that matters).

Donde hay confianza da asco.
Familiarity breeds contempt.

Quien bien te quiere te hará llorar.
He who loves you will make you cry.

Dios los cría y ellos se juntan.
Birds of a feather flock together.

Nadie nace enseñado.
Nobody is born educated.

Hablando del Rey de Roma, por la puerta asoma.
(Speaking of the King of Rome, he comes in through the door.)
Talk / Speak of the devil.

De tal palo tal astilla.
Like father, like son.

Dime con quién andas y te diré quién eres.
You know a man by the company he keeps.

136 Appearances

No es oro todo lo que reluce.
All that glitters is not gold.

El hábito no hace al monje.
(A monk's habit doesn't make you a monk.)
Don't judge by appearances.

137 Advice

A caballo regalado no le mires el diente.
Don't look a gift horse in the mouth.

El que no se arriesga no cruza la mar.
Nothing ventured, nothing gained.

A buen entendedor, pocas palabras.
A wise man needs few words.

Más vale lo malo conocido que lo bueno por conocer.
Better the devil you know.

No hay mal que por bien no venga.
Every cloud has a silver lining.

A quien madruga Dios le ayuda.
The early bird catches the worm.

Con paciencia todo llega.
A little patience goes a long way.

Quien con fuego juega se quema.
(If you play with fire, you'll get burned.)
Those who live in glass houses shouldn't throw stones.

Nunca digas de este agua no beberé.
Never say never.

A perro flaco todo son pulgas.
It never rains, but it pours.

Cuatro ojos ven más que dos.
(Four eyes are better than two.)
Two heads are better than one.

Nunca te acostarás sin saber una cosa más.
You learn something new every day.

Perro ladrador, poco mordedor.
His / Her bark is worse than his / her bite.

Cuando el río suena, agua lleva.
There's no smoke without fire.

Agua pasada no mueve molino.
(Water that has flown past cannot move a mill.)
Let sleeping dogs lie.

Los árboles no dejan ver el bosque.
You can't see the wood for the trees.

El que a buen árbol se arrima, buena sombra le cobija.
Choose your friends wisely.

Más vale tarde que nunca.
Better late than never.

El que siembra recoge.
As you sow, so shall you reap.

En abril aguas mil.
It always rains in April. / April showers.

Hasta el cuarenta de mayo no te quites el sayo.
(Don't leave off your coat till the fortieth of May.)
Ne'er cast a clout till May be out.

138 Food

A buen hambre no hay pan duro.
Hunger is the best sauce.

Al pan pan y al vino vino.
(Bread is bread and wine is wine.)
Call a spade a spade.

De lo que se come se cría.
We are what we eat.

A cada uno su parte.
Give everyone his due.

SPECIAL VOCABULARIES

Sections 139 to 148 provide selective vocabulary lists for ten important thematic areas. The first five are of general, everyday interest and are intended to take your vocabulary beyond the basic expressions common to most phrasebooks. Sections 144 to 148 are more specialized and, depending on whether you want Spanish primarily for business, keeping up with current affairs, scientific research, or literary and cultural studies, you will find one or more sections addressed to your needs. The vocabularies are of course not exhaustive on any topic, but offer you a practical resource for looking up terms you may meet, and for increasing your own word power.

139 Numbers and statistics

(a) Cardinal numbers

1	*un, uno / -a*	13	*trece*
2	*dos*	14	*catorce*
3	*tres*	15	*quince*
4	*cuatro*	16	*dieciséis*
5	*cinco*	17	*diecisiete*
6	*seis*	18	*dieciocho*
7	*siete*	19	*diecinueve*
8	*ocho*	20	*veinte*
9	*nueve*	21	*veintiuno*
10	*diez*	22	*veintidós*
11	*once*	30	*treinta*
12	*doce*		

★ Note that from number 30 onwards, 31, 32, etc., are written as three separate words.

31	*treinta y uno*	90	*noventa*
32	*treinta y dos*	100	*cien*
40	*cuarenta*	101	*ciento uno*
50	*cincuenta*	102	*ciento dos*
60	*sesenta*	200	*doscientos*
70	*setenta*	300	*trescientos*
80	*ochenta*		

1.000 *mil*
1.001 *mil uno*
1.100 *mil cien*
1.200 *mil doscientos*
10.000 *diez mil*
100.000 *cien mil*
1.000.000 *un millón*

For Spanish punctuation with figures, see section 3(iii).

★ In Spanish the word *millón* is a noun, not an adjective, so when followed by another noun, it needs the preposition *de: un millón de niños* a million children, but *cien libros* a hundred books.

(b) Ordinal numbers

1° primer, primero / -a 1st
     mi primer trabajo my first job
     el primero y principal the first and most important one

2° segundo 2nd
3° tercer, tercero / -a 3rd
4° cuarto 4th
5° quinto 5th
6° sexto 6th
7° séptimo 7th
8° octavo 8th
9° noveno 9th
10° décimo 10th
11° undécimo / decimoprimer(o) 11th
12° duodécimo 12th
13° decimotercero / decimotercio 13th
14° decimocuarto 14th
20° vigésimo 20th
21° vigésimo primero 21st
30° trigésimo 30th
31° trigésimo primero 31st
40° cuadragésimo 40th
41° cuarenta y uno 41st
100° centésimo 100th
101° ciento uno 101st
1000° milésimo 1000th

★ Note that, with dates, Spanish uses the ordinal number only for the 1st (although the cardinal *uno* can also be used):

> *el 1°/primero de agosto* 1 August

For other dates, use the cardinal number (always written as a numeral):

> *el 1 de enero* 1st January
> *el 14 de abril* 14th April

With the names of sovereigns Spanish uses the ordinal numbers when speaking, but Roman numbers in writing:

> *Carlos I (Carlos primero)* Charles the First

(c) Approximate numbers

There are several ways to express approximation. One of the most common is putting the word *unos/-as* in front of any number except 1:

> *unos cinco* about five

You can also give approximations adding the suffix *-tantos/-as* to indicate the English expressions 20 odd, 30 odd, etc.: *veintitantos/-as, treintaitantos/-as* or you can add *y pico* or *y algunos* after some numbers:

> *Tiene cuarenta y pico años.* He is about 40 years old.
> *cincuenta y algunos,* 50 or so.

The expression *un pico* < coll. > means 'quite a bit':

> *Te habrá costado un pico.*
> You must have paid quite a bit.

Adding *y muchos* to a number like 20, for example, is a colloquial way of saying almost 30:

> *veinte y muchos* almost 30 / getting on for 30

Another way of expressing approximation is adding *-ena* to units of 10 between 10 and 60, and to 100, e.g.:

> *una decena* about 10
> *una veintena* about 20 / a score
> *una sextena* about 60
> *una centena* about 100

Note the special meaning of *una quincena*. It is used to express a period of two weeks (i.e. 15 days) in expressions such as:

la primera quincena de agosto the first two weeks in August

but *15 días / dos semanas* is the common way of saying 'two weeks / a fortnight'.

Nos reuniremos dentro de 15 días.
We will meet in two weeks' time.

una docena a dozen
centenares hundreds
decenas dozens (approx.)
decenas de libros dozens of books (approx.)
miles thousands
un millón de a million

Había miles de personas en la plaza.
There were thousands of people in the square.

cientos de miles hundreds of thousands
unos cuantos several / a number (of)

(d) Idiomatic expressions with numbers

cada dos por tres constantly
las tres cuartas partes del tiempo most of the time
decirle cuatro verdades a alguien to tell someone a few home truths
estar en el séptimo cielo to be over the moon / in seventh heaven / on cloud nine
el séptimo arte the cinema
(de hoy) en una semana a week from today
uno a uno one by one
de (dos) en (dos) in (twos), by (twos)
uno sí y otro no every other one
una y otra vez time and again
Está a dos pasos de aquí. It's only a few steps away.
No hay dos sin tres. It never rains but it pours.

The numbers *cien* and *mil* are used to imply 'masses / a hundred and one':

Hay cien / mil maneras de hacerlo. There are 101 ways of doing it.

(e) Other numerical expressions

sumas y restas sums / additions and subtractions
tres más / y tres son seis three and / plus three is six
diez menos dos son ocho ten take away two is eight
seis (multiplicado) por tres son dieciocho three times six is eighteen
dos con cinco / dos coma cinco (2, 5) two point five

(f) Statistics and percentages

un estudiante de cada cinco one student / pupil in (every) five

El treinta por ciento (30%) de los empleados prefiere este sistema.
Thirty per cent of employees prefer this system.

Las previsiones varían entre 5.000 y 6.000 pesetas.
The estimates vary between 5000 and 6000 pesetas.

Hay 700 casos al año.
There are 700 cases a year.

Las inversiones superarán los 5 millones de dólares.
Investments will top / rise above 5 million dollars.

La cifra se elevará a 20.000 pesetas.
The figure / sum will amount to 20,000 pesetas.

El número de viajeros ha aumentado de 5.000 a 7.000.
The number of passengers has risen from 5000 to 7000.

Las cifras muestran un aumento de un 10%.
The figures show a 10% increase.

En lo que va del año, la inflación ha aumentado en un 5%.
Inflation has risen by 5% so far this year.

140 Times, dates, age and temporal expressions

(a) Giving the time

Remember that the 24-hour clock is used in all official timetables in
Spain and to express exact times, e.g. in public transport, working
hours, radio / T.V. programmes, airports, etc.

Notice that with the 24-hour system, to express minutes past the
hour Spanish uses the number of minutes and not *y cuarto / menos
cuarto* or *y media*:

Mi avión sale a las 15.50 (quince cincuenta).
My plane leaves at 15.50.

a las diez (en punto) de la mañana
at ten o'clock in the morning / at ten a.m. (sharp)

In everyday conversation, people use the 12-hour system with *de la mañana* for a.m. and *de la tarde / noche* for p.m.

a las cinco menos cuarto at a quarter to five
Son las tres y media. It's half past three.
Son las nueve pasadas / un poco más de las nueve. It's just after nine.
las doce (en punto) twelve o'clock (precisely)

Note the following abbreviations in conversation:

Son menos (cinco / diez).
It's (five / ten) to.

Son y media / y cuarto / menos cuarto.
It's half past / a quarter past / a quarter to.

To give an approximate time:

Serán las diez menos cuarto. It must be / It's probably about a quarter to ten.
hacia las tres (at) about three (o'clock)
Son casi las ocho. It's nearly eight.

Other expressions:

¿Qué hora es? What time is it?
¿Tiene(s) hora, por favor? Could you tell me the time, please?
Yo tengo las tres menos diez. I make it ten to three.
Este reloj se atrasa / adelanta. This watch is running fast / slow.
Se me ha parado el reloj. My watch has stopped.

(b) Dates

(See section 139a and b for use of cardinal and ordinal numbers.)

Note the word order in Spanish if you are giving a day and date:

el lunes 19 de julio Monday, 19 July

To ask the date:

¿Qué día / fecha es hoy?
¿A cuántos estamos? < coll. >
¿A qué día estamos?

Answer:

> *Hoy es 15 de julio de 1993.*
> *Estamos a 15 de julio, 1993.*

To refer to years:

> *Nacieron en 1960.*
> They were born in 1960.
> *El acontecimiento tuvo lugar en 1654.*
> The event took place in 1654. *(mil seiscientos cincuenta y cuatro)*
> *los años 20 / 30* (etc.) the 1920s / 1930s (etc.)
> *en (la década de) los 80* in the late 1980s

(c) Referring to the past

ayer	yesterday
antes de ayer / anteayer	the day before yesterday
el día anterior	the previous day / the day before
dos días antes	two days before
el año pasado	last year
el año anterior	the previous year, the year before
antaño < formal >	yesteryear / of times gone by
antes	previously, beforehand, before
antiguamente	formerly, in earlier times
entonces	then, at that time

(d) Referring to the present

hoy	today
hoy en día	at the present time, nowadays
en los tiempos que corren < formal >	at the present time, these days
actualmente	at present, currently
a veces	sometimes, occasionally
hasta ahora	(up) until now
últimamente	lately
ya	already, now

(e) Referring to the future

de ahora en adelante < formal >	henceforth
dentro de tres días	in three days' time / from now
dentro de unos días	in a few days' time
desde ahora	from now on
desde hoy	from today
desde mañana	from now on,
dentro de poco	soon, in a short time
al día siguiente	the next day
dos días después	two days later, the next day but one
en un futuro no lejano	in the not too distant future
mañana	tomorrow
pasado mañana	the day after tomorrow
de pascuas a ramos	once in a blue moon
pronto	soon

(f) Age

con el paso de los años as the years go by
envejecer to get older / to grow old
ir para noventa to be getting on for ninety
un niño / una niña de cinco años a five-year-old child
una persona de edad avanzada an elderly person
una persona de mediana edad a middle-aged person
quitarse años de encima to take years off oneself
rejuvenecer rejuvenate
la tercera edad over sixty (senior citizens)

¿Cuántos años tienes?
How old are you?

¿Cuántos años le echas?
How old do you think / reckon he is?

Están muy bien para su edad.
They're in very good shape for their age.

Le pesan los años.
His age is taking its toll of him.

No aparenta su edad.
He doesn't look his age.

Son adolescentes.
They are in their teens.

Tendrá unos cincuenta años.
He's about fifty / in his early fifties.

Tiene cincuenta y muchos < fam. >
He's well into his fifties.

Tiene veinte años.
He's twenty years old.

El tiempo pasa volando.
Time flies.

 # The weather

For the more common expressions relating to the weather based on
the verb *hacer*, see section 128.

(a) Expressions common in conversation

un chaparrón a shower, downpour
una ola de calor a heatwave
¿Qué tal hace? / Cómo hace? What's the weather like?
¿Has oído el tiempo? < coll. > Have you heard the weather forecast?
Hace un frío que pela. < coll. > It's freezing cold.
Se acerca una tormenta. There's a storm coming.
Ha empeorado el tiempo. The weather's got worse.
Hace fresco hoy. < coll. > It feels nippy / chilly today.

(b) Expressions used in weather reports

algunos claros por la tarde bright spells in the afternoon
ligera subida de las temperaturas temperatures slightly better
tiempo seco y soleado dry, sunny weather

No habrá cambios. / El tiempo se mantendrá sin cambios.
There will be little change in the weather.

Las precipitaciones serán abundantes. There will be heavy rainfall.

Aumento de la nubosidad en el norte.
Cloud cover will increase in the north.

Habrá peligro de heladas en las carreteras.
There will be danger of ice on the roads.

Habrá nubosidad de evolución diurna en el noroeste.
Cloudy weather will develop during the day in the north-west.

La niebla no ha levantado. The fog has not lifted.

temperaturas en descenso que alcanzarán, los 2° bajo cero en algunas zonas temperatures falling to 2° centigrade in some areas

En Santander se registraron 2 litros por metro cuadrado.
Two litres of rain per square metre were recorded in Santander.

temperaturas bajas / altas para esta época del año temperatures lower / higher than we would expect for this time of year

Los siguientes puertos están cerrados al tráfico.
The following mountain passes are closed to traffic.

Se recomienda el uso de cadenas en los siguientes puertos.
The use of snow chains is recommended in the following passes.

máximas de 30° en Sevilla; mínimas de 22 en Soria y Burgos maximum temperature 30 degrees centigrade in Seville; minimum temperature 22 in Soria and Burgos

Burgos dio la mínima con 6° C bajo cero.
The lowest recorded temperature was in Burgos with 6° C below zero.

142 Travel

(a) Cars

Parts of the vehicle:

el aire acondicionado	air-conditioning
los amortiguadores	shock-absorbers
la baca	roof-rack
la batería	battery
una bujía	spark plug
la caja de cambios	gearbox
el capó	bonnet
cierre centralizado	central locking
el cinturón de seguridad	seat-belt
el conversor catalítico	catalytic converter
el depósito de gasolina	petrol tank
la dirección	steering
los elevalunas eléctricos	electric windows
el espejo retrovisor	rear-view mirror
los faros	headlights
el freno	brake

el freno de mano	handbrake
el gato	jack
el intermitente	indicator
el limpiaparabrisas	windscreen wiper
las luces de cruce / cortas	dipped beams / headlights
las luces de posición	side-lights
la llave de contacto	ignition key
el maletero	boot
la marcha	gear
un motor diesel	diesel engine
el motor	engine
un pinchazo	puncture
la puerta	door (of car)
el salpicadero	dashboard
la tracción delantera	front-wheel drive

la válvula	valve
una velocidad	speed, gear
la ventanilla	window
el volante	steering wheel

Actions:

arrancar	to start up, to drive off
calarse	to stall
cambiar el aceite / la rueda	to change the oil / wheel
chocar contra	to collide with
dar el intermitente	to indicate
dar las luces / la ráfaga	to flash (headlights)
darse contra algo	to bang into something
embragar	to engage the clutch
frenar	to brake
llenar el depósito	to fill up (with petrol)
poner las luces	to switch the lights on
salir	to set off
soltar el embrague	to declutch / to let out the clutch
tener una avería	to break down
Se me ha calado el coche.	I've stalled my car.

Other vocabulary:

un atasco	traffic jam
el código de circulación	the highway code
una cola	tailback
una colisión múltiple	multiple pile-up
un control de velocidad	speed check / test / trap
un embotellamiento	traffic jam
el examen de conducir	driving test
firme inestable	worn-out road surface
un paso de cebra	zebra crossing
la prueba del alcohol	breathalyser / alcohol test
saltarse un semáforo (en rojo)	to go through a red light
saltarse un semáforo en ámbar	to go through an amber light
seguridad vial	road safety

(b) Roads

una autopista de peaje	motorway with toll
una autovía	a dual carriageway
una (carretera de) circunvalación	ring road / bypass
una carretera comarcal	B-road / secondary road
una carretera nacional	A-road / main road
un carril de aceleración	acceleration lane

un ceda el paso	give-way junction
un cruce	crossing / junction
un paso a nivel	level crossing
una rotonda	roundabout
un stop	junction with stop sign
un túnel	tunnel

For reports on road and traffic conditions listen to the information given by the *Dirección General de Tráfico* on local radio stations. In winter, the weather forecast on T.V. also provides information on the conditions of the roads and mountain passes, and there is a 24-hour telephone service (*Tele-ruta*) – call the operator to find the number, or look in the telephone book.

Please remember: another driver flashing his / her headlights at you is warning you; it does not mean 'After you'!

(c) Public transport

In big cities like Madrid, you can obtain a travel card by filling in the application form in any tobacconist's (*estanco*). This card will allow you to travel by bus, train or metro, changing as many times as you need. You will have to show this card to the conductor or to the ticket collector, together with a monthly pass or annual season ticket which you can get in the tobacconist's, underground or other transport booths.

Bus:

In most Spanish towns, books of ten bus tickets – *bonobús* – can be bought in advance. You have to get them stamped when you get on the bus and each ticket is valid for one line only. You can buy them in the tobacconist's (*estanco*), newsagent's (*kiosco*) or in any transport booth. There are also single tickets for one journey, which you get on the bus. Buses usually run from 6.00 to 24.00 and some big cities like Madrid offer a night service (*búho*) which runs every half hour from 1.00 to 3.00 a.m. and every hour from 3.00 to 5.00 a.m.

un autobús	bus, coach
un bonobús (bono de transporte)	book of (ten) tickets
el horario	timetable
una parada de autobús	bus stop
una parada facultativa	occasional / request stop
una tarifa reducida	reduced price ticket (e.g. for children)
dar la tarifa exacta	to give the exact money
picar el billete	to time-stamp ticket in a machine

Train and underground:

Train tickets can be purchased in advance at the station or from a travel agency. There are single or return tickets, as well as monthly travel cards and *bonotrén*. There are various reductions applicable if you are travelling as a family, group, or if you are a child or Senior Citizen (*ciudadano de la tercera edad*), and these usually apply to foreign tourists as well as Spanish nationals. There are certain days each month when all tickets are cheaper (*días azules*). Ask for advice before purchasing your ticket. In the main railway stations there is an office for the traveller (*servicio al viajero*) for complaints and other matters.

All the main railway stations in big cities are connected with the underground. Tickets for the underground in Madrid and Barcelona can be bought in advance. One ticket is valid for a single journey within the zone (*zona urbana*), however many times you change trains. There are also tickets for ten journeys (*bonometro*), which you can buy at the entrance to the stations, from the ticket office, or from machines.

el andén	platform
un billete abierto	an open ticket
un billete de ida y vuelta	a return ticket
la boca del metro	entrance to the underground
el coche-cama	sleeper
la consigna	left-luggage official
una consigna automática	automatic luggage locker
diario	daily
una estación de metro	underground station
un horario	timetable
litera	bunk
punctual	on time
con un retraso de 10 minutos	10 minutes late
un(a) revisor / -a	ticket collector
una taquilla	ticket office
un transbordo / cambio	change (of trains)
vagón cafetería / restaurante	buffet / restaurant car
venta de auriculares	sale of headphones
la vía	line
bajar(se) del tren	to get off the train
reservar un billete	to book a seat (on a train)
subir(se) al tren	to get on the train
taladrar / picar / perforar un billete	to date-stamp a train ticket (e.g. in a machine)

viajar en 1ª / 2ª clase	to travel 1st / 2nd class
el tren tiene parada en las siguientes estaciones:	train stopping at . . .
con parada en todas las estaciones de su recorrido . . .	
stopping at all stations to . . .	
próxima parada, Medina del Campo	next stop, Medina del Campo

El Intercity destino Madrid efectuará su salida del andén 4.
The Intercity service to Madrid will be departing from platform 4.

Planes:

el control de pasaportes	passport check
el embarque	boarding
el equipaje de mano	hand luggage
la facturación de equipajes	check-in
nada que declarar	nothing to declare
objetos a declarar	goods to declare
una puerta	departure gate
reclamación de equipajes	baggage claim
la sala de embarque	boarding area (within terminal)
una tarjeta de embarque	boarding pass
una terminal de aeropuerto	airport terminal
la tienda libre de impuestos	duty-free shop
aterrizar	to land
despegar	to take off
facturar	to check in
reclamar el equipaje	to reclaim luggage

Shopping

(a) Types of shops

una boutique	(small specialized) shop
un centro comercial	shopping centre (in or out of town)
un concesionario de coches	car dealer
un estanco	tobacconist's (also stamps and stationery)
una feria	occasional / special market
unos grandes almacenes	department store
un hipermercado	hypermarket / superstore
una farmacia	chemist's
un mercadillo	open market
la plaza / el mercado	(covered) market
un supermercado	supermarket

tener un comercio / una tienda	to run a shop / business
una tienda de artesanía	craft shop
una tienda de ultramarinos	grocer's
la venta catálogo	mail-order shopping

(b) Departments within stores

The general term for 'a department' is *un departamento* or *una sección de*, e.g. *el departamento / la sección de papelería* (stationery department).

alimentación	food
artículos de menaje	household items
bricolaje	D.I.Y.
la caja	checkout / till
ferretería	ironmongery / hardware
jardinería	gardening
lencería	lingerie
librería	books
menaje	kitchenware
muebles / mobiliario	furniture
ofertas	discounts / special offers
papelería	stationery
ropa	clothing
sección de caballeros	men's section
sección joven / de jóvenes	boys' section
sección de niños	children's section
sección de señoras	ladies' clothing section
tejidos	fabrics
vajilla y cristalería	china and glass
zapatería	shoeshop

(c) Methods of payment

(cantidad) total	total amount
un cheque	cheque
un cheque de viaje	traveller's cheque
la factura	bill
una tarjeta (de crédito)	(credit) card
un ticket de caja / compra, recibo	till receipt
un vale de compra	credit-note
dejar algo a deber	to purchase by deferred payment
dejar una fianza	to pay a deposit / to make a down payment
pagar al contado / en efectivo	to pay cash
pagar con cheque / talón	to pay by cheque
pagar a plazos	to pay in instalments

pagar con tarjeta de crédito / VISA	to pay by credit card / VISA
pagar hasta el último céntimo	to pay to the last penny
un pago mensual	monthly payment
teclear el número personal	to key in one's PIN number (for identification)

¿Tiene las 50? / ¿No tendrá las 50? / Si me da las 50 . . .
Would you have a 50 peseta coin?

¿A nombre de quién extiendo el cheque?
To whom should I make the cheque out?

Cárguelo a mi cuenta, por favor. / Apúntelo en mi cuenta, por favor.
Put it on my account, please.

(d) Sales and reductions

Exchanges are not usually possible when you buy articles in the sales, and some shops will not accept credit cards during the sales. Usually, all clothes alterations have to be paid for separately when items are purchased in the sales.

comprar algo en las rebajas to buy something in the sales
hacer un descuento del 10 por ciento 10 per cent reduction
liquidación total clearance sale
liquidación por cierre de negocio closing-down sale
no se admiten reembolsos ni cambios no refunds or exchanges
precios increíbles unbelievable prices
las rebajas sales
las rebajas de enero January sales
la semana blanca sale of bed linen
todo a (5.000) everything at (5 000 pesetas)
últimos días final days

Los pantalones de caballero están con el 10 (por ciento).
There is 10% off gents' trousers.

144 Commerce and finance

(a) Government spending and revenue

la administración pública	public administration, Civil Service
la balanza comercial	balance of trade
bonos del Tesoro	government bonds
la burocracia	bureaucracy
cobrar una pensión	to draw a pension
congelar las subvenciones del gobierno	to freeze government funding
la contribución a la Seguridad Social	National Insurance contribution
el contribuyente	the taxpayer
una declaración con derecho a devolución	tax return with right to rebate
una declaración conjunta	joint return
una declaración negativa	negative return
una declaración positiva	positive return
los derechos de herencia	death duties
la desgravación fiscal	tax relief
desgravar impuestos	to reduce tax liability
una devaluación del 5%	5% devaluation
la economía de libre mercado	free-market economy
la economía política	political economy
la economía sumergida	black economy
evadir impuestos	to dodge taxes
el gasto público	public spending
hacer la declaración de la renta	to make an income-tax return
Hacienda	Inland Revenue
los impuestos locales	local taxes (cf. Council Tax / rates)
el impuesto sobre el juego	betting tax
el impuesto sobre el patrimonio	wealth tax
el impuesto sobre la propiedad	property tax
el impuesto sobre la renta	income tax
el impuesto de sucesión	inheritance tax
el impuesto de valor añadido (I.V.A.)	value-added tax (V.A.T.)
la inflación	inflation
la intervención estatal	state intervention
libre / exento de impuestos, no imponible	tax-free
unas medidas restrictivas	restrictive measures
una moneda estable	stable currency
pedir una subvención	to ask for a grant
los pensionistas	pensioners
la política monetaria	monetary policy
una política proteccionista	protectionist policy

el presupuesto nacional	national budget
privatizar	to privatize
el recaudador de impuetos / contribuciones	tax collector
recaudar impuestos	to collect taxes
la reducción del déficit público	reduction in the public deficit
el sector de servicios	tertiary sector, service sector
el sector público / privado	public / private sector
la Seguridad Social	Department of Social Security
subvencionar a alguien	to give someone a subsidy, to subsidize
subvencionar un ente público	to subsidize a nationalized industry
sujeto a impuestos	taxable, subject to tax
el tesoro público	Treasury

(b) Salaries and income

If you are inquiring about Spanish salaries, be prepared for the fact that most companies will quote the annual salary: either *bruto* (gross) or *neto* (net), but you will usually get 14 payments per year (in most cases an extra payment at Christmas and in the summer).

There is a minimum rate of pay, authorized by the government, known as the *salario mínimo interprofesional* which is frequently referred to in pay negotiations.

There are various words for wages / salary:

los honorarios	fees
el jornal	(daily) wages
la paga	payment, pay, pocket money
el sueldo	salary (usually when paid monthly into a bank)
la antigüedad	length of service with employer
un(a) asalariado / -a	wage-earner
un aumento de sueldo	pay rise
la baja maternal	maternity leave
la baja por enfermedad	sick leave
buscar empleo / trabajo	to look for work / a job
la cartilla del paro	unemployment benefit card
la cartilla de la Seguridad Social	Social Security Card (medical treatment)
la congelación de salarios	wage freeze
un contrato permanente	fixed-tenure contract
un contrato prorrogable	renewable contract
un contrato válido hasta . . .	contract valid until . . .
la escala de salarios	(wage) scale

311

la estructura de salarios	salary structure
la extra / prima	bonus
el finiquito	notice of termination of contract
una gratificación	bonus / ex gratia payment
la jubilación anticipada	early retirement
media jornada	half day
el mercado de trabajo	labour market
el pluriempleo	having more than one job
un punto	a point (on salary scale)
la remuneración	remuneration
la renovación del contrato	renewal of the contract
el salario base	basic salary
un trabajo a tiempo completo	full-time job / post
un trabajo a tiempo parcial	part-time job / post
un trabajo fijo	a permanent job / post
cobrar el paro	to claim unemployment benefit / to be on the dole
estar parado / en (el) paro	to be unemployed
fichar	to clock in / out
hacer horas extra	to do overtime
ir a la huelga	to go on strike
las negociaciones	negotiations
pedir un aumento de sueldo	to ask for a pay rise
los sindicatos	trade unions
solicitar un empleo / puesto	to apply for a job
trabajar por horas	to work by the hour

(c) Banking and investment

un banco	bank
el banco emisor	issuing bank
la caja	cashdesk, till
una caja de ahorros	savings bank
un cajero automático	cashpoint (machine)
el cambio	exchange rate
una cantidad / suma	amount, sum
el capital	capital
una carta de crédito irrevocable	irrevocable credit note
un(a) cliente	customer
la comisión bancaria	bank commission
un crédito (bancario)	bank loan / credit
una cuenta corriente	(current) bank account
una cuenta a plazo fijo	a fixed rate account / a deposit account
un cheque al portador	uncrossed cheque
un cheque de viaje	traveller's cheque

un cheque sin fondos	cheque which will bounce
un(a) empleado / -a de banco	bank clerk
un endoso	endorsement
un extracto de cuenta	statement of account
una hipoteca	mortgage
un impreso	form
un ingreso	paying in (money)
los intereses anuales	yearly interest
una letra de cambio	bill of exchange
una libreta / cartilla de ahorros	savings account
un libro de cheques / un talonario	cheque book
los movimientos de una cuenta	bank account transactions
el número de cuenta	account number
un préstamo bancario	bank loan
un recibo	receipt
un saldo	balance (of bank account)
saldo a favor	credit balance
una sucursal (bancaria)	branch
una tarjeta de crédito	credit card
un tipo de interés	rate of interest
una transferencia (bancaria)	credit transfer
el vencimiento	falling due, expiry
una ventanilla	counter
abonar dinero en una cuenta	to pay money into an account
abrir una carta de crédito	to open a letter of credit
abrir una cuenta	to open an account
cambiar dinero	to change money
al cambio de hoy	at today's rate
cerrar una cuenta	to close an account
cobrar un cheque	to cash a cheque
domiciliar un pago	to authorize payment by direct debit
estar en números rojos	to be overdrawn / in the red
extender un cheque	to write a cheque
hacer un ingreso	to pay money in
hacer una transferencia	to make a transfer
meter dinero en la cuenta	to put money into one's account
pasar (una factura) por el banco	to pay by direct debit
pedirle dinero a alguien	to borrow money from someone
pedir un préstamo	to ask for a loan
Por favor, teclee su número personal.	Please key in your personal (PIN) number.
prestarle dinero a alguien	to lend money to someone
rellenar un impreso	to fill in a form
sacar dinero	to withdraw / take out money
una acción	share
un(a) accionista	shareholder

un(a) agente de bolsa	stockbroker
la Bolsa (de Valores)	the Spanish Stock Exchange
el cambio	exchange rate
una cartera (de valores)	portfolio
un corredor de bolsa	broker
un corredor de comercio	exchange broker
la cotización	quotation, price (on the Stock Exchange)
las divisas	foreign currency
una inversión segura	safe investment
el mercado de divisas	the foreign exchange market
los mercados bursátiles	the stock markets
una obligación	bond, debenture
las transacciones bursátiles	dealings on the Stock Exchange
el valor (de la peseta)	the value / rate (of the peseta)
los valores	stocks, securities
cerrar al alza	to close up
cerrar a la baja	to close down
Hay mucho movimiento en la bolsa.	There's heavy trading.

(d) Production

un almacén	warehouse
una cadena de montaje	assembly line
una cadena de producción	production line
carga y descarga	loading and unloading
un contratista	building contractor
los costes de producción	production costs
una empresa	firm, company
una fábrica	factory, plant
un fabricante	manufacturer
los gastos	expenditure
un grupo industrial	industrial group
la mano de obra	workforce
la materia prima	raw material(s)
un obrero	a worker
un obrero especializado	a skilled worker
una pieza de repuesto	spare part
el proceso de fabricación	manufacturing process
la producción en serie	mass production
un producto	product
el rendimiento	output
un taller	workshop
un tratante	subcontractor

(e) Sales and marketing

un aumento del capital	increase in capital, rights issue
la Cámara de Comercio e Industria (CCI)	Chamber of Commerce
un(a) cliente / -a	customer
la competencia	competitors, competition
un comprador	buyer
un concesionario	recognized dealer
un consumidor	consumer
un(a) detallista	retailer
un distribuidor	dealer
un intermediario	middle-man
un(a) mayorista	wholesaler
un proveedor	supplier
un(a) representante	sales representative
un(a) vendedor / -a a domicilio	door-to-door salesman / woman
el volumen de ventas	turnover
distribuir	to market / distribute
una inversión a corto / largo plazo	a short- / long-term investment
la investigación del mercado	market research
lanzar un producto (al mercado)	to launch a product
la marca (de un producto)	brand
una marca registrada	trade mark
una muestra	sample
la planificación	(forward) planning
la sociedad de consumo / consumista	consumer society

(f) Advertising and public relations

una agencia de publicidad	advertising agency
un anuncio / cartel publicitario	an advertisement
una campaña publicitaria	advertising campaign
un escaparate	window (display)
un lema	caption
un jefe de producto	product manager
un mensaje publicitario	advertisement, blurb
poner un anuncio	to run an advert
preparar el mercado	to prepare the market
promocionar un producto	to promote a product
la propaganda	advertising
las relaciones públicas	public relations
la sección de anuncios / anuncios por palabras	advertisements, classified advertising
un spot publicitario	publicity spot

145 Politics and current affairs

(a) Government

la administración pública	Civil Service
el / la alcalde(sa)	Mayor / Mayoress (Lord Mayor / -ess in London)
el Ayuntamiento	Town Hall
el Congreso de los Diputados	Congress of Deputies (cf. House of Commons)
el Consejo de Europa	Council of Europe
el Consejo de Ministros	Council of Ministers (cf. the Cabinet (Meeting))
la Constitución	the Constitution
la disolución del Parlamento	dissolution of Parliament
un(a) diputado / -a	an MP
un(a) funcionario / -a	civil servant
La Moncloa	official residence of the Prime Minister (used by journalists to indicate the Government, e.g. La Moncloa ha declarado que . . . cf. '10 Downing Street said . . .'
un ministerio	ministry
el ministerio de Agricultura	Ministry of Agriculture
el ministerio de Asuntos Exteriores	the Foreign Office
el ministerio de Cultura	Heritage Ministry
el ministerio de Defensa	Ministry of Defence
el ministerio de Economía y Hacienda	The Treasury
el ministerio del Interior	The Home Office
el ministerio de Justicia	The Lord Chancellor's Office
el ministerio de Obras Públicas y Urbanismo	Ministry of the Environment
el ministerio de Sanidad y Consumo	Ministry for Health and Safety
el ministerio de Trabajo	Ministry for Employment
el ministerio de Transportes	Transport Ministry
un(a) ministro / -a	minister
el / la Ministro / -a de Agricultura	Minister for Agriculture
el / la Ministro / -a de Asuntos Exteriores	Foreign Secretary
el / la Ministro / -a de Cultura	Heritage Secretary
el / la Ministro / -a de Defensa	Defence minister
el / la Ministro / -a de Economía y Hacienda	Chancellor of the Exchequer
el / la Ministro / -a de Educación	Education Secretary / Minister
el / la Ministro / -a del Interior	Home Secretary
el / la Ministro / -a de Justicia	Lord Chancellor

el / la Ministro / -a de Sanidad y Consumo	Minister of Health and Safety
el / la Ministro / -a de Trabajo	Employment Minister
el / la Ministro / -a de Transportes	Transport Minister
la oficina de empleo	JobCentre
el Parlamento	Parliament
el Parlamento autonómico	parliament of an autonomous region
el Parlamento Europeo	European Parliament
el / la Presidente / -a del Gobierno	Prime Minister
el presidente de la Junta (de Castilla y León)	President of the Council (of Castile and Leon)
el Rey	the King
el Senado	the Senate (House of Lords)
un(a) senador / -a	senator (peer of the realm)
el / la vice presidente del Gobierno	deputy prime minister

(b) Elections

abstenciones	abstentions
abstenerse	to abstain
alcanzar la mayoría (absoluta)	to get an absolute majority
aprobar (una ley)	to pass an Act
un(a) candidato / -a (por un partido)	candidate
el censo electoral	electoral register
una circunscripción	constituency
convocar elecciones	to call an election
el día de reflexión	day of reflection (i.e. day of no campaigning before an election, to allow time for thought)
dimitir	to resign
unas elecciones anticipadas	early elections / election brought forward
las (elecciones) autonómicas	elections in the autonomous regions
las (elecciones) europeas	elections for the European Parliament
las (elecciones) generales	general / parliamentary election
las (elecciones) municipales	local (town / city) council elections
las elecciones sindicales	trade union elections
elegir	to elect
una enmienda (a una ley)	an amendment
el escrutinio / recuento (de votos)	vote recount
un gobierno de coalición	a coalition government
mayoría absoluta / simple	absolute / simple majority
la oposición / el partido de oposición	the opposition (party)
la papeleta	ballot paper
presentar la dimisión	to resign

presentarse a las elecciones	to stand for election
el / la presidente / -a de mesa	officer in charge of the polling station
el primer / segundo escrutinio	first / second round of vote counting
un programa electoral	electoral manifesto
propaganda electoral	election propaganda
haber quorum	to have a quorum
un referendum	a referendum
retirarse	to stand down, withdraw
sellar las urnas	to seal the ballot boxes
ser candidato / -a a (la presidencia)	to be a candidate for (the presidency)
un sondeo de opinión	an opinion poll
las urnas	ballot boxes
el / la vocal	the declaring officer
una votación a mano alzada	ballot by show of hands
votar / ir a votar	to go to the polls
votar por correo	to vote by post
un voto	a vote
un voto en blanco	blank ballot paper
un voto nulo	void ballot paper
un voto secreto	secret vote

(c) Political debate

la agenda del día / el orden del día	the agenda, business of the day
el centro	the centre
la cohabitación	coalition / 'cohabitation'
continuar la discusión	to continue discussions
la derecha / izquierda	the right / left
hacer una intervención en el Parlamento	to make a speech in Parliament
una manifestación	protest march, demonstration
un(a) miembro del partido	(party) member
los militantes de base	grassroots members, rank and file members
un partido (de izquierdas)	a left-wing party
un partido político	political party
presentar una moción de censura	to put down a motion of censure
romper las negociaciones	to break off negotiations
ser de derechas	to be right-wing
someter (una enmienda) a votación	to vote on (an amendment)
tomar medidas en / a favor de (algo)	to take action in support of something

(d) Home affairs

un(a) asistente social	social worker
un atentado terrorista	a terrorist attack / outrage
la calidad de vida	quality of life
el ciudadano medio	average citizen / man in the street
cobrar una pensión	to draw a pension
un coche de policía	police car
una concesión	allowance
el Defensor del Pueblo	spokesman for the people, ombudsman
el desempleo	unemployment
un espacio abierto	open space / park
una familia numerosa	large family
una formación	training
un furgón de la policía	police van
un hospital de la Seguridad Social	National Health hospital
una huelga (de hambre)	(hunger) strike
ir a la huelga / ponerse en huelga	to go on strike
ir por la Seguridad Social	to go on the National Health
la jubilación	retirement pension
jubilación anticipada	early retirement
un(a) jubilado / -a	retired person
los marginados	the underprivileged
la población activa	labour force
la población ocupada	working population
la policía antidisturbios	riot police
prestaciones sociales	social security / benefit payments
la rehabilitación	social rehabilitation
la reinserción (en la sociedad)	re-entry into society
la renta per cápita	per capita income
la salud pública	public health
un sector de la población	sector of the population
un sindicato	trade union
los subsidios familiares	family allowances (e.g. child benefit, etc.)
el urbanismo	town-planning
un(a) urbanista	town-planner
la tercera edad	old age
una vivienda de protección oficial	(state) subsidized housing
una zona verde	green belt

(e) Foreign affairs

un bloqueo naval	naval blockade
un boicot	boycott

el Canal de la Mancha	English Channel
la C.E.E. (Comunidad Económica Europea)	E.E.C.
el comercio exterior	foreign trade
un consulado	consulate
una embajada	embassy
la emigración / inmigración	emigration / immigration
los emigrantes	emigrants
expulsar a alguien de un país	to expel someone from a country
una extradición	extradition
un(a) extranjero / -a	a foreigner
un(a) inmigrante ilegal	an illegal immigrant
la ley de extranjería	immigration laws
la O.N.U. (Organización de las Naciones Unidas)	U.N. (United Nations)
la O.T.A.N. (Organización del Tratado del Atlántico Norte)	NATO
un país en vías de desarrollo	developing country
un país subdesarrollado	underdeveloped country
el permiso de residente	residence permit
la política exterior	foreign policy
un(a) portavoz del gobierno	government spokesperson
un(a) residente	resident
romper las relaciones diplomáticas	to break off diplomatic relations
el Tercer Mundo	Third World

(f) The law and legal matters

el abogado de la acusación	counsel for the prosecution
el abogado defensor	counsel for the defence
absolver al acusado / a la acusada de . . .	to absolve the accused of . . .
el / la acusado / -a	the accused
acusar a alguien de algo	to accuse someone of something
una agresión	assault, violence
un agresor	attacker / mugger
apelar	to appeal
aprobar un proyecto de ley	to vote through a bill
un atentado	assassination attempt, outrage
el banquillo de los acusados	the dock
la brigada criminal	serious crime squad
cometer un delito	to commit an offence
una comisaría (de policía)	police station
comparecer (a juicio)	to appear (in court)
condenar a alguien a 5 años	to sentence someone to five years' imprisonment

un crimen	crime / murder
un(a) criminal	criminal / murderer
un chivatazo / soplo	undercover information, tip-off
encarcelar	to send to prison
entrar en vigor	to come into force (law)
una falta	lack / error
el / la fiscal	Crown Prosecutor
las fuerzas del orden	police (authorities), forces of law and order
los G.E.O. (Grupos Especiales de Orden)	special riot police, SAS
un(a) guardia / agente de tráfico	traffic warden
un homicidio	murder / manslaughter
incumplir una ley	to break a law
una infracción	offence
el / la juez / -a de instrucción	investigating magistrate
un(a) jurista	lawyer; jurist
levantar la sesión	to adjourn
llevar algo / a alguien a juicio	to bring / take (something / someone) to court
un macarra	hooligan, lout
un magistrado	magistrate
la magistratura	magistracy; judgeship
una multa	a parking ticket / fine
un notario	notary
un(a) oficial de policía	police officer
el palacio de justicia	the law courts
presentar una denuncia contra	to lodge an official complaint against
un / una preso / -a	prisoner
pronunciar un veredicto	to return / give a verdict
una proposición de ley	a private bill
un proyecto de ley	a bill
revocar una ley	to repeal a law
el raptor	kidnapper
un(a) rehén	hostage
un(a) reincidente	re-offender
un robo a mano armada	(armed) robbery
secuestrar un avión	to hijack a plane
una sirena de policía	police siren
testificar	to testify
un(a) testigo	witness
el tráfico de drogas	drug trafficking
un tribunal de primera instancia	Court of first instance
el Tribunal Supremo	Supreme Court (House of Lords)
una violación	rape
un violador	rapist

Computers and technology

(a) Computers

Much of the language of computers is international and rich in words imported from English. Sometimes, although there is a Spanish word, the English term is used just as frequently; in these cases, both words are given.

almacenar	to store
una aplicación del ordenador personal	P.C. function
un banco de datos	a data bank
binario	binary
un bit	bit
borrar	to delete
un byte / octeto	byte
un cartucho	cartridge
un circuito	circuit
compatible	compatible
una copia pirata	pirate copy
el cursor	cursor
un chip / una pastilla	chip
los datos	data
digital	digital
un disco blando / floppy	soft / floppy disk
un disco duro	hard disk
edición de textos	desktop publishing
formatear	to format
gráficos	graphics
una impresora	printer
una impresora laser	laser printer
la informática	computing / computer science, information technology
informatizar	to put on computer
introducir	to insert
un juego de ordenador	a computer game
un manual	manual
la memoria	memory
el menú	menu
modificar	to modify
el monitor	monitor
un ordenador	computer
un ordenador central	central computer
una pantalla	screen
poner / mandar un fax	to send a fax

portátil	portable
un procesador de textos	word-processor
procesar	to process
un programa	computer program
un ratón	mouse
una red	network
salvar un fichero / archivo	to save a file
el sistema operativo	operating system
el teclado	keyboard
una terminal	terminal

(b) Domestic technology and other recent technology

una antena parabólica	satellite dish
un (aparato) electrodoméstico	domestic appliance
un (aparato de) vídeo	video recorder
una batidora	mixer / blender
una cadena de música	hifi system
una central nuclear	nuclear power station
una cinta	tape
una cinta de vídeo	video tape
un compact disc / C.D.	compact disc, C.D. player
un congelador	freezer
un contestador automático	answering machine
un cuchillo eléctrico	electric knife
una lavadora	washing-machine
una lavadora-secadora	washer-drier
un lavaplatos / lavavajillas	dishwasher
un magnetófono	tape-recorder
un mando (a distancia)	remote control
un microondas	microwave oven
una nevera	refrigerator / fridge
una plancha de vapor	steam iron
una radio	radio
un radiocasete	radio cassette
una secadora	tumble-drier
la televisión por cable	cable T.V.
la televisión vía satélite	satellite television
el zápping	channel hopping

Si quiere dejar un recado, hágalo después de la señal.
If you want to leave a message, do so after the signal.

147 Cinema and the fine arts

(a) Cinema

The cinema is also known as *la pantalla grande* (the big screen) as opposed to *la pequeña pantalla* (i.e. the T.V.).

un actor/una actriz	actor, actress
la banda sonora	soundtrack
el cine de arte y ensayo	art-house cinema
un(a) cineasta	famous film director / film critic / film buff
un(a) cinéfilo / -a	keen cinema-goer, fan
un cortometraje	short film (especially documentary)
los dibujos animados	cartoons
un(a) director / -a	director
la distribución	distribution
doblar	to dub
un documental	documentary
encuadrar	to frame
la escenografía	setting
una estrella	star
un estreno total	new release
un(a) extra	extra / walk-on part
un festival de cine	film festival
la fotografía	camera work
la industria cinematográfica	the film industry
interpretar un papel	to play a role
Lleva dos semanas en cartel.	It has been running for two weeks.
llevar (una novela) al cine	to make a film of (a novel)
el montaje	editing
montaje de sonido	sound editing
la música de fondo	background music
una película en versión original	foreign film in original language (not dubbed)
poner	to be showing
un primer plano	close-up
un(a) productor / -a	producer
el reparto	cast
el rodaje	filming / shooting
rodar en exteriores	to shoot a film on location
sacar una película	to bring out a film

(b) Fine arts

una acuarela	water-colour
un(a) arquitecto	architect
un(a) artista	artist
un boceto	rough outline / sketch
el bordado	embroidery
un cuadro	painting, picture
el diseño	drawing, design
un(a) escultor / -a	sculptor
una escultura	sculpture
una exposición	exhibition
el fondo	background
un grabador	engraver
un lienzo	canvas
una litografía	lithograph
una maqueta	(scale) model
un marco	frame
un mecenas	patron
un mural	mural
un óleo	oil painting
un(a) pintor / -a	painter, artist
la primera línea	foreground
un tapiz	tapestry
las viñetas	cartoons

 Literature

(a) Writers and their craft

un(a) autor / -a	author
un(a) biógrafo / -a	biographer
componer	to compose
un(a) corrector / -a	proofreader
crear	to create/write
un crítico	critic
describir	depict, paint, describe
un(a) dramaturgo / -a	playwright, dramatist
un(a) ensayista	essayist

escribir	to write
un(a) escritor / -a	writer
un(a) escritor / -a de relatos cortos	short-story writer
evocar	to conjure up
un(a) filósofo	philosopher
un(a) historiador / -a	historian
un(a) lector / -a	reader
un(a) novelista	novelist
un(a) poeta	poet
un(a) redactor / -a, editor / -a	editor
relatar	to tell, relate

(b) Genres and works

★ Note that *la obra* = the complete works of an author, but *una obra* = one work.

una autobiografía	autobiography
una biografía	biography
un cuento de hadas	fairytale
una edición crítica	critical edition
edición de tapas blandas / en rústica	paperback
edición de tapas duras	hardback
un ensayo	essay
una fábula	fable
los géneros literarios	literary genres
una historia	story
la narrativa	literature / fiction
una novela	novel
una novela epistolar	epistolary novel
una novela histórica	a historical novel
una novela policíaca	detective story
una novela rosa	sentimental novel
una obra maestra	masterpiece
las obras completas	complete works
una obra de teatro	play
un poema	poem, epic poem
una poesía	poem
la poesía	poetry
la prosa	prose
un relato (corto)	short-story / tale

(c) Plays and acting

un actor / una actriz	actor, actress
un(a) apuntador / -a	prompter
el argumento	plot
un(a) cómico / -a	comic actor
una compañía de teatro	(theatre) company
el elenco	the cast
un(a) espectador / -a	spectator
hacer de	to play the part of
interpretar un papel	to play a part / role
un monólogo	monologue
montar una obra	to put on a play
el mundo del teatro	world of the theatre
una obra de teatro	play
una ópera	opera
los personajes	characters
en el primer acto	in / during the first act
el público	the audience
el reparto	the cast
una reposición	revival (of an earlier performance)
una representación	performance
una tragedia	tragedy
la trama	plot
el decorado	décor
el descanso / intermedio	interval
el escenario	stage
las luces	lights
un lleno	a full house
la noche de estreno	opening night, première
la puesta en escena	set
el vestuario	costumes
una butaca	seat (in the stalls)
la fila cuatro	row four
la galería	the gallery
un palco	a box

Dos entradas de butaca en la fila 10, por favor.
Two tickets for the stalls, row ten, please.

¿Quedan entradas para esta noche?
Are there any tickets left for tonight?

¿A qué hora empieza la función?
When does the performance start?

327

(d) Prose writing

un capítulo	chapter
la caracterización	characterization
un estilo elaborado	an elaborate style
un héroe	hero
una heroína	heroine
el narrador	narrator
un personaje principal	main character
un personaje secundario	minor / secondary character
el / la protagonista	protagonist
un tema árido	a dry theme
el tema central	main theme
un tema pasado <coll.>	hackneyed / well-worn theme
la temática (de la violencia)	the theme (of violence)
el tratamiento	treatment / handling (of a subject)
la última novela de	the latest novel by

(e) Poetry

la aliteración	alliteration
una balada	ballad
la cadencia	cadence
una canción	song
la cesura	caesura (pause in middle of line)
un cuarteto	rhyme scheme (ABBA), quatrain
una epopeya	epic
una estrofa	verse, stanza
una figura poética	poetic figure
la lírica	lyric poetry
la onomatopeya	onomatopoeia
un pareado	rhyming couplet (aa)
un poema corto	a short poem
un poema épico	epic poem
un poema lírico	lyric poem
la rima	rhyme
la rima interna	internal rhyme
el ritmo	rhythm
un soneto	a sonnet
tercetos encadenados	linked tercets (ABA BCB CDC)
un verso	line
un verso alejandrino	alexandrine (12-syllable line)
en verso blanco	in blank verse
en verso libre	in free verse

(f) Other elements

la crítica literaria	literary criticism
el estilo	style
el estructuralismo	structuralism
un eufemismo	euphemism
la expresión	expression
una figura retórica	rhetorical figure
el fondo y la forma	form and content
las imágenes	imagery
una hipérbole	hyperbole
la lectura	reading
el lenguaje	language
una metáfora	metaphor
la retórica	rhetoric
la semiótica	semiotics
un símbolo	symbol
un tópico	cliché
la tradición literaria	literary tradition

Appendix 1
The conjugation of *ser*, *estar* and *haber*

ser to be

PRESENT INDICATIVE
soy
eres
es
somos
sois
son

PERFECT INDICATIVE
he sido
has sido
ha sido
hemos sido
habéis sido
han sido

IMPERFECT INDICATIVE
era
eras
era
éramos
erais
eran

PLUPERFECT INDICATIVE
había sido
habías sido
había sido
habíamos sido
habíais sido
habían sido

PRETERITE INDICATIVE
fui
fuiste
fue
fuimos
fuisteis
fueron

PAST ANTERIOR INDICATIVE
hube sido
hubiste sido
hubo sido
hubimos sido
hubisteis sido
hubieron sido

FUTURE INDICATIVE
seré
serás
será
seremos
seréis
serán

FUTURE PERFECT INDICATIVE
habré sido
habrás sido
habrá sido
habremos sido
habréis sido
habrán sido

CONDITIONAL	CONDITIONAL PERFECT
sería	habría sido
serías	habrías sido
sería	habría sido
seríamos	habríamos sido
seríais	habríais sido
serían	habrían sido

PRESENT SUBJUNCTIVE	PERFECT SUBJUNCTIVE
sea	haya sido
seas	hayas sido
sea	haya sido
seamos	hayamos sido
seáis	hayáis sido
sean	hayan sido

IMPERFECT SUBJUNCTIVE	PLUPERFECT SUBJUNCTIVE
fuera / fuese	hubiera / hubiese sido
fueras / fueses	hubieras / hubieses sido
fuera / fuese	hubiera / hubiese sido
fuéramos / fuésemos	hubiéramos / hubiésemos sido
fuerais / fueseis	hubierais / hubieseis sido
fueran / fuesen	hubieran / hubiesen sido

FUTURE SUBJUNCTIVE	FUTURE PERFECT SUBJUNCTIVE
fuere	hubiere sido
fueres	hubieres sido
fuere	hubiere sido
fuéremos	hubiéremos sido
fuereis	hubiereis sido
fueren	hubieren sido

IMPERATIVE	INFINITIVE	GERUND	PAST PARTICIPLE
sé	ser	siendo	sido
sed			

estar to be

PRESENT INDICATIVE	PERFECT INDICATIVE
estoy	he estado
estás	has estado
está	ha estado
estamos	hemos estado
estáis	habéis estado
están	han estado

IMPERFECT INDICATIVE	PLUPERFECT INDICATIVE
estaba	*había estado*
estabas	*habías estado*
estaba	*había estado*
estábamos	*habíamos estado*
estabais	*habíais estado*
estaban	*habían estado*

PRETERITE INDICATIVE	PAST ANTERIOR INDICATIVE
estuve	*hube estado*
estuviste	*hubiste estado*
estuvo	*hubo estado*
estuvimos	*hubimos estado*
estuvisteis	*hubisteis estado*
estuvieron	*hubieron estado*

FUTURE INDICATIVE	FUTURE PERFECT INDICATIVE
estaré	*habré estado*
estarás	*habrás estado*
estará	*habrá estado*
estaremos	*habremos estado*
estaréis	*habréis estado*
estarán	*habrán estado*

CONDITIONAL	CONDITIONAL PERFECT
estaría	*habría estado*
estarías	*habrías estado*
estaría	*habría estado*
estaríamos	*habríamos estado*
estaríais	*habríais estado*
estarían	*habrían estado*

PRESENT SUBJUNCTIVE	PERFECT SUBJUNCTIVE
esté	*haya estado*
estés	*hayas estado*
esté	*haya estado*
estemos	*hayamos estado*
estéis	*hayáis estado*
estén	*hayan estado*

IMPERFECT SUBJUNCTIVE
estuviera / estuviese
estuvieras / estuvieses
estuviera / estuviese
estuviéramos / estuviésemos
estuvierais / estuvieseis
estuvieran / estuviesen

PLUPERFECT SUBJUNCTIVE
hubiera / hubiese estado
hubieras / hubieses estado
hubiera / hubiese estado
hubiéramos / hubiésemos estado
hubierais / hubieseis estado
hubieran / hubiesen estado

FUTURE SUBJUNCTIVE
estuviere
estuvieres
estuviere
estuviéremos
estuviereis
estuvieren

FUTURE PERFECT SUBJUNCTIVE
hubiere estado
hubieres estado
hubiere estado
hubiéremos estado
hubiereis estado
hubieren estado

IMPERATIVE	INFINITIVE	GERUND	PAST PARTICIPLE
está	*estar*	*estando*	*estado*
estad			

haber (auxiliary) to have

PRESENT INDICATIVE
he
has
ha (impersonal: *hay*)
hemos
habéis
han

PERFECT INDICATIVE
he habido
has habido
ha habido
hemos habido
habéis habido
han habido

IMPERFECT INDICATIVE
había
habías
había
habíamos
habíais
habían

PLUPERFECT INDICATIVE
había habido
habías habido
había habido
habíamos habido
habíais habido
habían habido

PRETERITE INDICATIVE
hube
hubiste
hubo
hubimos
hubisteis
hubieron

PAST ANTERIOR INDICATIVE
hube habido
hubiste habido
hubo habido
hubimos habido
hubisteis habido
hubieron habido

FUTURE INDICATIVE
habré
habrás
habrá
habremos
habréis
habrán

FUTURE PERFECT INDICATIVE
habré habido
habrás habido
habrá habido
habremos habido
habréis habido
habrán habido

CONDITIONAL
habría
habrías
habría
habríamos
habríais
habrían

CONDITIONAL PERFECT
habría habido
habrías habido
habría habido
habríamos habido
habríais habido
habrían habido

PRESENT SUBJUNCTIVE
haya
hayas
haya
hayamos
hayáis
hayan

PERFECT SUBJUNCTIVE
haya habido
hayas habido
haya habido
hayamos habido
hayáis habido
hayan habido

IMPERFECT SUBJUNCTIVE
hubiera / hubiese
hubieras / hubieses
hubiera / hubiese
hubiéramos / hubiésemos
hubierais / hubieseis
hubieran / hubiesen

PLUPERFECT SUBJUNCTIVE
hubiera / hubiese habido
hubieras / hubieses habido
hubiera / hubiese habido
hubiéramos / hubiésemos habido
hubierais / hubieseis habido
hubieran / hubiesen habido

FUTURE SUBJUNCTIVE	FUTURE PERFECT SUBJUNCTIVE
hubiere	*hubiere habido*
hubieres	*hubieres habido*
hubiere	*hubiere habido*
hubiéramos	*hubiéremos habido*
hubiereis	*hubiereis habido*
hubieren	*hubieren habido*

IMPERATIVE	INFINITIVE	GERUND	PAST PARTICIPLE
he	*haber*	*habiendo*	*habido*
habed			

Appendix 2
The conjugation of regular verbs

-ar verbs

PRESENT INDICATIVE
hablo (I speak)
hablas
habla
hablamos
habláis
hablan

PERFECT INDICATIVE
he hablado
has hablado
ha hablado
hemos hablado
habéis hablado
han hablado

IMPERFECT INDICATIVE
hablaba
hablabas
hablaba
hablábamos
hablabais
hablaban

PLUPERFECT INDICATIVE
había hablado
habías hablado
había hablado
habíamos hablado
habíais hablado
habían hablado

PRETERITE INDICATIVE
hablé
hablaste
habló
hablamos
hablasteis
hablaron

PAST ANTERIOR INDICATIVE
hube hablado
hubiste hablado
hubo hablado
hubimos hablado
hubisteis hablado
hubieron hablado

FUTURE INDICATIVE
hablaré
hablarás
hablará
hablaremos
hablaréis
hablarán

FUTURE PERFECT INDICATIVE
habré hablado
habrás hablado
habrá hablado
habremos hablado
habréis hablado
habrán hablado

CONDITIONAL
hablaría
hablarías
hablaría
hablaríamos
hablaríais
hablarían

CONDITIONAL PERFECT
habría hablado
habrías hablado
habría hablado
habríamos hablado
habríais hablado
habrían hablado

PRESENT SUBJUNCTIVE
hable
hables
hable
hablemos
habléis
hablen

PERFECT SUBJUNCTIVE
haya hablado
hayas hablado
haya hablado
hayamos hablado
hayáis hablado
hayan hablado

IMPERFECT SUBJUNCTIVE
hablara / hablase
hablaras / hablases
hablara / hablase
habláramos / hablásemos
hablarais / hablaseis
hablaran / hablasen

PLUPERFECT SUBJUNCTIVE
hubiera / hubiese hablado
hubieras / hubieses hablado
hubiera / hubiese hablado
hubiéramos / hubiésemos hablado
hubierais / hubieseis hablado
hubieran / hubiesen hablado

FUTURE SUBJUNCTIVE
hablare
hablares
hablare
habláremos
hablareis
hablaren

FUTURE PERFECT SUBJUNCTIVE
hubiere hablado
hubieres hablado
hubiere hablado
hubiéremos hablado
hubiereis hablado
hubieren hablado

IMPERATIVE	INFINITIVE	GERUND	PAST PARTICIPLE
habla	*hablar*	*hablando*	*hablado*
hablad			

-er verbs

PRESENT INDICATIVE
como (I eat)
comes
come
comemos
coméis
comen

PERFECT INDICATIVE
he comido
has comido
ha comido
hemos comido
habéis comido
han comido

IMPERFECT INDICATIVE
comía
comías
comía
comíamos
comíais
comían

PLUPERFECT INDICATIVE
había comido
habías comido
había comido
habíamos comido
habíais comido
habían comido

PRETERITE INDICATIVE
comí
comiste
comió
comimos
comisteis
comieron

PAST ANTERIOR INDICATIVE
hube comido
hubiste comido
hubo comido
hubimos comido
hubisteis comido
hubieron comido

FUTURE INDICATIVE
comeré
comerás
comerá
comeremos
comeréis
comerán

FUTURE PERFECT INDICATIVE
habré comido
habrás comido
habrá comido
habremos comido
habréis comido
habrán comido

CONDITIONAL
comería
comerías
comería
comeríamos
comeríais
comerían

CONDITIONAL PERFECT
habría comido
habrías comido
habría comido
habríamos comido
habríais comido
habrían comido

PRESENT SUBJUNCTIVE
coma
comas
coma
comamos
comáis
coman

PERFECT SUBJUNCTIVE
haya comido
hayas comido
haya comido
hayamos comido
hayáis comido
hayan comido

IMPERFECT SUBJUNCTIVE	PLUPERFECT SUBJUNCTIVE
comiera / comiese	*hubiera / hubiese comido*
comieras / comieses	*hubieras / hubieses comido*
comiera / comiese	*hubiera / hubiese comido*
comiéramos / comiésemos	*hubiéramos / hubiésemos comido*
comierais / comieseis	*hubierais / hubieseis comido*
comieran / comiesen	*hubieran / hubiesen comido*

FUTURE SUBJUNCTIVE	FUTURE PERFECT SUBJUNCTIVE
comiere	*hubiere comido*
comieres	*hubieres comido*
comiere	*hubiere comido*
comiéremos	*hubiéremos comido*
comiereis	*hubiereis comido*
comieren	*hubieren comido*

IMPERATIVE	INFINITIVE	GERUND	PAST PARTICIPLE
come	*comer*	*comiendo*	*comido*
comed			

-ir verbs

PRESENT INDICATIVE	PERFECT INDICATIVE
vivo (I live)	*he vivido*
vives	*has vivido*
vive	*ha vivido*
vivimos	*hemos vivido*
vivís	*habéis vivido*
viven	*han vivido*

IMPERFECT INDICATIVE	PLUPERFECT INDICATIVE
vivía	*había vivido*
vivías	*habías vivido*
vivía	*había vivido*
vivíamos	*habíamos vivido*
vivíais	*habíais vivido*
vivían	*habían vivido*

PRETERITE INDICATIVE	PAST ANTERIOR INDICATIVE
viví	*hube vivido*
viviste	*hubiste vivido*
vivió	*hubo vivido*
vivimos	*hubimos vivido*
vivisteis	*hubisteis vivido*
vivieron	*hubieron vivido*

FUTURE INDICATIVE	FUTURE PERFECT INDICATIVE
viviré	*habré vivido*
vivirás	*habrás vivido*
vivirá	*habrá vivido*
viviremos	*habremos vivido*
viviréis	*habréis vivido*
vivirán	*habrán vivido*

CONDITIONAL	CONDITIONAL PERFECT
viviría	*habría vivido*
vivirías	*habrías vivido*
viviría	*habría vivido*
viviríamos	*habríamos vivido*
viviríais	*habríais vivido*
vivirían	*habrían vivido*

PRESENT SUBJUNCTIVE	PERFECT SUBJUNCTIVE
viva	*haya vivido*
vivas	*hayas vivido*
viva	*haya vivido*
vivamos	*hayamos vivido*
viváis	*hayáis vivido*
vivan	*hayan vivido*

IMPERFECT SUBJUNCTIVE	PLUPERFECT SUBJUNCTIVE
viviera / viviese	*hubiera / hubiese vivido*
vivieras / vivieses	*hubieras / hubieses vivido*
viviera / viviese	*hubiera / hubiese vivido*
viviéramos / viviésemos	*hubiéramos / hubiésemos vivido*
vivierais / vivieseis	*hubierais / hubieseis vivido*
vivieran / viviesen	*hubieran / hubiesen vivido*

FUTURE SUBJUNCTIVE	FUTURE PERFECT SUBJUNCTIVE
viviere	*hubiere vivido*
vivieres	*hubieres vivido*
viviere	*hubiere vivido*
viviéremos	*hubiéremos vivido*
viviereis	*hubiereis vivido*
vivieren	*hubieren vivido*

IMPERATIVE
vive
vivid

INFINITIVE
vivir *haber vivido*

GERUND
viviendo *habiendo vivido*

PAST PARTICIPLE
vivido

Appendix 3
The conjugation of reflexive verbs

A reflexive verb is conjugated with the same endings as regular verbs. Any irregularities in the present, the preterite or the past participle will also apply. Take particular notice of the reflexive pronouns.

PRESENT INDICATIVE
me lavo
te lavas
se lava
nos lavamos
os laváis
se lavan

PERFECT INDICATIVE
me he lavado
te has lavado
se ha lavado
nos hemos lavado
os habéis lavado
se han lavado

IMPERFECT INDICATIVE
me lavaba
te lavabas
se lavaba
nos lavábamos
os lavabais
se lavaban

PLUPERFECT INDICATIVE
me había lavado
te habías lavado
se había lavado
nos habíamos lavado
os habíais lavado
se habían lavado

PRETERITE INDICATIVE
me lavé
te lavaste
se lavó
nos lavamos
os lavasteis
se lavaron

PAST ANTERIOR INDICATIVE
me hube lavado
te hubiste lavado
se hubo lavado
nos hubimos lavado
os hubisteis lavado
se hubieron lavado

FUTURE INDICATIVE
me lavaré
te lavarás
se lavará
nos lavaremos
os lavaréis
se lavarán

FUTURE PERFECT INDICATIVE
me habré lavado
te habrás lavado
se habrá lavado
nos habremos lavado
os habréis lavado
se habrán lavado

CONDITIONAL

me lavaría
te lavarías
se lavaría
nos lavaríamos
os lavaríais
se lavarían

CONDITIONAL PERFECT

me habría lavado
te habrías lavado
se habría lavado
nos habríamos lavado
os habríais lavado
se habrían lavado

PRESENT SUBJUNCTIVE

me lave
te laves
se lave
nos lavemos
os lavéis
se laven

PERFECT SUBJUNCTIVE

me haya lavado
te hayas lavado
se haya lavado
nos hayamos lavado
os hayáis lavado
se hayan lavado

IMPERFECT SUBJUNCTIVE

me lavara / lavase
te lavaras / lavases
se lavara / lavase
nos laváramos / lavásemos
os lavarais / lavaseis
se lavaran / lavasen

PLUPERFECT SUBJUNCTIVE

me hubiera / hubiese lavado
te hubieras / hubieses lavado
se hubiera / hubiese lavado
*nos hubiéramos / hubiésemos
    lavado*
os hubierais / hubieseis lavado
se hubieran / hubiesen lavado

FUTURE SUBJUNCTIVE

me lavare
te lavares
se lavare
nos laváremos
os lavareis
se lavaren

FUTURE PERFECT SUBJUNCTIVE

me hubiere lavado
te hubieres lavado
se hubiere lavado
nos hubiéremos lavado
os hubiereis lavado
se hubieren lavado

IMPERATIVE	INFINITIVE	GERUND	PAST PARTICIPLE
lávate *lavaos*	*lavarse*	*lavándose* (or other reflexive pronoun)	*lavado*

Appendix 4
The conjugation of irregular verbs

(i) Spelling changes which occur in order to keep the original pronunciation do not make a verb irregular. Examples of this are the change of *g* to *j* in front of *a* or *o* in cases like *coger: cojo, coja;* of *c* to *qu* in front of *e* in cases like *buscar: busque;* of *g* to *gu* in front of *e* in cases like *pagar: pague;* of *gu* to *gü* in front of *e* in cases like *averiguar: averigüe;* of *z* to *c* in front of *e,* in cases like *cruzar: cruce.* Note that, from the phonetic point of view, these verbs are perfectly regular.

(ii) In the overall pattern of irregularities, note than an irregularity in the present indicative affects the present subjunctive and the imperative; that an irregularity in the preterite affects the imperfect and the future subjunctive; and that an irregularity in the future affects the conditional.

(iii) The irregularities found in Spanish verbs can be conveniently summarized as follows:

* Diphthongizing verbs
There is a group of verbs in which the *e* of the stem changes to *ie*, and the *o* of the stem changes to *ue* in the forms of the present indicative where the vowel bears the stress:

pensar to think	**contar** to count
pienso	*cuento*
piensas	*cuentas*
piensa	*cuenta*
pensamos	*contamos*
pensáis	*contáis*
piensan	*cuentan*

The present subjunctive will therefore be *piense*, etc., and *cuente*, etc., and the imperative will be *piensa* and *cuenta* (but *pensad* and *contad*, with unstressed stem vowel).

To this category also belong one verb with *u* in the stem (*jugar* to play) and two ending in *-irir* (*adquirir* to acquire and *inquirir* to inquire) which change to *ue* and *ie*, respectively: *juego, adquiero, inquiero.*

- **Vowel-weakening verbs**

These are the verbs which change the *e* in the stem to *i* in the stressed forms of the present indicative and in the third persons of the preterite:

pedir to ask (for)

PRESENT INDICATIVE	PRETERITE INDICATIVE
pido	pedí
pides	pediste
pide	pidió
pedimos	pedimos
pedís	pedisteis
piden	pidieron

Verbs in this category weaken the vowel throughout the present subjunctive, the imperfect and the future.

- **Diphthongizing and vowel-weakening verbs**

Some verbs diphthongize the stem vowel in the present indicative, and weaken it not only in the third persons of the preterite but also in the unstressed forms of the present subjunctive and in the imperfect and the future subjunctive:

sentir to feel

PRESENT INDICATIVE	PRETERITE INDICATIVE
siento	sentí
sientes	sentiste
siente	sintió
sentimos	sentimos
sentís	sentisteis
sienten	sintieron

PRESENT SUBJUNCTIVE	IMPERFECT SUBJUNCTIVE	FUTURE SUBJUNCTIVE
sienta	sintiera / sintiese	sintiere
sientas	sintieras / sintieses	sintieres
sienta	sintiera / sintiese	sintiere
sintamos	sintiéramos / sintiésemos	sintiéremos
sintáis	sintierais / sintieseis	sintiereis
sientan	sintieran / sintiesen	sintieren

In a similar category are the verbs *dormir* to sleep and *morir* to die, which diphthongize *o* into *ue* and weaken it to *u* in the same cases as *e* to *ie*, and *e* to *i* in verbs like *sentir*. (Both will be found in the Appendix.)

- **Irregular futures**

Some verbs lose the first vowel of the ending, like *habré*, *podré*, *sabré*. When, in the evolution of Spanish, the loss of this vowel created the group *-lr-* or *-nr-*, a *d* was added: *valdré*, *saldré*, *pondré*. Finally, special shortened forms occur in *diré* (from *decir* to say) and *haré* (from *hacer* to make, to do). These irregularities apply to the conditional.

- **Consonant-adding verbs**

Verbs ending in *-acer*, *-ecer*, *-ocer* and *-ucir* add a *z* in front of the *c* of the present (*conducir: conduzco*). Some common verbs with *n* or *l* in the stem add a *g* in the present (*tener: tengo; salir: salgo*). Verbs ending in *-uir* add *y* before the personal endings of the present in the three singular persons and in the third plural. The most usual of these verbs will be found in the Appendix.

- **Strong preterites**

See section 42a. Instead of the regular preterite with stress on the last syllable (*hablé*, *comí*, *viví*), some verbs have a preterite with the stress on the penultimate syllable. This is usually known as a strong preterite. The same irregularity will apply to imperfect and future subjunctive. All these verbs can be found in the Appendix.

- **Irregular past participles**

See section 48c. Some verbs have an irregular past participle and a fairly large number have two participles, one regular and one irregular, in which case the regular form is used for the compound tenses of the verb. See section 48c(v) for details of the irregular past participle used as adjectives.

(iv) Here is a list of common irregular verbs, showing their irregularities:

advertir to warn
(as for *divertir*)

andar to walk

PRETERITE INDICATIVE		IMPERFECT SUBJUNCTIVE
anduve	anduvimos	anduviera / anduviese
anduviste	anduvisteis	etc.
anduvo	anduvieron	
		FUTURE SUBJUNCTIVE
		anduviere
		etc.

atender to help, to listen
(as for *tender*)

caber to fit, to be contained

PRESENT INDICATIVE	PRETERITE INDICATIVE	FUTURE INDICATIVE	CONDITIONAL
quepo	cupe	cabré	cabría
cabes	cupiste	cabrás	etc.
cabe	cupo	cabrá	
cabemos	cupimos	cabremos	
cabéis	cupisteis	cabréis	
caben	cupieron	cabrán	

PRESENT SUBJUNCTIVE	IMPERFECT SUBJUNCTIVE	FUTURE SUBJUNCTIVE
quepa	cupiera / cupiese	cupiere
quepas	etc.	etc.
quepa		
quepamos		
quepáis		
quepan		

caer to fall

PRESENT INDICATIVE	PRETERITE INDICATIVE	PRESENT SUBJUNCTIVE
caigo	caí	caiga
caes	caíste	caigas
cae	cayó	caiga
caemos	caímos	caigamos
caéis	caísteis	caigáis
caen	cayeron	caigan

IMPERFECT SUBJUNCTIVE	FUTURE SUBJUNCTIVE	GERUND
cayera / cayese	cayere	cayendo
etc.	etc.	

cerrar to close

PRESENT INDICATIVE	PRESENT SUBJUNCTIVE	IMPERATIVE
cierro	cierre	cierra
cierras	cierres	cerrad
cierra	cierre	
cerramos	cerremos	
cerráis	cerréis	
cierran	cierren	

colgar to hang, to hang up

PRESENT INDICATIVE	PRETERITE INDICATIVE	PRESENT SUBJUNCTIVE
cuelgo	colgué	cuelgue
cuelgas	colgaste	cuelgues
cuelga	colgó	cuelgue
colgamos	colgamos	colguemos
colgáis	colgasteis	colguéis
cuelgan	colgaron	cuelguen

IMPERATIVE
cuelga
colgad

concluir to finish

PRESENT INDICATIVE	PRETERITE INDICATIVE	PRESENT SUBJUNCTIVE
concluyo	concluí	concluya
concluyes	concluiste	concluyas
concluye	concluyó	concluya
concluimos	concluimos	concluyamos
concluís	concluisteis	concluyáis
concluyen	concluyeron	concluyan

IMPERFECT SUBJUNCTIVE	FUTURE SUBJUNCTIVE	IMPERATIVE	GERUND
concluyera / concluyese etc.	concluyere etc.	concluye concluid	concluyendo

conducir to drive

PRESENT INDICATIVE	PRETERITE INDICATIVE	PRESENT SUBJUNCTIVE
conduzco	conduje	conduzca
conduces	condujiste	conduzcas
conduce	condujo	conduzca
conducimos	condujimos	conduzcamos
conducís	condujisteis	conduzcáis
conducen	condujeron	conduzcan

IMPERFECT SUBJUNCTIVE	FUTURE SUBJUNCTIVE
condujera / condujese etc.	condujere etc

conocer to know

PRESENT INDICATIVE	PRESENT SUBJUNCTIVE
conozco	conozca
conoces	conozcas
conoce	conozca
conocemos	conozcamos
conocéis	conozcáis
conocen	conozcan

construir to build

(as for concluir)

convertir to convert

(as for divertir)

contar to count, to tell

PRESENT INDICATIVE	PRESENT SUBJUNCTIVE	IMPERATIVE
cuento	cuente	cuenta
cuentas	cuentes	contad
cuenta	cuente	
contamos	contemos	
contáis	contéis	
cuentan	cuenten	

costar to cost

(as for contar)

dar to give

PRESENT INDICATIVE	PRETERITE INDICATIVE	PRESENT SUBJUNCTIVE
doy	di	dé
das	diste	des
da	dio	dé
damos	dimos	demos
dais	disteis	deis
dan	dieron	den

IMPERFECT SUBJUNCTIVE
diera / diese
dieras / dieses
diera / diese
diéramos / diésemos
dierais / dieseis
dieran / diesen

FUTURE SUBJUNCTIVE
diere
etc.

decir to say, to tell

PRESENT INDICATIVE	PRETERITE INDICATIVE	FUTURE INDICATIVE	CONDITIONAL
digo	*dije*	*diré*	*diría*
dices	*dijiste*	*dirás*	etc.
dice	*dijo*	*dirá*	
decimos	*dijimos*	*diremos*	
decís	*dijisteis*	*diréis*	
dicen	*dijeron*	*dirán*	

PRESENT SUBJUNCTIVE	IMPERFECT SUBJUNCTIVE	FUTURE SUBJUNCTIVE	IMPERATIVE
diga	*dijera / dijese*	*dijere*	*di*
digas	etc.	etc.	*decid*
diga			
digamos			
digáis			
digan			

GERUND	PAST PARTICIPLE
diciendo	*dicho*

destruir to destroy
(as for *concluir*)

divertir to amuse

PRESENT INDICATIVE	PRETERITE INDICATIVE	PRESENT SUBJUNCTIVE
divierto	*divertí*	*divierta*
diviertes	*divertiste*	*diviertas*
divierte	*divirtió*	*divierta*
divertimos	*divertimos*	*divirtamos*
divertís	*divertisteis*	*divertáis*
divierten	*divirtieron*	*diviertan*

IMPERFECT SUBJUNCTIVE	FUTURE SUBJUNCTIVE	IMPERATIVE	GERUND
divirtiera / divirtiese etc.	*divirtiere* etc.	*divierte* *divertid*	*divirtiendo*

dormir to sleep

PRESENT INDICATIVE	PRETERITE	PRESENT SUBJUNCTIVE	IMPERFECT SUBJUNCTIVE
duermo	*dormí*	*duerma*	*durmiera / durmiese*
duermes	*dormiste*	*duermas*	etc.
duerme	*durmió*	*duerma*	
dormimos	*dormimos*	*durmamos*	
dormís	*dormisteis*	*durmáis*	
duermen	*durmieron*	*duerman*	

FUTURE SUBJUNCTIVE	IMPERATIVE	GERUND
durmiere etc.	*duerme* *dormid*	*durmiendo*

elegir to choose
(as for *pedir*)

empezar to begin
(as for *cerrar*)

encontrar to find
(as for *contar*)

escribir to write

PAST PARTICIPLE
escrito

hacer to do, to make

PRESENT INDICATIVE	PRETERITE INDICATIVE	FUTURE INDICATIVE	CONDITIONAL
hago	*hice*	*haré*	*haría*
haces	*hiciste*	*harás*	etc.
hace	*hizo*	*hará*	
hacemos	*hicimos*	*haremos*	
hacéis	*hicisteis*	*haréis*	
hacen	*hicieron*	*harán*	

PRESENT SUBJUNCTIVE	IMPERFECT SUBJUNCTIVE	FUTURE SUBJUNCTIVE	IMPERATIVE
haga	hiciera / hiciese	hiciere	haz
hagas	etc.	etc.	haced
haga			
hagamos			
hagáis			
hagan			

PAST PARTICIPLE
hecho

instruir to instruct

(as for *concluir*)

ir to go

PRESENT INDICATIVE	IMPERFECT INDICATIVE	PRETERITE INDICATIVE	FUTURE INDICATIVE
voy	iba	fui	iré
vas	ibas	fuiste	irás
va	iba	fue	irá
vamos	íbamos	fuimos	iremos
vais	ibais	fuisteis	iréis
van	iban	fueron	irán

CONDITIONAL	PRESENT SUBJUNCTIVE	IMPERFECT SUBJUNCTIVE
iría	vaya	fuera / fuese
etc.	vayas	fueras / fueses
	vaya	fuera / fuese
	vayamos	fuéramos / fuésemos
	vayáis	fuerais / fueseis
	vayan	fueran / fuesen

FUTURE SUBJUNCTIVE	IMPERATIVE	GERUND	PAST PARTICIPLE
fuere	ve	yendo	ido
etc.	id		

Contrary to the rule given in section 47(ii), *id* is exceptional in keeping its *d* when the reflexive pronoun *os* is added: *idos*.

llover to rain

PRESENT INDICATIVE	PRESENT SUBJUNCTIVE
llueve	llueva

merecer to deserve

(as for *conocer*)

morir to die

(as for *dormir*)

PAST PARTICIPLE
muerto

mover to move

PRESENT INDICATIVE	PRESENT SUBJUNCTIVE	IMPERATIVE
muevo	*mueva*	*mueve*
mueves	*muevas*	*moved*
mueve	*mueva*	
movemos	*movamos*	
movéis	*mováis*	
mueven	*muevan*	

nacer to be born

(as for *conocer*)

nevar to snow

PRESENT INDICATIVE	PRESENT SUBJUNCTIVE
nieva	*nieve*

oír to hear, to listen

PRESENT INDICATIVE	PRETERITE INDICATIVE	PRESENT SUBJUNCTIVE
oigo	*oí*	*oiga*
oyes	*oíste*	*oigas*
oye	*oyó*	*oiga*
oímos	*oímos*	*oigamos*
oís	*oísteis*	*oigáis*
oyen	*oyeron*	*oigan*

IMPERFECT SUBJUNCTIVE	FUTURE SUBJUNCTIVE	IMPERATIVE	GERUND
oyera / oyese	*oyere*	*oye*	*oyendo*
etc.	etc.	*oíd*	

pedir to ask (for)

PRESENT INDICATIVE	PRETERITE INDICATIVE	PRESENT SUBJUNCTIVE
pido	*pedí*	*pida*
pides	*pediste*	*pidas*
pide	*pidió*	*pida*
pedimos	*pedimos*	*pidamos*
pedís	*pedisteis*	*pidáis*
piden	*pidieron*	*pidan*

IMPERFECT SUBJUNCTIVE	FUTURE SUBJUNCTIVE	IMPERATIVE	GERUND
pidiera / pidiese	*pidiere*	*pide*	*pidiendo*
etc.	etc.	*pedid*	

pensar to think

(as for *cerrar*)

perder to lose

PRESENT INDICATIVE	PRESENT SUBJUNCTIVE	IMPERATIVE
pierdo	*pierda*	*pierde*
pierdes	*pierdas*	*perded*
pierde	*pierda*	
perdemos	*perdamos*	
perdéis	*perdáis*	
pierden	*pierdan*	

poder 'can', to be able

PRESENT INDICATIVE	PRETERITE INDICATIVE	FUTURE INDICATIVE	CONDITIONAL
puedo	*pude*	*podré*	*podría*
puedes	*pudiste*	*podrás*	etc.
puede	*pudo*	*podrá*	
podemos	*pudimos*	*podremos*	
podéis	*pudisteis*	*podréis*	
pueden	*pudieron*	*podrán*	

PRESENT SUBJUNCTIVE	IMPERFECT SUBJUNCTIVE	FUTURE SUBJUNCTIVE
pueda	*pudiera / pudiese*	*pudiere*
puedas	etc.	etc.
pueda		
podamos	IMPERATIVE	GERUND
podáis	*puede*	*pudiendo*
puedan	*poded*	

poner to put

PRESENT INDICATIVE	PRETERITE INDICATIVE	FUTURE INDICATIVE	CONDITIONAL
pongo	*puse*	*pondré*	*pondría*
pones	*pusiste*	*pondrás*	etc.
pone	*puso*	*pondrá*	
ponemos	*pusimos*	*pondremos*	
ponéis	*pusisteis*	*pondréis*	
ponen	*pusieron*	*pondrán*	

PRESENT SUBJUNCTIVE	IMPERFECT SUBJUNCTIVE	FUTURE SUBJUNCTIVE
ponga	*pusiera / pusiese*	*pusiere*
pongas	etc.	etc.
ponga		
pongamos		
pongáis		
pongan		

IMPERATIVE	PAST PARTICIPLE
pon	*puesto*
poned	

preferir to prefer
(as for *sentir*)

querer to want

PRESENT INDICATIVE	PRETERITE INDICATIVE	FUTURE INDICATIVE	CONDITIONAL
quiero	*quise*	*querré*	*querría*
quieres	*quisiste*	*querrás*	etc.
quiere	*quiso*	*querrá*	
queremos	*quisimos*	*querremos*	
queráis	*quisisteis*	*querréis*	
quieren	*quisieron*	*querrán*	

PRESENT SUBJUNCTIVE	IMPERFECT SUBJUNCTIVE
quiera	*quisiera / quisiese*
quieras	etc.
quiera	
queramos	
queráis	
quieran	

FUTURE SUBJUNCTIVE
quisiere
etc.

IMPERATIVE
quiere
quered

reír to laugh

PRESENT INDICATIVE	PRETERITE INDICATIVE	PRESENT SUBJUNCTIVE
río	*reí*	*ría*
ríes	*reíste*	*rías*
ríe	*rió*	*ría*
reímos	*reímos*	*riamos*
reís	*reísteis*	*riáis*
ríen	*rieron*	*rían*

IMPERFECT SUBJUNCTIVE	FUTURE SUBJUNCTIVE	IMPERATIVE	GERUND
riera / riese	*riere*	*ríe*	*riendo*
rieras / rieses	etc.	*reíd*	
riera / riese			
riéramos / riésemos			
rierais / rieseis			
rieran / riesen			

saber to know

PRESENT INDICATIVE	PRETERITE INDICATIVE	FUTURE INDICATIVE	CONDITIONAL
sé	*supe*	*sabré*	*sabría*
sabes	*supiste*	*sabrás*	etc.
sabe	*supo*	*sabrá*	
sabemos	*supimos*	*sabremos*	
sabéis	*supisteis*	*sabréis*	
saben	*supieron*	*sabrán*	

PRESENT SUBJUNCTIVE	IMPERFECT SUBJUNCTIVE	FUTURE SUBJUNCTIVE
sepa	*supiera / supiese*	*supiere*
sepas	etc.	etc.
sepa		
sepamos		
sepáis		
sepan		

salir to go out

PRESENT INDICATIVE	FUTURE INDICATIVE	CONDITIONAL	IMPERATIVE
salgo	saldré	saldría	sal
sales	saldrás	etc.	salid
sale	saldrá		
salimos	saldremos		
salís	saldréis		
salen	saldrán		

seguir to follow
(as for *pedir*)

sentarse to sit down
(as for *cerrar*)

sentir to feel

PRESENT INDICATIVE	PRETERITE INDICATIVE	PRESENT SUBJUNCTIVE
siento	sentí	sienta
sientes	sentiste	sientas
siente	sintió	sienta
sentimos	sentimos	sintamos
sentís	sentisteis	sintáis
sienten	sintieron	sientan

IMPERFECT SUBJUNCTIVE	FUTURE SUBJUNCTIVE	IMPERATIVE	GERUND
sintiera / sintiese	sintiere	siente	sintiendo
sintieras / sintieses	etc.	sentid	
sintiera / sintiese			
sintiéramos / sintiésemos			
sintierais / sintieseis			
sintieran / sintiesen			

soñar to dream
(as for *contar*)

tender to hang

PRESENT INDICATIVE	PRESENT SUBJUNCTIVE	IMPERATIVE
tiendo	tienda	tiende
tiendes	tiendas	tended
tiende	tienda	
tendemos	tendamos	
tendéis	tendáis	
tienden	tiendan	

tener to have, to possess

PRESENT INDICATIVE	PRETERITE INDICATIVE	FUTURE INDICATIVE	CONDITIONAL
tengo	*tuve*	*tendré*	*tendría*
tienes	*tuviste*	*tendrás*	etc.
tiene	*tuvo*	*tendrá*	
tenemos	*tuvimos*	*tendremos*	
tenéis	*tuvisteis*	*tendréis*	
tienen	*tuvieron*	*tendrán*	

PRESENT SUBJUNCTIVE	IMPERFECT SUBJUNCTIVE	FUTURE SUBJUNCTIVE
tenga	*tuviera / tuviese*	*tuviere*
tengas	*tuvieras / tuvieses*	etc.
tenga	*tuviera / tuviese*	
tengamos	*tuviéramos / tuviésemos*	
tengáis	*tuvierais / tuvieseis*	
tengan	*tuvieran / tuviesen*	

IMPERATIVE
ten
tened

traducir to translate
(as for *conducir*)

traer to bring

PRESENT INDICATIVE	PRETERITE INDICATIVE	PRESENT SUBJUNCTIVE
traigo	*traje*	*traiga*
traes	*trajiste*	*traigas*
trae	*trajo*	*traiga*
traemos	*trajimos*	*traigamos*
traéis	*trajisteis*	*traigáis*
traen	*trajeron*	*traigan*

IMPERFECT SUBJUNCTIVE	FUTURE SUBJUNCTIVE	GERUND
trajera / trajese	*trajere*	*trayendo*
trajeras / trajeses	etc.	
trajera / trajese		
trajéramos / trajésemos		
trajerais / trajeseis		
trajeran / trajesen		

tronar to thunder

PRESENT INDICATIVE	PRESENT SUBJUNCTIVE
truena	*truene*

valer to be worth

PRESENT INDICATIVE	FUTURE INDICATIVE	CONDITIONAL	PRESENT SUBJUNCTIVE
valgo	*valdré*	*valdría*	*valga*
vales	*valdrás*	etc.	*valgas*
vale	*valdrá*		*valga*
valemos	*valdremos*		*valgamos*
valéis	*valdréis*		*valgáis*
valen	*valdrán*		*valgan*

venir to come

PRESENT INDICATIVE	PRETERITE INDICATIVE	FUTURE INDICATIVE
vengo	*vine*	*vendré*
vienes	*viniste*	*vendrás*
viene	*vino*	*vendrá*
venimos	*vinimos*	*vendremos*
venís	*vinisteis*	*vendréis*
vienen	*vinieron*	*vendrán*

CONDITIONAL	PRESENT SUBJUNCTIVE	IMPERFECT SUBJUNCTIVE
vendría	*venga*	*viniera / viniese*
etc.	*vengas*	*vinieras / vinieses*
	venga	*viniera / viniese*
	vengamos	*viniéramos / viniésemos*
	vengáis	*vinierais / vinieseis*
	vengan	*vinieran / viniesen*

FUTURE SUBJUNCTIVE	IMPERATIVE	GERUND
viniere	*ven*	*viniendo*
etc.	*venid*	

ver to see

PRESENT INDICATIVE	IMPERFECT INDICATIVE	PRESENT SUBJUNCTIVE	PAST PARTICIPLE
veo	veía	vea	visto
ves	veías	veas	
ve	veía	vea	
vemos	veíamos	veamos	
veis	veíais	veáis	
ven	veían	vean	

vestirse to get dressed

(as for *pedir*)

volar to fly

(as for *contar*)

Suggestions for further reading

If you wish to follow up some of the areas covered in this book, you may like to consult the reference works listed below.

(1) Dictionaries

Cassell's Spanish–English, English–Spanish Dictionary, Cassell, London
Collins Spanish–English, English–Spanish Dictionary, Collins, Glasgow, third edition (1992)
Moliner, M., *Diccionario de uso del español* (reprinted 1990)
Real Academia Española, *Diccionario manual e ilustrado de la lengua española*, fourth edition (1989)
Real Academia Española, *Diccionario de la lengua española*, twenty-first edition (1992)
Seco, M., *Diccionario de dudas y dificultades de la lengua española*, ninth edition (1990)
Vox, *Diccionario general ilustrado de la lengua española*, Vox (1987)

(2) Phonology

Alarcos Llorach, E., *Fonología española*, fourth edition (1965)
Navarro Tomás, T., *Manual de pronunciación española*, twenty-fourth edition (1990)
Macpherson, I. R., *Spanish Phonology: Descriptive and Historical* (1975)
Quilis, A. and J. A. Fernández, *Curso de fonética y fonología españolas para estudiantes angloamericanos*, twelfth edition (1989)

(3) Grammar and usage

Alcina Franch, J. and J. M. Blecua, *Gramática española*, seventh edition (1989)
Butt, J. and C. Benjamín, *A New Reference Grammar of Modern Spanish* (1988)
Gili Gaya, S., *Curso superior de sintaxis española*, fifteenth edition (1989)
Lorenzo, E., *El español de hoy, lengua en ebullición*, third edition (1980)
Pratt, C., *El anglicismo en el español peninsular contemporáneo* (1980)
Ramsden, H., *An Essential Course in Modern Spanish*
Real Academia Española, *Esbozo de una nueva gramática de la lengua española* (1973)
Seco, M., *Gramática esencial del español,* second edition (1989)
Seco, R. (revised by M. Seco), *Manual de gramática española*, eleventh edition (1989)
SGEL, *Problemas básicos del español*

Index